Proceedings of the 1972 Annual Spring Meeting
of the American Ethnological Society

Learning and Culture

Solon T. Kimball
Jacquetta H. Burnett
Symposium Organizers and Co-Editors

AMERICAN ETHNOLOGICAL SOCIETY
Robert F. Spencer, General Editor

Distributed by the University of Washington Press
Seattle and London

Library of Congress Cataloging in Publication Data

American Ethnological Society.
    Learning and culture.

    (Its Proceedings of the annual spring meeting, 1972)
    Includes bibliographies.
    1. Ethnopsychology--Congresses. 2. Learning,
Psychology of--Congresses. 3. Socialization--
Congresses. I. Kimball, Solon Toothaker, ed.
II. Burnett, Jacquetta H., ed. III. Title.
IV. Series.
GN273.A43 1973   301.1   73-9920
ISBN 0-295-95305-5

PREFACE

The 1972 Annual Spring Meeting of the American
Ethnological Society was held in connection with the annual
meeting of the Society for Applied Anthropology in Montreal,
Que., between April 5th and 9th. The AES theme for the
meeting was Learning and Culture, reflecting a joint effort
on the part of the Society and of the Council for Anthropology
and Education (CAE). The organization of the symposium, the
results of which are published here, was undertaken by Dr.
Jacquetta H. Burnett, representing the Council for Anthropology
and Education, and Dr. Solon T. Kimball, representing the
American Ethnological Society.

The Society also expresses its pleasure at the interest shown by students in submitting papers for competition for
the Elsie Clews Parsons prize. The 1972 medalist and winner
was Miss Carol S. Holzberg, Boston University, whose paper,
"Friendship: The Affective Manipulation," appears with this
volume. William L. Partridge, University of Florida, was
awarded second prize for his paper, "City and Region: Contrasting Urban Cultures in Colombia."

Robert F. Spencer, Editor
American Ethnological Society

University of Minnesota
March, 1973

CONTENTS

PERSPECTIVES ON LEARNING AND CULTURE

Solon T. Kimball
University of Florida

Jacquetta H. Burnett
University of Illinois

I. Introduction

Despite past achievement and continuing advance it does not seem unreasonable to assert that we are still a long way from fully understanding the processes of learning.

The problem is a complex one and the knowledge we gain is due in part to the way we define it as well as the means we use to secure answers for the questions we ask. Thus, those who direct their energies to intricately devised experiments for rats, dogs, pigeons, and other symbol lacking animals may gain great insight into animal psychology but still possess evidence of doubtful validity for humans. Those who seek to elucidate the maturational sequences, as did Gesell, provide us with ordered descriptions of behavioral stages but we do not learn much about the explanatory processes. Others, like Piaget and Bruner who are concerned with cognitive development, have opened further vistas into the human mind and its stages of growth.

The conclusions about learning can be significantly different depending upon the perspective which shapes the research effort. If the environment, physical and human, is viewed as patterned systems then its effects upon the individual would not be treated as discrete and isolated causation, but in the context of mutually influencing interconnections. The significance of this latter approach should be fully understood.

Once we expand our focus from one which probes the individual only to one in which both environment and individual are viewed as linked in a dynamic relationship, then the questions we ask and the precedures we utilize are modified. For example, anthropologists view the regularities of behavior manifested in custom and belief as the culture of a people. The ways in which they group themselves to accomplish communal goals we label social structure. Both of these aspects can be examined as systems and together with their interconnections they constitute the human environment. We assume the human infant at birth possesses the capabilities for responding to these influences and that during the long period of dependency there is an uneven but continuous progression toward a maturity which we call adulthood. The variabilities within and between cultures are reflected in the differential consequences of individual experience. The problem of elucidating the learning process becomes set by such empirical considerations. Specifically in what manner and with what effect does the environment shape the individual? Furthermore, to what extent is the process of learning itself culturally prescribed? If our evidence should establish the cultural discreteness of process, as it already has been demonstrated for cultural variability, then we must agree that each cultural system requires a distinct learning theory (Kimball 1965).

The justification for such a view is supported by a number of facts and assumptions. If the learning process were genetic and invariable then variation or modification of the cultural environment would have no effect on it. But if the consistencies of the learning process differ from one culture to another then are we not justified in assuming a cultural variable in the incorporation and organization of experience? And if the learning process is a cultural variable then what is the effect upon established theories which assume universal applicability? There are other and even more intriguing challenges that would have to be examined eventually. Before we proceed further in this direction, however, let us have a quick look at the widely prevalent explanation of learning as found in stimulus-response formulation.

We are deeply indebted to all those whose persistent and laborious work did so much to clarify the relationship between stimulus and response as a learning mechanism. Among such men Thorndike, Pavlov, and Skinner occupy a preeminent place. The originality of their ideas and the force of their findings have brought in their wake a revolution in our understanding of the learning process and, indeed, in our perception of the world. That their respective research results were mutually compatible and not contradictory gave added weight to their credibility.

The relatively rapid spread and acceptance of the ideas of this neurally based, mechanistic approach to learning can be attributed to many factors. Chief among them, however, was that the explanations they offered gave scientific justification to so many practices that were then already current. Educators had no difficulty in understanding or accepting a theory of learning based upon rewards and punishments, although they did not recognize, then or now, that in most instances the application of such sanctions were primarily for behavioral rather than intellectual problems. Concepts of associationism and reinforcement supported other practices. In retrospect the congruence between research results and accepted practices is not surprising, because the newly won scientific formulations were simply more precise statements of common sense experience.

Let us also recall that these findings found acceptance beyond the circle of education. Those who wanted to shape men's minds or exploit their needs, utilized this new science of the mind for their own purposes. Advertisers and propagandists called in the experts to advise them on the application of this new scientific knowledge and those who espoused political or religious creeds believed that once they captured the instruments of education that they could bring their utopias into being.

The response to these new ideas, however, was not wholly unanimous. Our intellectual humanists were among the first to recoil in horror at the prospect of the consequences to humanity which a dictatorial state might bring with the conscious application of the new science of the mind. In Brave New World, Aldous Huxley describes for us the amusing, all too possible, but also terrifying portrait of a dehumanized utopia. That there were obvious correspondences between the existing system of social classes and the scientifically created castes of his fantasy caused some to view his writings as satire. It may well have been just that, but it must also be viewed as a serious attempt to warn us about the future.

Arthur Koestler's message in Darkness at Noon is of the same kind, but the setting is the grim reality of the present. You will recall that when the tragic hero of his story meets his jailors he discovers that he encounters brutish repositories of doctrinal inculcation, men who showed no evidence of the high ideals which revolutionary reform had promised. The account which George Orwell gives us in Animal Farm and in "1984," is little different from these others in its implications--the awful power to shape and reshape humanity by those who systematically utilize the conditioning process. That these anxieties were something more than either fiction or fantasy was brought home to us with jolting clarity when we first learned of the brainwashing of some of the American soldiers who had become prisoners of the Chinese in the Korean War.

If through this mechanism of learning we hold the power to both create as well as to destroy humanity, then it behooves us to know exactly the nature of the force with which we live. No one can deny the practical importance of those discoveries which demostrate how certain aspects of experience are patterned through association, repetition, and reinforcement. They provide both theoretical and empirical support for teaching practices which are now current, and for programmed instruction. In fact, it is not uncommon to encounter those who draw an analogy between humans and computers when they refer to the effects of environment upon the individual as the process of programming. In such an analogy the individual may be thought of as a complicated electronic device whose performance is a function of new stimuli or input upon a previously established patterning derived from its environment. Such a representation of human behavior possesses certain advantages. It is simple. It is congruent with much of what we know about the learning process and it conforms with our prevalent tendency to project our knowledge about mechanics onto humans. This is, in effect, a psychological version of the input-output theory which when joined with that of the black box of mechanical engineering gives us a simple and fascinating formula that has recently become quite popular among social scientists. We should remind ourselves, however, of the many who have cautioned that there are significant differences between the human brain and the computer. The ease with which the latter solves complicated mathematical problems is indeed impressive, but the machine as well as the problems originate with man. Let us also remind ourselves that the experiments of Thorndike, Pavlov, or Skinner on rats, dogs, or pigeons did not originate with these animals, nor could the significance of their findings ever be communicated to those creatures who were the subjects of them.

In some ways we are now at the heart of our problem. Homo Sapiens differs from other forms of animal life in one crucial aspect, namely, his capacity for acquiring and transmitting culture. Now the learned behavior which we subsume under culture includes many things, some of which we share with other animals, but the symbolism associated with articulate speech and its use in cognitive thought sets man sharply apart. Language is the instrument of the higher mental processes. It is fundamental for orderly discrimination, for categorizing the objects and events of experience, for reasoning, and for problem solving. We cannot assert that other animals lack the capacity for cognition, the reported instances of insightful behavior would lead us to believe otherwise, but only man possesses the tools which permit him to transmit experience in symbolic form.

The problem then is to formulate a learning theory which can account for the process of enculturation--the consequences of the relation between the human organism and its characteristics and culture viewed as environment. We shall gain an inadequate and distorted solution, however, if we assume that either organism or environment are constants. We know, for example, that the human foetus, in ways not yet clearly specified, responds to the culturally prescribed behavior of human motherhood. Each society offers its own rules of appropriate diet, activity, and relationships for the mother and frequently also for those in intimate association with her. Other rules cover delivery and reception of the new-born infant as well as the behavior expected of the mother and other members of the family. In such manner humans convert the physiology of pregnancy and birth into culturally defined processes. The subsequent periods of infancy and childhood are also surrounded with cultural prescriptions. In fact, we now believe that it is impossible for the human infant to achieve full humanity in either an organic or symbolic sense outside of a cultural environment.

In the beginning, more than a million years ago, man linked his destiny to a developmental process which intermeshed the maturation of physical capacities with a cultural environment. The pervasiveness of the interconnection is seen most dramatically in the effect of the environment upon the mind. It becomes manifest in the pattern of response to all forms of stimulation, including those which originate within the organism as well as those which are external to it. Indeed, we might conclude that the basic cultural perspective becomes firmly embedded during the first few months of life even before the acquisition of articulate speech or the sense of self. Such a view contains far reaching implications for a theory of learning. It challenges some of the implicit assumptions which accompany the stimulus-response theory, and requires new explanations of cognitive learning and its processes. Before describing the specific research from which these conclusions have been taken, a quick resumé of the meaning of cultural environment is needed.

The cultural world into which each individual is born and comes to maturity provides him with a conceptual framework which permits him to organize his experiences in a meaningful manner. He learns to identify things, the relationships between them and him, and specifies his own behavior in the events in which he participates. The language which he learns provides the specific terms with which he identifies, categorizes, and evaluates. In its entirety this learning constitutes a system of thought and feeling which explains the working of the universe. It makes meaningful to him the natural phenomena, the rhythms of nature, and the origin and future of life. It also accounts for a cosmic order as found in mythological tales of miraculous creation, or in scientific explanations of the inexorable working of nature's laws.

This system of thought and its body of knowledge is called the world view. It gives to the members of each specific society their distinctive perspective. Hence the meaning of items, acts, or events must be sought within the context of each specific culture and learning theory which fails to recognize this fact is inadequate. For example, we can no longer reckon any single stimulus as a constant. Its effect is a function of an already existing pattern of response. Stated differently there is a perceptual screen, either conscious or unconscious, which modifies each stimulus in the direction of already existing responses. For example, if we proceed from a purely mechanical model of input-output the prediction of results is based upon an assumption of constancy in stimuli as well as in the mechanism of reception, but where we postulate an organic-cultural model, both stimulus and consequence must be viewed as

variables. The common sense of this statement can be attested
to by every teacher who has observed the differential response
of students to a lesson in grammar, arithmetic, or other subject. We are correct in attributing to individual differences
the variation in response, but it is a variation based upon the
perceived meaning of the teaching act. Fortunately, studies
which illuminate how infants incorporate world view are available.

The research by William Caudill and his associates
demonstrates the importance of the pattern of child care in
shaping the responses of the infant to its environment (Caudill
1970). This pattern, in turn expresses in subtle and persistent
ways the world view of the caretakers. Through observation and
interview Caudill gathered data on thirty American and thirty
Japanese middle-class families, each one having a first born
infant of from three to four months of age. He noted that the
basic caretaking activities around sleep and nutrition were
approximately the same, but that there were considerable differences in other aspects of the relationship. These differences
could be accounted for, at least in part, by the contrast between American and Japanese views of the position of the individual in ordinary family life. Based upon earlier research
and a review of the literature Caudill explained that:

> The relative conception of the infant would seem to
> be somewhat different in the two cultures. In Japan,
> the infant is more seen as a separate biological
> organism which from the beginning, in order to
> develop, needs to be drawn into interdependent re-
> lations with others. In America, the infant is more
> seen as a dependent biological organism which, in
> order to develop, needs to be made increasingly
> independent (1970:42).

Caudill offers the usual cautions about the need for
more work before definite conclusions can be made, but then
states that some major dimensions are clear. He says:

> There is an area of basic similarity for the infant
> and caretaker in both cultures centered around the
> infant's needs for sleep, food, and clothing, and the
> mother's caring for these needs. Beyond this, however,
> and in line with our predictions at the beginning of
> this paper, the greatest contrast, for both the infant
> and the mother, are between the two cultures. The
> American baby is more alone, is more active in the
> manipulation of his body and in the use of objects
> and is higher in vocalization. The American mother
> talks to her baby more, and seems more to encourage
> hime toward response and activity. The Japanese baby
> is less alone, and is both physically and vocally
> more quiet. The Japanese mother rocks her baby more
> and talks to him less. Her actions seem directed to

soothing and quieting the baby rather than encouraging
response and activity. These differences between the
cultures do not occur as isolated characteristics of
behavior but rather are interwoven in such a way that
the general patterning of behavior is different in the
two cultures (1970:69).

The question which now concerns us is the relevance of
these findings to our central problem, namely, the relation
between the environment, particularly cultural environment, and
the development of the individual. Caudill believes that in the
day by day repetition of the simple routines of life the differences in the patterning of behavior and emotional expression
leads "to different psychological and social results as a child
grows to be an adult in the two cultures." This conclusion is,
in itself, of major importance. It confirms the intricate
interdependence of organic and cultural processes in the initial
stages of being. Furthermore, it suggests that the direction
and pattern of subsequent stages of development have already
been set by the distinctive mould of cultural environment and
under normal circumstances this pattern will be extended and
strengthened as the individual moves through childhood.

Can we, however, extract a deeper understanding by
asking about the relationship between patterning and world view?
The evidence from anthropology leads us to accept congruences
between all aspects of culture, and between culture and personality. For example, the work of Bateson and Mead (1942)
among the Balinese showed how the dangerous consequences of the
free expression of emotion are successfully contained by child
rearing practices which direct and reward ritualized responses.
Bali is a society which prescribes rigid rules of behavior for
members of the social castes and status rankings within each
and also provides severe penalties for those who violate these.
In this society appropriate theatricality poses no threats nor
does it involve the individual emotionally, but compassion
evokes confusion and embarrassment. In Bali, as elsewhere,
the congruences between social structure, behavior, and personality become apparent to us.

The differential effect of the environment on the
infant established by Caudill for Americans and Japanese, and
substantiated by child training practices among the Balinese
may be verified at a simple level of observation for all cultures in definitions of maleness and femaleness through the
differential assignment of tasks, or in the distribution of
prestige associated with status ranking. Sex and status are
important components of a family system and are symbolically
expressed in juridical and religious formulations. These
conceptualizations may be counted as a part of the value system
and with time we might trace their congruences with other
values and their relationship with the social structure. From
such a description and analysis we could then abstract the

world view. The important point for us to recognize, however, is that there is a connection between the simple routines of life, such as those which are used in the care of infants, and the overarching conceptualizations which give meaning to behavior.

As the child acquires the facility of speech he also acquires the means by which he can abstract upon his experience, but always within the context which his culture prescribes. Language is itself a cultural instrument which in its vocabulary and structure reflects the identities, structure, and process of a world view. It is from the environment then that the infant and child acquires the kinesthetic, evaluative, and cognitive learning that he brings with him when he encounters the systematized learning of formal education. These learnings are congruent with the world view of those who were his caretakers as an infant and his other associates as he progressed into childhood.

When we come to examine the learning process in the schools, however, we are beset with a tangled situation. The environment of formal schooling may be, in its organization and culture, at greater or lesser variance with that from which the student comes and, if so, we may expect tensions and the need for adaptation which can take the form of rejection.

Those who teach have always been aware of differences in performance of their students. Some were bright, others dull, some were energetic and others lazy. When intelligence tests began to be used extensively about a half century ago the sorting of students on the basis of their performance gave us a presumed scientific basis which helped to explain the variation in the academic record. Unfortunately, the problem of individual differences turned out to be a bit more complex than could be met by this device. For one thing cultural variability was ignored. Allison Davis and others called attention to the fact that these tests favored children from one background and discriminated against those from another (Davis and Hess 1948). Then later Martin Mayer's survey of American schools turned up the fact that individual differences among teachers also had to be taken into account (Mayer 1961). His case study showed that when you joined an imaginative teacher with a group of students that the results could be extraordinary. Other studies indicate that children of middle class background respond to the school setting more favorably than those who are culturally divergent such as children of lower socio-economic classes or ethnic origin. The problem that confronts us is to determine if these responses are a function of the school environment and its curriculum, of the intelligence of children, of the background of the children, or of some determinable combination of the three.

The controversy surrounding intelligence and background has a tangled history spanning several decades of controversy.

The work of Allison Davis and Martin Deutsch is familiar to
anthropologists interested in the area. For example, Allison
Davis cites several studies which show that there is a general
increase in the average IQ test scores of Negro children which
correlates with length of residence in the city and the acquisition of linguistic skills (Davis 1951). The work of Martin
Deutsch with three and four year old Negro slum children in
New York gives us further insight. In an experimental program
which increased the manual and linguistic skills and enlisted
the sympathetic aid of parents, he was able to prepare these
children to enter their first year of school at a level of
readiness equal to that of the average child (Deutsch 1967).
Its basic assumption was that the cultural environment of low-
status children was deficient in preparing them for successfully meeting the requirements of formal schooling and hence a
special preliminary program was required.

        The most recent eruption in the continuing controversy
is Jensen's conclusion that performance of children on intelligence tests is a function of racial background or genetics.
An important symposium of the AAA challenged the logic of
Jensen's position and procedural assumptions which he employed
in his statistical analysis of presumably racial groups (Brace,
et al. 1971). More recent careful statistical studies of family
background in relation to intelligence performance have confirmed an opposite view that certain key variables of the background of children, when held constant, do account for variable
performance on IQ tests. Thus, Mercer discovered that when
certain sociocultural characteristics such as coming from less
crowded homes; having mothers who expected them to be educated
beyond high school; living in a home where head of household had
more than ninth grade education; when English was spoken all or
most of the time, and where the family was buying or owned its
own home, were the same for Chicanos, Blacks, and Anglos, the
measure of intelligence scores of the children were not different (Mercer 1971). In another study, Mayeske (1971) re-examined
the Coleman data and discovered that racial-ethnic differences
in composite scholastic achievement increasingly disappear as
one takes into account (holds constant) more and more social
conditions of children's environment. These studies do not
answer but only raise the question of the relationship between
the cultural perspective acquired in the family setting and the
adaptation to the school environment. For this purpose we draw
upon the Gans (1962) study of a West Side Boston settlement of
Italians and for contrast an upper-middle class suburb near
Toronto (Seeley, et al. 1956).

        The Italian residents in Boston preserved many details
of the village life from which they or their parents came,
particularly evident in the formation and functioning of the
family, in child rearing, and in their view of economic and
governmental institutions. These latter, external to and

controlled by those outside the local group, are viewed as
potentially disruptive and as exploitative and hence to be dealt
with cautiously and to be exploited in turn. Education and the
schools are seen in much the same perspective and it is recognized that their influence can lead an individual to deny his
allegiance to his group. Schooling is valued only as it prepares for vocational goals, and if it is successful here then
the adolescent turned adult is assured of an adequate income to
meet the needs of family and peer group. To the extent that
education conforms to the values of the group it is positively
valued, to the extent that it opposes or threatens the group its
values are rejected. If education proves to be the instrument
which provides for individual advancement it is disruptive of
group cohesion. Thus, in a perspective which honors adherence
to group values and perpetuation of the group, education as an
end in itself is of little consequence and to the extent that it
alienates the individual from the group it is objectionable.

The middle class values of the residents of Crestwood
Heights provide a distinctly different educational climate from
that encountered among the West End Italians. For these sub-
urbanites the schooling their children receive is an integral
part of the life career which, when combined with the cultural
perspective absorbed from within the bosom of the family, prepares each individual as an adult to participate in the public
world and to found his own family. In their equal concern for
individual achievement the school and the home possess complementary functions. There is none of the suspicious tension
which characterizes the view of education held by the Italian
villagers. In fact, the economic, governmental, and professional institutions provided the arena within which the Crestwood
Heights fathers, and eventually their sons when grown to man-
hood, contend for the honors and rewards of their society.

Although we lacked the specific information to compare
the organization and curriculum of the schools to which the
parents of these two groups sent their children, it seems safe
to assume that the apparent similarity between them is much
greater than any difference. Nevertheless, no matter how similar
in external detail, there is a vast difference between them
which appears as a function of the population they serve. These
differences are contained within the contrasting concepts of an
Italian or suburbanite family and its relations to the formal
institutions of the community, in the definition of life goals
and the resulting career patterns, and in the definition of the
purpose of formal education. When we examine these views, the
behavior associated with them, and the values to which they give
expression, we encounter a part of their world view. This
specific material was included in order to show how world view
shaped the response to institutions as instrumentalities of a
society and in this instance how the substance of formal education must be seen in its dynamic relationship with world view.

Enough has been said now for us to return to the problem of learning theory and its explanation of individual development. However adequate the stimulus-response paradigm may be for explaining the relationship between animal behavior and learning, if applied to humans, it fails to take into account the cultural dimension. The evidence contained within these several examples here utilized convincingly suggests that we need a new theory which accounts for environmental factors expressed through culture.

II. The Symposium

The symposium on "Learning and Culture" provided an opportunity for a representative sample of those who are deeply involved in the study of conditions and processes associated with the acquisition and transmission of culture to report their problems and their progress. The participants were drawn from several sub-areas within anthropology and across disciplinary boundaries and express the variety and range of work and thought now boiling up from the relatively young field of anthropology of education.

This symposium, however, is not a review of the field. It selectively samples from the growing edges of the field. (Some might argue that there is no substantial center from which a growing edge might extend; indeed it might be argued that the whole area of study is a raw growing edge.) We invited partici-pants to give papers who themselves are deeply involved in research at those growing edges and asked them to address them-selves to significant problems as they are viewed from the vantage point of their own work. The papers of the symposium, then, are rather like a stratified sampling of contributions drawn from the various sub-fields of anthropology which focus upon the theme of learning and culture. As is true of most new areas within the social sciences, the symposium is inter-disciplinary. Thus two of our participants claim an initial affiliation with psychology and sociology respectively, and only secondarily with anthropology. Others, who count themselves primarily as anthropologists may also identify with some closely associated discipline such as biology, linguistics, or sociology. Despite the variety of perspectives and emphases among these social scientists in their approach to problems of education to culture, we find overlapping conceptual discoveries and common problems. In these areas of overlapping concept, problem de-finition, and discovery can be discerned the shadow of a new profile of explanation and understanding in the field.

Although there is considerable variety in the kinds of problems which the separate contributors have chosen it also seems to us that there is an overriding communality among them in their general focus on learning and culture. It is possible, however, to distinguish three major sub-areas of concern. For

example, Poirier, Brukman, and Cole examine basic aspects of the
process of learning in its biologic, linguistic, and cognitive
dimensions. Another cluster of papers, those by Von Mering,
Moore, Howard, and Harrington, look at the process of socialization in the context of institutions and their rituals. The
raw contrast between situation in which socialization rituals
are appropriate and congruent and where they are alien and
enforced offers us the opportunity for a deeper perspective on
the consequences of the learning environment. There is a final
group of four papers whose authors are concerned with the
significance of understanding the educational process in the
context of social change. While Wax and Chance utilize cross-
cultural situations involving schooling, Cohen traces the
transformations which schools undergo due to deep societal
shifts, and Wilson encompasses all mankind in the broad evolutionary theory he advances.

Another dimension of culture and learning from which
the papers can be viewed is that of a continuum ranging from
undirected to directed learning. For example, Poirier, Brukman,
and Cole focus more on the processes of and methodologies for
examining learning rather than inducement or organized stimulation by older members of a social unit. While Von Mering,
Moore, Howard, and Harrington do not ignore undirected learning
they focus on widely employed devices such as rituals, arranged
situations, or patterned social relationships which induce,
direct, and stimulate certain "learnings." The papers by Wax,
Chance, and Cohen carry us further along this continuum to the
explicit and organized directed learning, with its consequent
emphasis, even predominant emphasis, on teaching and on organized
arrangements to increase the possibility of the occurrence of
certain kinds of learning. Wilson offers a clear delineation of
this continuum by grouping in broad categories all experiences
of the individual through social awareness and socialization to
education. Education, he says is set off from the others, not
by learning, but by teaching. A similar continuum has been
formulated in other ways (Herskovitz 1954; Wallace 1961; Cohen
1971), but Wilson's statement of it is a useful one to use in
comparing types of cultures and types of education. This
cursory analysis suggests that any proposed conceptual framework of culture and learning must also address itself to consideration of the degree to which learning is directed by others.

This quick overview should assist in comprehending the
contextual relevance of the fuller commentaries which follow.
For each group of papers, of course, there are specific considerations which should be kept in mind. In order to make
explicit the dynamics of the learning process, for example, the
research must explore the relationships between the setting or
external environment, genetic capabilities and maturational
sequences, the social structure and activities of the group, and
where human societies are concerned the culture. From such an

xviii

examination should come explanations of phylogenetic adaptions, ontogenetic development, and comparative variation. It seems eminently sensible that our search should begin with the non-human primates.

What can careful scrutiny of the learning process and socialization patterns among non-human primates contribute to our understanding of humans? Poirier's comparative sweep of the non-human primates firmly establishes the biological base of behavior, but he also establishes that the development of genetic capabilities are a function of several other variables. These include the ecology or conditions of the setting; the interactive pattern of nurturance and dependence (primarily with the mother); the play with peers to establish sex identity, behavioral maturity, and dominance ranking; the response to social structure and status through contact with the adult males; and the group wisdom deposited in habituated responses. Basically, however, socialization is a consequence of interaction. Initially it arises from the reciprocal stimulation between mother and infant in their linked nurturant-dependence roles followed by play activity with peers when skills mature, sex identity is established, and the dominance hierarchy emerges. From adult males the young learns the social structure of the group with its status hierarchy.

The inseparability of biology and learning are manifested in many different ways. Poirier points out, for example, that as one progresses toward the human end of the primate continuum there is encountered a lengthened period of dependency and an expanded opportunity and need for learning. Certainly the behavior associated with the more complex social groups calls for a greater flexibility and wider range of adaptive behavior. Even the shortened nipple length may have been a contributing factor in primate evolution.

But it is to the crucial role of peer-group play activity that Poirier directs our attention. It is through interaction with one's peers that the young takes the first hesitant steps which eventually lead to the dissolution of its dependent bond with the mother. The repetitive activity shapes responses and establishes identities. In fact, Poirier suggests that the freely expressed curiosity and high activity level associated with play may account for the phylogenetic position which primates have achieved and that the "human child may be at the apex of this pyramid, as demonstrated by its many and varied play activities."

When we come to examine the learning process among humans we must take into account a new and significant variable-- language as symbols. Man's propensity for culture and for the use of language as a vehicle of socialization expands enormously his adaptive capability beyond the habituated responses acquired through interaction of non-human primates. We do not suggest any loss in the potency of learning from interaction, but the use of language for teaching and learning introduces a new element of fluidity in the choice of social settings in which learning occurs, as Brukman's paper makes clear.

Although Brukman directs his discussion toward methodological questions, his approach harbors a position on language acquisition that could give rise to waves of controversy were it set forth explicitly and extended by analogy to culture acquisition. He metaphorically phrases his position by saying that "all normal human children are language learning machines preequipped with an apparatus which generates theories about the linguistic structures that they are exposed to." This position is grounded already in an enormous body of research but a persuasive fact in its favor is the observation that by about six years of age, "the child has mastered the essentials of his native language," without, as well as with, benefit of directed instruction regarding phonology, morphology, or syntax (Langacker, 1968). From this point of view the function of experience is not to shape language, for not only the capability but also the essential structures of language is innate; but that experience activates the linguistic competence with which we are born.

This radical rationalistic reversal in the empiricistic direction of our research and thinking on the relationship between language acquisition and learning, as well as culture acquisition and learning, sets us off in new directions in search of answers to new problems, and sets in motion new thoughts about old conclusions. Thus, consider the cultural ethnographers long reliance on "imitation" as the main and predominant process to describe culture acquisition. In the heyday of behavioral theories of learning based on expericicistic assumptions this explanation seemed simple minded, naive, even lazy-headed. But, in light of the idea that language learning is an ontogenetic process, one could reconsider this bias toward "imitation." One might reflect on the proposition that culture acquisition, or acquisition of some significant set domains of culture is based on the same inborn cognitive structures that language acquisition depends upon. This is not the occasion for following out the full analogical implications of this line of thought, but there is no doubt that the prospect is exciting and potentially significant for a theory of culture acquisition.

Brukman raises a methodological problem inherent in the research procedures usually employed to investigate language, when one is interested in understanding and explaining language acquisition among children. The characteristic introspective methodology employed by linguistics in exploring features of language acquisition and its relationship to context, Brukman suggests, cannot be used when one is investigating very young children particularly at the ages at which they are behaving in a most interesting way with respect to acquisition of language, for example, at the ages of 1, 2, 3, and 4. Moreover, as

Brukman points out directed teaching of language behavior in other cultures seems to be concerned mainly with teaching that certain language characteristics, and the attendant behaviors, must be associated with certain social situations. Contrary to expectations based on studies of language acquisition, primarily among middle-class families speaking English, French, or Russian, the acquisition by children of correct speech is not a matter of concern of the adults in many other societies. Thus the assumption that language competency is primarily a function of directed teaching reflects our society's emphasis on directed teaching, and is one more instance of the extent to which our own cultural categories and assumptions flow into our scientific endeavors. At the same time Brukman emphasizes that we can't confine attention even in our own society to the mother-child or even adult-child relationship, and hope to explore all the experiences in language that have significant learning value for the young.

When we come to the paper presented by Michael Cole we encounter an entirely new dimension of the problem. Among the several lively issues which he provokes, the central one concerns the relationship between anthropology and psychology in their respective approaches to the study of cognition and culture. (There is a fundamental disagreement between these two disciplines respecting the relative merits of experimental versus natural history approaches in research.) Utilizing examples based upon his own research among the Kpelle of Liberia he demonstrates the mutual advantage which arises from such collaboration. His findings also lend support to the anthropological contention that learning is structured, albeit situational and patterned. It has been from this vantage that the anthropological challenge has come which questions the worth of tests which measure performance but which psychologists use to erect schemes of developmental levels or compare groups. Although Cole recognizes the validity of the challenge he still contends that rapprochement can lead to a sounder base for understanding intellectual processes.

To assert that anthropology has nothing to learn from psychology would constitute an arrogance based on ignorance. But whether or not psychological procedures can contribute to the problems as defined within anthropology requires an examination of contrasting assumptions and defined problems. For example, no rapprochement is possible as long as cognition is treated as a property or attribute. And there is no evidence that psychologists can or will abandon the immense investment they have made in performance determination, nor in the theories of cognition which support such a position. Cole recognizes the dilemma although it is not clear that he has resolved the issue, but where he invents experiments based on natural situations he may well make a contribution of immense significance. It is possible, even probable, that in the process he will decide that the terminological identities which psychologists have created are a culture-bound burden and must also be dumped.

Cole implies this possibility when he suggest that the experimental routines for eliciting information on cognition and intellect are themselves culturally based. The studies of cognitive anthropologists have made us aware of emic categories, but Cole points out that an adequate cross-cultural experimental psychology requires equally careful attention to the situations that elicit certain categories and their attendant meanings.

* * * * * *

The papers we have grouped in Part II, The Rituals of Socialization, are widely divergent from each other in many respects. Their authors examine behavioral pieties among Euro-American middle class families, the process which inducts the children of a Guatemalan elite to an aristocratic life style, the contrasting and often conflicting experiences and behavioral expectations of native Hawaiian children in their families and in school, and the unintended socialization of ethnic slum children in a New York City school. Although there are great geographical and social distances which separate the subjects of these various researches, and although the specific focus of each author is distinct, these differences become superficial when we compare the conceptual problems with which they are all concerned.

The core problems with which each author wrestles exhibit a remarkable similarity among them. For example, there is a common concern with the relationship between the process of socialization in its situational setting and the consequences as manifested in behavior and the acquisition of a world view. There are problems of learning related to inter- and intra-generational and to cross-cultural situations. There are questions of situationally defined behavior and its adaptive or maladaptive consequences. There are questions of the appropriateness of culture-linked rituals in cross-cultural socialization. There are contrasts in the power of symbols and behavior learned fron one's intimates and those which are deployed from formal institutions. In sum, we have here a set of papers which offer rich comparative pickings.

In the first of these papers Von Mering carries us to the behavioral heart of the socializing functions of the primary group to reveal for us the significances of ordered and repetitive ritual activity. He classifies behavior as routine, procedure, or program if associated with problem-solving, and labelled habitual stance, transactional performance, and behavioral piety or social message if associated with learnings of social identity. His classificatory scheme, however, is only intended to be a device to explore a much larger and more fundamental question, namely, understanding the ordered process through which humanity is learned and transmitted. In this search he comes to view behavioral pieties as the micro-mirrors of widely prevalent social realities which, in their iterative expression within the primary group, provide a fundamental socialization of the individual not elsewhere obtainable. If such a view is validated by research we are in possession of an insight of immense consequence. Not only does it add further support to the view that learning is a culturally realized process, but also that the patterning of learning is specific to the social and cultural context. Furthermore, acknowledgement of such a dynamic would bring extensive restructuring of the developmental life-cycle of the individual, and of prevalent programs of consciously directed socialization, some of which we would discard as being either ineffectual or harmful. So also would our search for the causes of abnormal behavior be redirected and remedial programs be reconstituted.

Von Mering also directs attention to the use of ritual in socialization. He emphasizes the teaching possibilities of ritual, particularly in small family households in contemporary society. The ritual behavior, what he calls iterative activities, can become the basis of both personal character as well as of the transmission and maintenance of specialized or generalized social response systems throughout life. Defining socialization as "a matter of learning about man-made structure," he considers for us how family ritual can be used as a practical way of teaching children about social reality and at the same time can provide a means of family control and continuity. However, as he points out, in order to do this the family must maintain some schedule of availability of its differing members for one another. He suggests that the household scheduling of persons in time and space is a fundamental feature of social organization that might well be used in cross-cultural comparisons of transmission.

Ritual, of course, represents a regularized scheduling of activity and personnel in time and space. Insofar as family customs carry the mark of a particular sociocultural class or ethnic heritage, family rituals bear on the question of continuity of cultural diversity within the private family world in complex cultures. Thus, although in the public world there may appear to have been the complete disappearance of a cultural tradition, it may be maintained and continued in the private world of family ritual.

Moore's analysis also examines family ritual or iterative behavior but in the contrasting context of an elite in Guatemala. He describes how traditions appropriate to an aristocratic position and life style are perpetuated. Enculturation and continuity are managed by means of small scale rituals that include of course the critical scheduling of people in certain places at certain times. He also points out how new conditions of life, which disrupt the scheduling, may indeed lead to the modification of certain elements of the enculturated pattern. He illustrates then the continuing tension between intra-generational adaptation and inter-generational transmission in changing societies, and thus perhaps in all societies.

Some transmitted patterns which may have been adaptive in the past continue to be valued and rationalized thus insulating them from the selective effects of adaptive efficiency. Although some of the younger generation pick up intra-generational adaptive behavior they may themselves transmit to their own children valued traditional modes of patterned behavior and perception which they received from another generation but which are no longer adaptive. Thus Moore suggests that the functional assumption that maladaptive cultural patterns will cease to be transmitted within the generation in which they are maladaptive, may be too easy an explanation. Cultural transmission is not always the handmaiden of adaptive selectivity.

The evidence from Moore's analysis suggests that cultural transmission, or enculturation--conscious and unconscious arrangements for learning--may present the younger generation with some cultural patterns that are ill adapted to new conditions of life, as well as with patterns that are nicely adapted to that generation's life conditions. Under these circumstances there may be intra-generational adaptation that appears as a discontinuity in the behavior of the new generation. But it must also be recognized, that that generation may attempt to transmit the earlier pattern rather than the intra-generationally adapted pattern to its own succeeding generation. Thus while one might insist that in the long run the patterns transmitted will be adaptive, in the short run, perhaps of several generations and certainly within one generation, a different picture of the nature of adaptation could emerge.

Recognition of the uneven course of culture transmission and our hidden assumptions concerning transmission and acquisition has arisen because culture transmission does not ordinarily occur in a homogeneous cultural setting. In the contemporary world transmission, particularly directed teaching, more often involves a cultural interface of at least two, and sometimes several cultures or sub-cultures. Thus to investigate the conditions for learning and culture one must, as we have already suggested, take into account the conditions which affect the transmission of culture.

Howard's discussion of the 'Aina Punehana raises the question of just what culture transmission means when native Hawaiian children experience the cultural assault of a formal school setting. In that context it is clearly affected by the political stratification along ethnic lines which is also paralleled in the economic institutions in the uneven distribution of access to occupations and income. A similar pattern turns up in the educational institutions which are administered and dominated not by those from 'Aina Punehana but by others who are either of Caucasian or Japanese-American ancestry. Can this be counted as an example of transmission in which an older generation inducts a younger generation into a cultural system? Not only are the transmitters in this instance of Caucasian and Japanese ancestry, but they transmit a set of behavior patterns associated with middle-class Americana, according to Howard. In the past we have viewed teaching under these conditions not as culture transmission, but as some form of acculturation or assimilation. This mode of dealing with the problem, however, can stifle our progress in understanding the nature of culture transmission in complex and pluralistic cultures.

If we begin with a different assumption, the assumption that children are capable of learning more than one cultural system simultaneously, under certain conditions, then our attention is directed to examining the conditions under which the children encounter each of the traditions they might learn.

Thus, whether learning a cultural tradition is culture transmission or assimilation, is not a question of whether the tradition is drawn from a second culture, but is an expression of the structural conditions affecting the relationships between (and among) the social groups which carry the traditions. If those relationships are tolerant, accepting, and peaceful, then children may simultaneously learn, and learn to keep situationally separate, two or even more than two cultural systems. If social relationships between the social groups bearing the cultures are hostile, then learning the initial one may be a case of transmission, but learning the second involves assimilation and rejection of the first. Howard provides us with an instance of the latter case when he describes the denigration of the child's primary cultural tradition in the school setting. Thus the interface at which another cultural tradition is presented to the children is experienced as a hostile encounter. Moreover the intent of the school personnel and strangers to the children is to modify behavior instilled by the primary culture. Under these conditions, as Howard points out, children who are already well along the way in the acquisition of a primary culture engage in certain strategies and tactics to resist the school's transmissions. In their resistance to middle-class Americana they become defenders of the continuity of their primary culture. Indeed the resistance to the secondary culture is a political act, for the children in doing so are concerned with the external relations of their primary group.

Much of what has been said about the relationship between the social setting and school organization of 'Aina Punehana in Hawaii applies with equal pertinency to the schools serving the multi-ethnic working class ghetto area in New York City which provides the locale for the paper by Harrington although his explicit focus on political socialization differs from that chosen by Howard. Harrington's contextual problem was to discover if the programs of the schools developed some political efficacy that would redress the failure of their parents to compete successfully for the rewards which a society offers. He concluded that there was very little positive good that schools contributed; instead they did much harm.

However valuable the findings of the research by him and his associates may be the significant contribution of their efforts for our purposes is lodged in their analytical procedures. They examined the socialization processes in the setting of the classroom, in the peer groupings of playground and lunchroom, in situations contrasting symbolic definitions versus objective reality, and in the content analysis of textbooks used to instruct about political and governmental processes. Only in situations involving peer groups did the learning experience approximate the reality of the situation so that playground, for example, provided the setting for learning both the rules and practice of political skills. In contrast, the aggressive resistance of many pupils to the demands of the classroom limited greatly, if it did not inhibit, achievement of formal teaching objectives. There were continual discrepancies between the ritual formulations of the school authorities and actual experience, contradictions that impressed on students that their role was to be docile and that in the allocation of premiums some were privileged and some not. Furthermore, textbooks presented an idealized version of politics that was counter to experience. Significantly, Harrington suggests that the peer system provided the flexible cushion that permitted the rigid school structure to be perpetuated.

Harrington states that the democratic aspects of schools are functionally important to a society if the controlling segment in that society must anticipate resorting to undemocratic acts to control citizens. This is accomplished, he says, because the undemocratic features of schools build in a sense of legitimacy for such means. Another curiosity that Harrington points our regarding the political socialization of minority and ethnically different groups is that the political ideas which they are taught are more mythologized, more idealized and less realistic, than are the political ideas taught to those who are children of people of superior economic and political positions. Harrington describes the special character of some of the "myth-making" that is involved in dressing up the reality of political situations. Thus, not only are political leaders presented to the poor and disadvantaged as being always honest, always dependable, etc., but educators in these settings engage in and spread the illusion that all goes well. At the same time, the extracurricular opportunities of middle and upper-class schools, in the form of peer dominated activities and subsystems, assure that these children will have the opportunity to learn the organizational patterns that will be used and subsequently maintain position and control (Burnett 1968).

The structures and currents that contribute to the complexity of the socialization process are indeed impressive.

But recurring similarities of basic problems presented in this paper and in the preceeding ones should be noted. These are the questions about the importance of situation, inter- and intra-generational interactions, the congruency between ritual and practice, cross-cultural perspectives, and the contrast between behavior learned in natural groups and that received from formal institutions.

* * * * * *

The study of the transmission and acquisition of culture cannot be separated from the main body of anthropological concepts and theory, from relevant developments in other behavioral sciences, nor from the changes and social movements of the world in which we live. Thus one of the objectives of this symposium was to seek the contribution of those who would address themselves to some of these aspects. The papers of this section do just that. They range from a critical reevaluation by Wax of some basic anthropological concepts as they bear upon ethnic studies programs, to a program oriented analysis of educational strategies available to minority peoples by Chance, to a careful analysis of the sweeping structural changes in American society and their implications for education by Cohen, and to a carefully constructed evolutionary schema embracing all levels of societal complexity by Wilson. These papers not only broaden the perspective of the field of anthropology and education but they add to our knowledge and illuminate the contextual implications of some of the micro-studies reported upon earlier.

Ethnic studies programs, Wax suggests, specifically Indian studies programs, bear directly on the question of their relation to the preservation of cultural traditions. While ethnic studies programs within the schools are geared to redress long neglect and denigration of the children's native background, or at least this should be their primary function according to Wax, the programs themselves offer positions and economic resources that in some ways help improve the economic position of Indians as compared with other groups in society. Wax insists that the purpose of such programs is not to enculturate the younger generation of Indians "to return to an outmoded or deteriorated reservation environment." In giving the young Indian an idea of who he is and who his ancestors were, the Indian defines himself to the other groups. Thus ethnic studies programs symbolize a respect by the educator for the skills, traditions, and perceptions which the child does bring with him from his home as representative of his community. But ethnic studies programs contribute more than this. Multicultural transmission efforts in complex societies present optional modes of adaptation when situations demand alternative ways of customary behavior.

In the course of his discussion, Wax raises the knotty problem of the concept of cultural continuity. He points out that anthropologists once tended to believe that existing culture traits or trait-complexes were virtually impregnable to change. He notes that ethno-historians have begun to discover that change is continuous, and a people in the sense of a continuing group may exist as a social and political entity beyond the point-in-time at which it stops practicing what anthropologists may regard as definitive traits of the culture of its ancestors.

The view that Indian cultures of the United States are becoming extinct or are degenerating into a culture of poverty is a position based on this assumption regarding continuity of traits. But this conception is a static one and it tends to discount the significance of adaptation in the continuity of culture. Thus when the North American Indians of the 18th and 19th century worked out a variety of adaptations to their new and changing biological and social environments, adaptations that incorporated and involved syncretic processes were then regarded as something less than authentic culture. This position denigrates the present strivings of these people to create new adaptations. Yet, says Wax, "Those whose grandchildren survived are still Indians, or Native Americans but they no longer practice exactly (italics are ours) the same ways of their ancestors."

In light of Wax's critical comments, it is a hard truth but one we must consider, that anthropologists have contributed to what Chance calls the "culture of silence" of minorities, particularly Indian minorities in Canada and the United States. Indeed along with minorities demythologizing their understanding of the reality of the relationship between their own culture and other dominant sub-cultures in the society, anthropologists may need to and may be in the process of demythologizing those theories that have helped rationalize the kind of anomic silence in which most Indian groups have moved until recent times. These minorities have recently been going through changing levels of self-consciousness and self-definition. At the level of silence such groups are convinced that they are descended from an "authentic" culture, as they survive and adapt to conditions of control by a more powerful social group.

Under certain conditions Chance believes these groups reorient their conceptions of themselves vis-a-vis a dominant culture and begin to demythologize their conceptions of a society that has created their dependency. As Chance notes educators have actually helped to feed these groups' sense of dependency and deficiency. But insofar as education aids economic access, and part of the demythologizing has been to recognize the significance of access to economic resources, education in the minds of such minorities becomes a lever to raise themselves to the third level of consciousness. They are now ready to attempt

to transform the social institutions and cultural rules that
affect their lives. They escape from their former dependency
as they gain control over their own group life. This control
is in part realized through control of education. Even more
important is the effort to control channels of access to new
social, economic, and political resources within the society
through schooling. In summary then both Wax and Chance agree
on the significant role that formal education may play in the
transformation of ethnic relations in complex industrial
societies.

Both Cohen and Chance point to the curious paradox that
individualization, and the emphasis on individual performance,
assures greater conformity than does performance and work based
on groups or shared productivity. Chance also believes that
individualization leads to greater control by adults and greater
conformity from the students. Earlier, Harrington had noted
that individualized competition was not used to organize resources on playgrounds, a situation where students themselves
were in control of the rules. Considering swings as a scarce
resource, an associate of his found that in times of greatest
demands kids act not to "maximize possession of a swing, but
rather to maximize access to a swing." From another aspect
Cohen argues that individualization while designed to promote
individual learning rates of the pupils does little to enhance
characteristics linked to ethnic origins or to common histories.

Cohen argues further that public school organization,
and its associated pedagogical ideology has been historically,
and is at the moment, a reflection of the technological characteristics of the society -- specifically its occupational
structure. In recent years school functions have been expanded
to incorporate new services to serve special populations, such
as the physically and mentally handicapped. At the same time
there was a shift in emphasis from the transmission of knowledge and skills to one of service to formerly neglected groups,
such as the poor. The schools were organized otherwise in the
era of primary industry (agriculture) or secondary industry
(factories); but now that tertiary industries, that is, the
service occupations dominate the society one finds the school
increasingly reflecting service orientation in its objectives.
Cohen associates learning with this condition of the environment
on the assumption that cognitive expectations and the methods of
cognitive and language organization are reciprocally supportive
of the methods and patterns of social organization. She also
asks, however, if special welfare and social service functions
which have risen to such prominence in school structure in most
urban settings at least will act as a divisive force in sub-
cultural identity or whether they will, on the contrary, assist
in increasing the sense of sub-cultural identity. If we accept
Chance's position we would conclude that a service approach will
assist minorities gain control of culture transmission and access

to the resources of certain other institutions in the society. On the other hand it can be argued that if the minorities begin to control the process of transmission and the content of transmission in the schools, that they will decrease, not increase, their chances of access to economic and political resources of the society.

While these later papers in some ways seem far removed from the theme of learning and culture, they do focus on the consequences which flow from the organization of teaching and learning. Indeed they are clearly part of the problem of culture transmission and of the problem of understanding the conditions of the nature of transmission itself. In the final paper Wilson's evolutionary schema reminds us that evolution of education has been characterized not just by emergence of new forms, but that complex societies of the modern era are mainly characterized by a whole range of modes of transmission and education. Thus his work suggests that while we concentrate on some important conceptual problems and the relationship of learning and teaching to culture, we might also assess our tendency to focus mainly on directed teaching and formal situations for teaching in modern industrial states to the neglect of the other modes of learning.

Since Wilson looks at culture and education in both time depth and in comparative perspective, it will be useful to take note of certain important propositions that his evolutionary schema generates, propositions that invite further empirical inquiry and testing. His typology of education is based on two conditions, each of three factors: the first is a specialization or nonspecialization of the teacher involved in transmitting culture; the second factor is whether all individuals of a given age-sex category, or only some individuals of a given age-sex category, receive the transmission; the third factor is the social purpose of the culture transmission, or whether it is intended to equip the individual for a specific, or specialized, position in his society, or to equip him for a position in the society that all individuals of a given age-sex category will hold (e.g. father, voting citizen, housewife, etc.). The system of categories which Wilson presents is generated by relating types of levels of cultural development to his typology of education, a scale which reflects increasing structural differentiation and increasing functional specialization. He finds that it is not entirely true that the least differentiated forms of education are found at the lowest levels of cultural development, because this sequence does not hold in a unilineal fashion throughout the scale. Yet this result is consistent with the discovery by others that sub-systems of culture do not follow a unilinear course of development. But speaking in general he did find the following propositions to be well grounded enough to invite further research.

Once a type of education emerges it tends to persist,

xxx

and is found at higher levels of cultural development
as well as lower levels of cultural development.
New types of education are additive rather than
substitutive, with some exceptions. (See types 3
and type 7 in Wilson's paper)
Each culture level is associated with a new emergent
type of education, with the exception of the family
and apprentice types of education, both of which are
found in some societies at the earliest cultural
levels.
Each higher culture level is associated with more
types of education than the immediately preceding
culture level; or no culture level has fewer types
of education than the immediately preceding level.

These propositions add up to the observation that new
educational practices appear with the development of new culture levels, and it underlines the importance of determining
what are the functional requisites at a given level of culture
which generate, or give rise to a different type of education.
This problem invites us to develop a general theory of education
in culture that can be tested first through retrodiction, prior
to testing by prediction.

The framework offered by Wilson also allows us to view
many of the papers in this symposium as empirical "stuff" for
exploring the problem of functional prerequisites. Thus Cohen's
paper spells out the proposition that the social organization of
schools and their linguistic and cognitive characteristics reflect the changing occupational structure complements and complements and further details Wilson's discussion of the same
level of culture. Wilson points out that education of teacher-
all individuals-general type is related to the societal conditions of a rapidly changing, highly developed technology that
requires that people be trained for a wide variety of specializations, many of which cannot be anticipated during the period
of education. Cohen suggests additionally that this type of
education has also been put to providing, or trying to provide,
services to special groups within the society, a function which
she is not yet sure can be handled by schools engaged in Wilson's
type 8 education. The type of education that was suited to
providing specialized services of this sort, is type 5, teacher-
some individuals-general, a type that first appears with the
development of advanced nuclear centered cultures; that is, the
stage which we usually described as emergent civilization. This
type of education continues to exist in our society, but mainly
in the form of private education, e.g. Groton, not in the public
educational sector. Eventually, however, the validity of
Wilson's scheme must be tested by further research and by its
heuristic value in assisting a meaningful overview of the
problem.

*   *   *   *   *   *

The papers, as we warned in the opening paragraph, range widely, and thereby, make a summary a hard task indeed; but that reflects the very difficulty facing the anthropological study of education at its present stage. The variety and range of that study requires a simplified conceptualization that casts wide ranging descriptive accounts, seemingly contradictory conclusions, and miscellaneous generalizations, into new and meaningful interrelation and integration with one another. Our symposium suggests the processes of culture transmission will flower in new discoveries and understanding provided language and culture acquisition receive special research attention; provided we develop new, ingenious methodologies for studying children in natural settings in the process of acquisition; provided we are not prevented by past prejudices and habituation from combining naturalistic field study with culture-wise and culture-fair experimentation, and vice-versa; provided we do not confine our conceptualization to a uniclutural setting, but instead face squarely the conditions of cultural pluralism, culture continuity, and culture change; provided we incorporate into our thinking consideration of the genetic and the physiological in relation to the cognitive and affective dimensions of culture; and finally provided we give careful conceptual consideration to the social, structural, and ecological conditions that vary and determine the relationships among the facts of transmission. We also must recognize that in the main our papers have focused on problems of eidos and less upon ethos of culture. This symposium then has emphasized culture and cognition, much more than culture and affective development, in contrast to what might have been true ten years earlier, even with the same thematic title, learning and culture. This probably reflects a general focus of the various disciplines that bear on and contribute to this domain. Insofar as the anthropology of education, involves culture transmission and insofar as culture transmission concerns the relationship between culture and the individual. The emphasis in the immediate future will be on the cognitive aspects of that relationship, rather than upon the affective aspects of that relationship. Eventually, however, when we solved a significant set of cognitively based problems, we shall no doubt circle back around, clothed with new understanding, to address ourselves, to old problems we never solved but merely left behind for a time.

REFERENCES

Bateson, Gregory
    1958   Naven. Stanford, Stanford University Press.

Bateson, Gregory and Margaret Mead
    1942   Balinese Character: A Photographic Analysis.

New York, New York Academy of Sciences.

Brace, C. L., G. R. Gamble, and J. T. Bond, eds.
     1971   Washington, D.C., Anthropological Studies, No.
                   8, AAA.

Burnett, Jacquetta
     1968   Ceremony, Rites, and Economy in the Student
                   System of an American High School. In Human
                   Organization, Vol. 28, No. 1, Spring, 1969,
                   pages 1-8.

Caudill, William and Helen Weinstein
     1970   Maternal Care and Infant Behavior in Japanese
                   and American Urban Middle Class Families. In
                   Families in East and West: Socialization
                   Process and Kinship Ties, ed. by Reuben Hill
                   and René Konig. The Hague, Mouton.

Cohen, Y.
     1971   The shaping of Men's Minds: Adaptations to
                   the Imperatives of Culture: In Anthropological
                   Perspectives on Education, Murray Wax, et al.
                   eds, New York, Basic Books pages 19-50.

Davis, Allison
     1951   Intelligence and Cultural Differences: A Study
                   of Cultural Learning and Problem-solving.
                   Chicago, University of Chicago Press.

Davis, Allison and Robert Hess
     1948   Social Class Influences upon Learning.
                   Cambridge, Harvard University Press.

Deutsch, Martin
     1967   The Disadvantaged Child. New York, Basic Books.

Gans, Herbert J.
     1962   The Urban-Villagers: Group and Class in the
                   Life of Italian-Americans. New York, Free Press
                   of Glencoe.

Herskovits, M.
     1954   Man and His Works. New York, Alfred Knopf.

Kimball, Solon T.
     1965   The Transmission of Culture. In Educational
                   Horizons, Vol. 43. Washington D.C. Pp. 161-
                   186.

Langacker, Ronald W.
    1968   Language and Its Structure. New York, Harcourt
                Brace and World, Inc.

Mayer, Martin
    1961   The Schools. New York, Harper and Brothers.

Mayeske, G. W.
    1971   Exploration of Racial-Ethnic Differences in
                Achievement Test Scores, Washington, D.C.,
                Office of Education.

Mercer, J. R.
    1971   Pluralistic Diagnosis in the Evaluation of
                Blacks and Chicanos, A Procedure for Taking
                Sociocultural Variables into Account in Clinical
                Assessment; Paper presented at meetings of the
                American Psychological Association, Washington,
                D.C.

Seeley, John R., R. Alexander Sim, and Elizabeth W. Loosley
    1956   Crestwood Heights: A Study of the Culture of
                Suburban Life. New York, Basic Books.

Wallance, A
    1961   Culture and Personality. New York, Random
                House.

I. THE LEARNING PROCESS

SOCIALIZATION AND LEARNING AMONG NONHUMAN PRIMATES

Frank E. Poirier
Ohio State University

Introduction

This paper discusses some of the processes and results of socialization and learning among nonhuman primates. The task is to isolate some of the variables to help build an evolutionary scheme. Until recently, potential contributions of biologically-oriented explanations of social development, and social behavior generally, were largely ignored or misunderstood. Simmel (1970) notes that as an interest in the biological aspects of socialization has increased, and its importance recognized, there has been an acceleration of interdisciplinary research and communication. Such cooperation has raised the level of sophistication in the use of biologically oriented concepts and explanations. Furthermore, the attitude that it is not useful to search for origins of the socialization process in the behavior of other animals, especially nonhuman primates, because they cannot be shown to possess culture is not germane. In fact, the denial of culture among some nonhuman primates is arguable. In any event, such biases impair understanding the nature of socialization and learning (i.e., Clausen, 1968; Goslin, 1969; Shimahara, 1970).

It is often harder to define the nonhuman primate socialization process than it is to isolate its consequences. The major limitation for establishing a theoretical framework is the lack of longitudinal behavioral studies. Except for some laboratory studies, and studies by Japanese primatologists (i.e., Itani, 1958, 1959; Itani, et al., 1963; Kawai, 1958a, 1958b; Kawamura, 1958), and on the Cayo Santiago rhesus colony (i.e., Koford, 1963; Sade, 1965, 1967; Vessey, 1971), where most animals and genealogies are known, most nonhuman primate field studies last between 12 and 24 months. This hardly gives enough time to fully comprehend the socialization and learning processes. Therefore, much of our theoretical framework is derived from socialization studies on humans (Child, 1954; Clausen, 1968; Erickson, 1950; Freud, 1923, 1930), dogs (Scott, 1945, 1950, 1958), cats (Rosenblatt, et al., 1961), goats (Collias, 1956), sheep and other ungulates (Altmann, 1956). This is a highly diverse group of subjects, at best.

Original models of the socialization process dealt pri-

3

marily with the critical periods hypothesis expounded by Lorenz
(1937), Scott and Marston (1950), Scott (1958), and Riesen (1961).
Lorenz's critical periods model, based on his work with geese,
seems too simplistic an approach when dealing with nonhuman primates. There is, after all, no inherent reason why data on cats,
fish, ducks, chickens, etc. can be applied equally well to complex social animals such as the nonhuman primates. There are
significant differences between such vertebrates and the nonhuman primates, differences which are exemplified in the complex
primate social orders. Complex nonhuman primate social groups
add dimensions not present in many phylogenetically lower animals. Studies of sensory functions and imprinting when compared with studies of primate infants suggest that the critical
periods become less fixed in time and more diffuse in nature as
one moves across the phylogenetic scale.

The socialization process refers to an exceedingly wide
range of complex phenomena. As used here, socialization refers
to the sum total of an individual's past social experiences
which, in turn, may be expected to shape future social behavior.
Socialization is that process linking an ongoing society to a
new individual. Through socialization, a group passes its social traditions and life-ways to succeeding generations. Socialization insures that adaptive behavior will not have to be
"rediscovered" anew each generation.

The factors impinging upon the socialization process
are complex and varied. Since the individual is the outcome,
the "product", of a given socialization process, it is appropriate to investigate the impinging variables vertically (in
terms of time) and horizontally (in terms of social interactions).
The consequences of socialization depend not only upon the individual's original genetic material and the degree to which
climate, nurturance, and other factors permit realization of
that potential, but also upon the behavior of others with whom
the individual is or has been in regular contact (Poirier,
1972).

The Importance of Social Living

Primate socialization, and learning, is influenced by
certain social and biological characteristics. Most primates
live in highly complex, bisexual, year-around social groups of
varying size. Group characteristics vary, and the degree of
sociality, dominance, sexuality, and interanimal relationships
differ; however, most primates spend most of their lives in
close association with conspecifics. Within the social group
an animal learns to express its biology and adapt to its sur-
roundings. Differences in primate societies depend upon the
species' biology, and to a great extent upon the circumstances
in which an individual lives and learns. The composition of
the social group, and the particular balance of interanimal

4

relationships, constitutes the nature of the social environment within which a youngster learns and matures.

Troop, or social life, is not equally important for all primates. Amongst Nilgiri langurs social relations are not oriented primarily toward individual protection by cooperative group action, but instead by an individual's dashing through the nearest tree. Why then does the Nilgiri langur, if the animals do not take full advantage of the opportunities which group living normally offers in the form of grooming, play and protective behavior, still live in social groups? Washburn and Hamburg (1965) suggest that a primary raison d'etre for a group existence is learning. The group is the center of knowledge and experience far exceeding that of its individual constituents. Within the group experience is pooled and generations linked. In the social context an animal learns what foods to eat, what behavioral patterns to employ, who the existing predators are, and the correct usage of the communication matrix. An animal learns its mode of survival by living in a troop where it benefits from the shared knowledge of the species (Poirier, 1970a, 1971). Slow development in isolation means disaster for the individual and extinction for the species (Harlow, 1963; Mason, 1963, 1965).

Social living is requisite for a young monkey, ape, or human to perform effectively as an adult member of its species. Animals with restricted social experience, for example, those raised in isolation, show strikingly abnormal sexual, grooming, and aggressive behavioral patterns (Mason, 1960, 1961a, 1961b, 1963). Restricted monkeys are not attracted to conspecifics, nor are others attracted to them. Laboratory studies suggest that full development of an animal's biological potentialities requires the stimulus and direction of social forces that are usually provided in the social group (Harlow, 1963, 1965; Mason, 1963, 1965).

Biological Bases of Primate Socialization

Primate socialization is influenced by certain primate biological characteristics. Washburn and Hamburg suggest that group life is the sociological response to the primate biological adaptation of prolonged immaturity.[1]

> Since the prolongation of pre-adult life is biologically expensive for the species, there must be major, compensatory advantages in the young's remaining relatively helpless for so long. (Washburn and Hamburg, 1965, p. 620)

The compensation is learning. Despite the restraints imposed upon the social order, the long period of infancy has a selective advantage:

> ...it provides the species with the capacity to learn the behavioral requirements for adapting to a wide variety of environmental conditions. (Ibid.)

5

With retardation of growth and a longer period of infant dependency, there is a clear tendency for individual experiences to play a more subtle role in shaping behavior into effective patterns. The extended dependency period enhances the amount and complexity of learning possible and increases the opportunities to shape behavior to meet local environmental conditions. Flexibility of behavioral patterns may be one of the principal benefits of the long period of infant dependency (Poirier, 1969a, b, 1970a, b, 1972). There appears to be a definite relationship between prolonged post-natal dependency and the increasing complexities of adult behavior and social relationships. A prolonged period of youth allows for learning in infant and juvenile play groups and provides more time for regular contact with adults which probably promotes the socialization process and helps integrate young animals into the social group. Learning thus appears to be very important for the proper social development of nonhuman primates (cf. Mason, 1965; Washburn and Hamburg, 1965).

Schultz (1956) has shown a progressive increase in length of infant and juvenile periods from prosimian to monkey to ape and to human. The result of this prolongation has been the extension of time available for learning and socialization. Prolongation of youth is also evidenced in the hominid fossil record. Simons and Pilbeam, for example, have suggested that there are direct fossil evidences (rates of tooth wear and eruption) of significant differences in maturation rates, and therefore in the learning processes, between the extinct pongid Dryopithecus indicus and its possible hominid contemporary Ramapithecus punjabicus.

Other biological characteristics probably linked with prolongation of youth and influencing primate socialization are: primate mothers normally bear one infant each parturition; much of the primate infant's early perceptions of the world are from the mother's stomach or back; and a primate mother nurses her infant.

There is also the possibility that certain immediate post-partum activities help bind the new primate infant to its mother and vice-versa. We know, for example, that among some mammals, such as sheep, rabbits, cats, and rats, that a mother's post-partum licking and cleaning of her infant leads to proper maternal-infant attachment and to such activities as proper evacuation of the bowels. Material on immediate post-partum primate activity is limited, primarily because few observers (even under laboratory conditions) have witnessed the birth of an infant. A recent and comprehensive review of this subject is found in Brandt and Mitchell's 1971 article.

The available evidence suggests a rather consistent pattern, at least among prosimians and monkeys, in which the mother licks both herself and her infant clean soon after birth. Many primate mothers also consume the placenta and umbilical cord soon after expulsion. Among the few births witnessed among

6

lorises, the mother consumes the afterbirth within an hour or two after delivery following which her activity generally declines (Doyle, et al., 1967). A similar pattern occurs among lemurs (Petter-Rousseaux, 1964). In another prosimian, the galago, the mother generally consumes the placenta and then attends to the newborn.

New World primates also eat the placenta. Takeshita (1961) reports that the third phase of squirrel monkey delivery behavior is consuming of the placenta. Hopf (1967) notes that squirrel monkeys also consume the umbilical cord. Williams (1967) reports that the woolly monkey may nibble at the umbilical cord, but in neither of the two observed parturitions did the female eat the placenta.

Similar patterns emerge among Old World monkeys. Rosenblum and Rosenblum (reported in Brandt and Mitchell, 1971) report that a guenon mother began to handle and lick the head of a newborn as soon as it emerged. Upon expulsion the infant was cradled and then licked, groomed, and mouthed. Afterwards, the mother consumed the placenta. A similar pattern is reported for the mona monkey (Takeshita, 1961). A patas mother has been observed to lick her infant soon after birth and a half-hour later she had eaten the cord and placenta (Goswell and Gartlan, 1965). Gillman and Gilbert (1946) report that a baboon mother licked and groomed her infant clean. She often fingered the umbilical cord and consumed the placenta. Rhesus mothers have been reported to consume both the umbilical cord and placenta (Hartman, 1928; Tinklepaugh and Hartman, 1930). Meier (1965) reported that surgically-delivered infants of some laboratory-reared rhesus females are not accepted by their mothers. In contrast, surgically-delivered infants of six feral mothers were cared for. Certainly this has something to do with their relative contacts with the birth process. The question arises, however, as to whether a mother deprived of consuming the placenta treats her infant differently. Presumably, stumptail macaques also eat the placenta (Bertrand, 1969).

The pongid condition is less clear, primarily because few ape births have been witnessed. However, it has been reported that chimpanzee mothers may consume the afterbirth. An orangutan mother has been reported to suck the fetal membranes, but she did not try to eat them (Graham-Jones and Hill, 1962).

Although we can't say with any certainty what role, if any, the licking and cleaning of an infant and eating of the placenta play in the initial attachment of the mother to the infant, it appears that such behavior helps form the initial attachment.

Socialization Variables

In this section we briefly review some variables influencing primate socialization, specifically those of age, sex, and interanimal relationships. First, the age variable. Although socialization is a continuous process occurring at all developmental stages, age may be a variable. The importance of any specific social event may vary according to the age at which the animal experiences it. The specific or average age of an individual may be a significant antecedent variable in two ways. (1) There may be a simple causal relationship between age and some dependent variable. In some species, early socialization may have more pronounced effects than later socialization. (2) There may be a more complex effect of age, not to be expressed in simple quantitative terms. The socialization process may have qualitatively different kinds of effects at various life cycle periods.

The primate growth cycle may be divided into four periods (Harlow, 1966; Scott and Marston, 1950). During the first or neonatal period, locomotor and ingestive behavioral patterns are suitable only for infantile life. During this stage, mother-infant contact is continuous, close, and of long duration. The importance of the neonatal period in the socialization process is directly related to the amount and kind of maternal protection and solicitude afforded the infant. During the second period, the transitional period, adult locomotor and ingestive patterns overlap, at least in unskilled manifestations, infantile forms. This period terminates when the young leave the regular company of their mothers. The transitional period is usually gradual and extends over several months. However, considering the total life span, the relative time span is short. During the third period, peer socialization, the youngster contacts individuals other than its mother, especially the mother's prior offspring, older females, and age mates. Peer socialization is characterized by the gradual subsidence of infantile behavioral patterns and is marked by the weaning process. Prior to full adult participation in the social group, an animal passes through the juvenile/subadult period, when infantile patterns disappear and adult behavioral patterns, such as sexual behavior, are practiced. The length of the juvenile/subadult period depends upon the animal's sex (nonhuman primate females assume adulthood earlier than males) and the species' longevity.

Four main elements of socialization are discernible for each life cycle period. These are: (1) the typical life condition, or style, dominating the attention of the adults and their offspring; (2) the agents of socialization, those individuals and social units playing a role in the socialization process; (3) objectives which these agents follow or set as goals, and (4) the main learning tasks facing the individual, the problems to be solved or skills to be learned.

General behavioral theory, as applied to humans, views personality development as influenced by learning in social relationships. It also suggests that what is learned depends upon the agents and processes of socialization. Some variation among dif-

8

ferent socializing agents is a matter of individual idiosyncrasies, but some may be associated with social status
characteristics. The socializing effects of an adult may
differ markedly from those of peers and elder siblings. Interactions with one's parents may have different results than
similar interactions with adult nonrelatives. We must conclude that the several variables defined for the human situation, such as sex, age, status of the socializing agents,
and degree of social intimacy are equally inportant aspects
in the nonhuman primate socialization process.

The Mother-Infant Dyad--
An Early Basis of Socialization

The ties of a newborn with its mother are the earliest,
become the strongest, and last the longest of any. This is
based upon the biological considerations noted earlier. For
varying lengths of time, depending upon the rate of neuro-
muscular development, a mother serves as the infant's locomotor organ and neocortex and so determines the nature of the
basic socialization environment. The neonatal infant, while
clinging to its mobile mother, forms an attachment to her and
through her to virtually her whole ecological-social setting.
Most mammalian young learn to make social accommodations according to the behavioral modes of the mother. Although physiological and morphological states influence the nature and extent of
the early mother-infant relationship, psychological factors and
social habits formed during infancy influence the nature and extent of social tendencies that persevere later (Tinklepaugh,
1948). Later attachments may simply be differentiations and
specializations of this early and relatively amorphous dyadic
state (Porirer, 1972).

Some variability witnessed in mother-infant relationships is phylogenetically related; the relationship tends to
become more complex and longer lasting in higher primates.
However, other factors such as habitat and social organization
may affect the relationship. These possibilities can be investigated on a group of closely related primates to see whether
variations in these factors are accompanied by variations in
the mother-infant pattern. Chalmers (1972) has attempted such
a study on cercopithecines.

The maternal relationship is the youngster's first affectional bond (Harlow, 1962, 1963). (Other bonds include the
peer affectional system, the heterosexual bond, and the bond
between older and younger animals [Harlow, 1966]). Possibly as
clinicians report for humans, the relationship between older
animals is simply an elaboration and redirection of the initial
maternal attachment (Jolly, 1966). With the formation of an
attachment to the mother, favorable conditions prevail for social learning, for social learning commences with the mother.

9

Occasions for such learning are multiplied as the growing animal moves outward from its mother. Experimental investigations have paid little attention to the task of specifying how this experience contributes to normal social development. However, one of the primary functions of contacts with other animals may be to sharpen, strengthen, or generalize the learned behavior originating in the mother-infant relationship.

There are notable differences in how nonhuman primate mothers handle and the amount of time they are in contact with their infants (Jay, 1962; Poirier, 1968, in press; Tinklepaugh and Hartmen, 1932, among others). Most field studies report that a mother and her newborn form the center of a cluster of interested group members; the mother and infant are especially attractive to other group females. Among baboons (DeVore, 1963) and Japanese macaques (Sugiyama, 1965), this interest may be limited to peering at or trying to touch the infant. In other species the mother permits group members to hold and carry her infant. This occurs, to varying degrees, among langurs (Jay, 1962; Poirier, 1968; Sugiyama, 1965), vervets (Gartlan, 1969; Struhsaker, 1967), and chimpanzees (van Lawick-Goodall, 1967). Similar interest in infants has been reported in laboratory studies of a rhesus macaque colony (Hinde and Spencer-Booth, 1967; Rowell, Hinde and Spencer-Booth, 1964; Spencer-Booth, 1968).

From birth, in neonate mammals, behavior is typified by reciprocal stimulation between parent (more specifically mother) and offspring. The infant attracts the female's attention who presents the newborn with a variety of tactile, thermal, and other stimuli, typically of low intensity and primarily approach-provoking. Socialization commences on this basis. Behavioral development is essentially social from the beginning. The principal factors in this development involve the perceptual development of the female, processes of individual perception of the young, and the reciprocal stimulative relationships between a female and her young.

The dependent nature of the mother-infant bond demands that the participants arrive at a mutually satisfying pattern of interaction whose consistency and flexibility allow the physical and social maturation of both to follow their respective courses. The interaction pattern derives its original form and later alterations from the characteristics of the pair itself and the social and physical environment. The mother's age and maternal experience affect her behavior from the very beginning, including her degree of "restrictiveness" or "permissiveness," as well as the success with which she satisfies her own and her infant's needs with ease and economy of effort.

Certain stimuli seem to elicit a female's solicitous reactions towards an infant. Many newborns look different than adults. For the first few months of life they possess a natal coat, e.g. the hair coloring prior to darkening or the acquisition of the adult coat color. The natal coat may be an essential

10

element in releasing the female's maternal behavior (Booth, 1962; Jay, 1962). It is generally present during the first months of life when an infant most requires its mother's protection and nourishment. It is almost certainly more than mere coincidence that the duration of the natal coat coincides with a period of great dependency, when it is essential for the youngster to be sheltered and protected by older animals (Poirier, 1968).

Gartlan (1969) has pointed out that within the old World genus Cercopithecus, forest-dwelling species lack a natal coat.[2] He suggests that in species where a natal coat appears, it may reflect a special vulnerability of small infants to environmental dangers. The contrasting coat color marks the small infant as an object of special interest and concern. Little is known about the behavior of species in which there is no contrasting natal coat, but these infants may keep in closer body contact with the mother for a much longer period of its development.

Is there a corollary to a natal coat among human primates? One might argue that the soft, silky, baby-powdered smell of a human infant functions rather like an approach-provoking natal coat. It is common for a human adult to remark about the qualities of a baby's skin and to respond to the urge to make contact.

There are so many variables affecting the mother-infant relationship that some are likely to be overlooked. In a recent study of feral baboons, Ransom and Rowell (1972) reported that nipple length could affect the maternal-infant relationship. Nipples of multiparous baboon mothers are usually much longer (2-3 inches in length) than those of primiparous mothers (1/2 inch in length). During the first few days of life, a baboon infant needs assistance in finding and maintaining nipple contact. Its ability to cling in a tightly flexed position against her upper chest, whether the mother is sitting or walking, is limited and the mother frequently assists the infant. A firstborn infant, unable to maintain contact with its mother's short nipple, soon begins to struggle and search for it. An infant born to a multiparous mother, however, can retain her longer nipple and often sleeps in a slumped position. During the first few days, young females frequently interrupt their own feeding and social activities to assist their firstborn to reach and maintain nipple contact. Young mothers are also likely to experience nipple discomfort, due to stretching, and continually set their infants down for short periods. These infants experience frequent frustration due to interruption of feeding and severance of body contact. The early interaction between a multiparous mother and her infant is more harmonious and secure. These infants retain nipple contact when the mother is seated or walking without having to maintain tight flexion, and thus make fewer demands for attention and support. Multiparous females are less disturbed by the infant's manipulation of the nipple, and are less likely to put their infant down. A small difference in nipple length may produce extensive variation in the early experiences of infants, and in the development of the mother-infant relationship.

11

A. Acquisition of Social Status: Behavior expressing social ranking seems also to be learned by the infant from its mother. Reports from long-term studies on macaques indicate that infants mimic their mothers' social interactions with other adults and infants of high status mothers count on their mothers' support in case of trouble. The psychoanalytic concept of identification has been introduced into non-human primate studies to explain the fact that Japanese macaque infants with dominant mothers tend themselves towards dominance (Imanishi, 1957). Infants of higher ranking Japanese macaque mothers had substantial contact with and identified successfully with troop leaders. Offspring of lower-ranking mothers had minimal contact with troop leaders and were unable to identify with them during childhood; in the Takasakiyama troop they became peripheralized or deserted the troop (Itani, et al., 1963). Koford's (1963) and Sade's (1965, 1967) reports on the Cayo Santiago rhesus macaques indicate that adolescent sons of the highest-ranking females hold a high rank in the adult male hierarchy. Baboon infants of lower-ranking mothers exhibited considerable insecurity in the form of a greater frequency of alarm cries and more contact demands on the mother, leading to an intensification of the mother-infant bond. Offspring of higher-ranking females, however, acted more secure and exhibited more freedom from their mother (DeVore, 1963). In a recent baboon study (Ransom and Rowell, 1972) it has been suggested that a mother's status is one factor determining her infant's position within the dominance hierarchy.

A different situation obtains among some arboreal colobids, for example, Nilgiri langurs (Poirier, 1968a, b, 1970a, b), in which dominance is infrequently expressed. Dominance is not an important feature in an adult Nilgiri langur female's life and her status was seldom apparent in daily activities. There is no indication that a mother's status had any measurable effect upon her infant's social behavior. A mother's status was probably less important for her infant's social development than was her "temperament," which may have affected the total pattern of her maternal behavior (see also Jay, 1962). Every Nilgiri langur infant has free access to every other infant; females of all ranks have free access to all infants, and infants and females have minimal contact with adult males (Poirier, 1968). The Nilgiri langur infant is reared in a different environment and by a different process than the macaque and baboon infant (Poirier, 1972).

B. Weaning: Weaning is one aspect of the nonhuman primate maternal-infant behavioral system which is largely ignored, except on the gross level. During weaning

...there is a gradual transition of the dyadic relationship in monkeys and apes from an initial period of virtually continuous physical attachment and co-directed attention, through several transitional

stages, to an ultimate stage of independent and separate functioning of the offspring and mother. Such
independence is obviously necessary for the infants
to enter into the adult activities of the species,
and for the mother to turn her attention to the next
offspring when it comes (Kaufman and Rosenblum, 1969).
Weaning encompasses the physical and emotional rejection of the
infant by its mother, who, although she once was the major source
of comfort, warmth, and food, now is hostile and denying. The
severity of rejection depends upon the temperament of both mother
and infant. Some mothers reject their infants more positively
than others, and some infants are more persistent in their attempts
to resist rejection. Multiparous females may wean their infants
with less effort than primiparous, younger females (Jay, 1962).
Dominant females seem to have less trouble weaning their infants,
who seem less reluctant to leave them, than do subordinate females.
     There is a wide range of weaning behavior, not only in
procedure, but in moment of onset, among nonhuman primates. Some
laboratory and field studies suggest that gender influences weaning. Among laboratory groups of pig-tailed macaques, M. nemestri-
na, male infants left the mother more often than female infants,
and mothers left male infants more than they left female infants
(Jensen, et al., 1967). Reports on feral Japanese macaques agree;
male infants left their mothers to form male peer groups at an age
when young females remained with their mothers (Itani, 1959).
Such differences are ultimately related to adult roles. On the
other hand, a feral study of Nilgiri langurs suggested no sexual
differences in weaning (Poirier, 1968). The lack of sexual differences in weaning among Nilgiri langurs, contrasted with the
Japanese macaque situation, may somehow be related to the greater
behavioral variation noted for Japanese macaque males and females
when compared to Nilgiri langur males and females.
     Variations in weaning behavior may ultimately be related
to ecological variables. Among terrestrial baboons, the infant
appears to be rather conservative, the mother innovative in the
initiation of independent behavior (Ransom and Rowell, 1972).
Rhesus macaque mothers play the major role in facilitating the independence of their infants during early stages of weaning (Hinde
and Spencer-Booth, 1967). In a comparative study of four cercop-
ithecine groups, Chalmers (1972) found that infants of the more
terrestrial vervet and DeBrazza's monkey left their mothers at an
earlier stage than infants of the more arboreal mangabey and Sykes
monkey. A vervet or DeBrazza's infant which stumbles or is clumsy, will come to little harm if it is near or on the ground.
Therefore, it can leave the mother without facing this risk. A
clumsy arboreal infant, however, is likely to be harmed if it falls.
Even if it did not kill or injure itself, it might be impossible
for the mother to locate or retrieve it. It is clearly advantageous for an arboreal infant to stay close to the mother.
     What are the possibilities; what might an investigation

13

of weaning behavior reveal? One possibility has been pointed out
by M. Mead in her book "Sex and Temperament in Three Primitive
Societies" (1935), where she remarked on the association of adult
aggressiveness with rough and abbreviated nursing habits in contrast to the gentle and prolonged nursing in a more cooperative
tribe. Heath, in an unpublished experiment on early weaning and
aggressiveness in rats, found a significantly higher degree of
aggressiveness in nine early weaned rats compared to nine rats
remaining with the mother.

Anthoney (1968) suggests an ontogenetic development of
grooming from nursing and weaning behavior. Grooming first becomes important for the infant when it is weaned; although the
mother disallows nursing, she usually tolerates the infant's attempts to groom her. Thus, whenever the weaned infant is frigh-
tened or otherwise needs security, it comes to groom rather than
nurse. There may be some link between the amount of grooming
and the length of the nursing period.

Infant-Male Relationships

Perhaps the most variable relationship, in terms of a-
mount and time of contact, which an infant has is with the adult
males of a group. An up-to-date review of the subject is found
in Mitchell, 1969 and Mitchell and Brandt, 1972. A male primate
may kill a youngster (as among south Indian langurs, Sugiyama,
1967), he may have little or no contact with it (Nilgiri langurs),
or he may participate to a greater degree than the female in its
care (Gibraltar macaques). In some species adult male-infant
contact is minimal, in others it is extensive. In some species
males play the role of group protector, in others they play an
important role in the socialization process. In some species
the male's role is passive, in others it is active. The role of
the adult male seems to be influenced by the amount of role
learning necessary, the nature of the social structure, ecology,
(e.g. arboreal vs. terrestrial) one male versus multiple male
troops, and the phylogenetic position of the species. This diversity is hardly surprising given the variability within the
order Primates of many factors such as ecology and social structure. Generally males of Old World species do not appear to
care for infants as extensively as males of New World species.

Social structure influences the amount and type of adult
male-infant contact. This may be illustrated by comparing Nilgiri
langurs (Poirier, 1969a, b, in press) and Japanese macaques. Nilgiri langur groups are organized into fairly consistent subgroup
assemblages, each of which is a social aggregate of individuals
of similar age and/or sex. Most social interaction occurs within
rather than between subgroups. Infants and juveniles rarely interact with adult males, especially when females in the subgroup
give birth. All Nilgiri langur infants have minimal association

14

with adult males, who are largely peripheral (physically and socially) to the group. On the other hand, Japanese macaque troops are comprised of central and peripheral protions. Infants that are born into the central part of the troop identify with troop leaders; they in turn become leaders. Whereas all Nilgiri langur infants go through a similar rearing process, some Japanese macaque infants receive special attention from leader males, passing through a different rearing process than infants on the troop's periphery.

The adult male's role varies according to his age, dominance, specific social group, and individual idiosyncrasies. The roles most often assumed are protection and directing neutral responses towards young infants, but this is variable in both pattern and extent (DeVore, 1963; Chalmers, 1968; Lahiri and Southwick, 1966; Mitchell, 1969). Most paternal care is directed to youngsters once they acquire the adult coat color. A male who assumes a nurturing or protective role is likely to be subadult or fully adult, sometimes of fairly high-rank. Paternal roles are not reported for young, low-ranking males excepting when a young male is protective of his young sibling (Kaufman, 1966; Koford, 1963; Sade, 1965, 1967; van Lawick-Goodall, 1967).

Some interesting cases of paternal behavior are found among hamadryas baboons (Kummer, 1968), where young males adopt young females who later become their sole consorts, among Gibraltar macaques (Burton, 1972; MacRoberts, 1971), and among Japanese macaques. Itani (1959) reports that dominant Japanese macaque males adopt yearlings when the females are bearing new infants. This behavior is very frequent in some groups and rare or absent in others. Burton (1972) reports that from the 14th to 20th day after birth, subadult Gibraltar macaque males become a predominating influence in an infant's life. Subadult males follow the leader male who often carries the infants. Once the infant begins to walk, mothers allow subadult males to take it. Subadult males carry the infant as far as 200 yards from the mother during troop progressions. The subadult male acts like a "baby sitter," he conveys youngsters over any walking distance greater than five feet, or over any jumping distance greater than a foot. Subadult males also remove young infants from dangerous situations. The socialization of infant Gibraltar macaques (from 15 days to 3 months) occurs largely within the framework of the relationship to the subadult male, but it is not confined to it. Like most relationships, age, season, breeding status, and temperament affect the duration, intensity, and even nature of the relationship. During their association, infants learn the appropriate responses for specific vocalizations from the subadults. This process seems to be a conditioning one, a function of the differential behaviors of the subadult male. The infant soon learns to recognize negative signals (e.g., a warning bark or threat) from being picked or

15

scooped up by the subadult male. On the other hand, when a positive signal is given (i.e., a greeting call or contentment noise) the subadult male makes no specific response.

The adult leader male plays a major role in the socialization of the young Gibraltar macaque, the mother acts primarily to reinforce learning. Consistently the day after the adult male encourages a young infant to walk or climb dorsally, the mother does the same. No female did these things before the male. The Gibraltar macaque adult male assumes four primary socializing roles: (1) to encourage the infant to develop motor abilities permitting social interaction, (2) to reorient the infant away from himself to other troop members, (3) to reinforce socially acceptable behaviors by not interfering, or by giving a positive reward (embracing, for example), and (4) to punish inappropriate behaviors by chasing or threatening the youngster.

The demeanor of individual adult males may also affect the infant's development. For example, Simonds (1971) notes in his study of feral bonnet macaques that the idiosyncracies of the leader adult male in some troops strongly influence the infant's social development. Similar observations were made among Japanese macaques.

Possibly one reason we know so little about the male's socializing role, or assume it is minimal, is because we simply are not accustomed to watch for it. The male's socializing role may be passive in contrast to the active role assumed by the mother. Chalmers (1972) notes that the physical removal of an adult male Sykes monkey results in increased restrictiveness of the mother towards the infant, whereas removal of an adult male patas does not. Two possibilities are suggested. One is that removal of the male disturbs the mother and she reacts in a more cautious and protective manner towards her infant than she would when relaxed. Another is that removal of the male upsets the social equilibrium of the group, dissolving dominance dependent relationships (Imanishi, 1960) under which the mother might have gained protection from the adult male's presence. Differences in maternal reaction may also be linked to genuine species-specific behavioral differences. Patas monkeys live in one male group in which the adult male is independent of other group members, interacting rarely with the adult females. Studies of captive patas support this (Hall, Boelkins, and Goswell, 1965). That the absence of an adult male from a captive patas group might not upset the mothers is therefore not surprising.

The Role of Play Behavior

Although there is some difficulty defining exactly what play is, most observers agree that play helps socialize the youngster. (See Loizos, 1968, for a comprehensive discussion of primate play behavior.) Behavioral patterns common to sexual and dominance relationships are practiced in the play group. An animal may learn its position in the dominance hierarchy during play-fighting bouts.

A young primate's earliest contacts beyond the mother are with its peers; a large portion of this early contact occurs as play behavior. Play first begins as a nonsocial activity and then develops into a peer group activity (Poirier, in press). Infants seem to adjust to their fellows and learn to become effective group members with the help of play behavior (Mason, 1965). Through trial and error, through constant repetition of play behaviors, an animal learns the limits of its self-assertive capabilities. The play group is a context for such learning because its members, mostly peers, are young and their teeth are neither sharp nor long enough to inflict damage. The basic adult dominance hierarchy may be formed in the play group wherein youngsters compete for food, sleeping positions, or the easiest arboreal pathways. Within the play group, juveniles establish close social bonds which later help maintain group unity. Infants learn to mix within the play context, by playing with peers they develop a fully integrated personality. Surrogate-reared infants allowed twenty minutes of play daily with their peers were considerably better adjusted (as adults) than infants raised with mothers alone (Harlow, 1971, among others). There is strong supporting clinical evidence that peer group interactions are both necessary and sufficient for development of normal adult social behaviors.

The period of maximal nonhuman primate social play may correspond to the brief period of avian imprinting. During play an animal learns which species it belongs to. Far from being a "spare-time," superfluous act, play at certain crucial early life stages seems necessary for the occurrence and success of later social life. The very quality of play, exaggeration of movement, ensures maximal energy expenditure, increasing the strength of the learning process. The longer the period of infant dependency the more vulnerable the infant is to influences and interactions adversely affecting its social development. Therefore, the more essential it is that there be a means of ensuring continous and corrective interactions with its species. Play might serve this function (Loizos, 1968).

There may be a relationship, perhaps indirect, between phylogenetic position and the amount, duration, and diversity of play behavior (Beach, 1945; Loizos, 1968). There may also be a distinction between animals whose mode of survival is highly specialized, structurally or behaviorally, and those who are "opportunistic" (Lorenz, 1956; Morris, 1964). The latter are characterized by their restless curiosity, what Morris calls their neophilia, or love of the new. These animals, of which primates are the supreme examples, generally maintain higher activity levels than more specialized species. The human child may be at the apex of this pyramid, as demonstrated by its many and varied play activities. The importance of play behavior for the full development of the human child has not been adequately appreciated.

Even though play is an important item in a young primate's life, there is a great deal of variability between the amount of play and the participants which does not solely reflect phylogenetic or ecological conditions. Nilgiri langurs, for example, are not very playful (Poirier, 1969a, 1970a; Tanaka, 1965). In contrast to the dearth of play behavior Poirier noted among Nilgiri langurs, e.g. one play sequence per 6.9 hours of observation, north and south Indian langur youngsters spend considerable time in vigorous play behavior. Possibly the limited number of playmetes available in the smaller Nilgiri langur groups influences behavioral development. A maturing youngster in an average Nilgiri langur group has fewer peer social interactions than the common langur, baboon, and macaque infant maturing in troops containing 15 or 20 young playmates. Play may serve a less important function in the behavioral development of Nilgiri langurs than among common langurs, baboons, and macaques.

The Influence of the Social Structure

Primates are group-living, social animals; therefore, to fully comprehend the socialization process it must be viewed within the context of the social structure. The development of primate infantile behaviors involves the interaction of a genetically determined base with a set of environmental conditions. We must remember that the environmental context of primate infants is largely social. Group structure reflects and influences individual behavior (Poirier, 1969 b, in press). Not only the form of group organization, but group life itself is dependent upon the early environment of individual animals. Presumably, any given form of social organization is sustained as an adaptation to the ecology, but socialization is relevant.

The reciprocal relationship between socialization and social structure is not necessarily one of discrete interactions, but may take the form of cycles or other sequences prolonged over substantial time periods. Primate social groups differ according to many variables, but with few exceptions the animal learns to use its biology efficiently and adapt to its environment within the group (Washburn and Hamburg, 1965). Differences in primate societies are due not only to biology, but to the social circumstances in which the individual lives and learns. The species-specific troop social structure determines which animals an infant will or will not contact. For example, Nilgiri langur subgroup assemblages allow an infant an inordinate amount of contact with its mother, other females and peers, and little contact with the adult male or males. Some of the social differences characteristic of Indian leaf-eating monkeys are partially due to the amount of contact animals have with others

18

(Poirier, in press).

Summary - Future Research

The task of discovering those factors, and intricate combinations, that direct the form and development of social behavior has begun in a number of field and laboratory studies. A major outcome of these studies is the realization that more long-term observation, experimental manipulation, and analysis of primate behavior and group structure will be well worthwhile. In the future, the most effective socialization studies will involve long-term investigation of the following (Crook, 1970): (1) The extent of mother-exclusive care of young in comparison to "aunt" behavior and "baby-sitting" by peers, siblings, and older group members (males and females). (2) The rate of maternal attitudinal change to the infant preceding and subsequent to weaning. (3) The extent, manner, and frequency of peer interactions, especially in play groups. (4) The extent, manner, and frequency of heterosexual contact. (5) The patterns of interaction between juvenile males approaching puberty and adult males and females. (6) The manner and extent of exclusion of adult males from the breeding units (Itani, 1972). (7) The pattern of "friendship" relations. (8) The influence of consanguineal ties (Kawamura and Kawai, 1956; Sade, 1965, 1967). (9) The development of male alliances, leadership, and interactive "policing" of troops. (10) The effects of parental roles and status on the behavioral development of youngsters (i.e., Kawai, 1958 a, b). Others can be added to this list.

Primate Learning

A. The Biological and Evolutionary Background

In order to fully understand the processes involved in socialization and learning, I have chosen to deal with them separately. Learning is at an optimum for primates for, from an evolutionary viewpoint, selection is for successful behavior. Structure, physiology, and social life all result from selection, and the structure-physiology-behavior of primate populations are adapted to one another and to a way of life. Some parts of this complex are almost entirely based upon heredity with a minimum dependence upon environment, whereas others are heavily influenced by learning. Primates inherit an ease of learning, rather than fixed instinctive patterns; they easily, almost inevitably, learn behaviors essential for survival. Primates do learn to be social, but they are so constructed that under normal circumstances this learning always occurs. For lower vertebrates, as for primates, "evolution, through selection, has built the biological base so that many behaviors are easily, almost inevitably learned" (Washburn and Hamburg, 1965:613). Learning processes

19

serve and are an extension of the evolutionary process. Comparative primate studies are practically useless if they ignore the
biological frame of reference. Assessments of relative learning
or "intelligence" among primates are usually irrelevant and inaccurate because they ignore this fact, as well as for other
methodological reasons (Hall, 1963).

Kummer (1971) suggests that in contrast to the highly
specialized but rigid skills common to the lower vertebrates,
primates have a potential for learning broad sets of tasks which
neither they nor their ancestors previously encountered in this
specific form. "This flexibility, and not a specialized but
genetically fixed skill, prepared the way for culture" (147).

In primate social systems, and presumably in most higher
mammalian systems, individual behavior is largely controlled by
a continuous process of social learning arising from group interactional patterns. Learning is extremely important, for animals
whose behavioral traits do not conform sufficiently to that of
the group's norms are less likely to reproduce and may be ejected.
Social selection of this type must have a strong stabilizing
effect upon the genetic basis of temperamental traits and motivational thresholds. Primate societies seem to determine the genetic basis of individual social responses (Crook, 1970).

Learning during socialization and the emergence of a
social role has a preponderant effect in shaping individual
behavior. Social conformity and the maintenance of a group structure results primarily from the adoption of traditional behaviors
characteristic of the total social system. This is primarily
accomplished by three interacting groups of factors (Crook, 1970):
(1) the species repertoire of biologically programmed neonate
reflexes and social signals, together with innate factors affecting temperament and tendencies to learn some responses more
readily than others, (2) the behavior of individuals comprising
the relevant social milieu, which partly controls the emergence
of individual role playing, and (3) direct environmental effects
such as availability of need-reducing commodities and consequent
behavioral learning that exploits the world in the manner ensuring greatest individual survival.

Diamond and Hall (1969) specify the association cortex
as the neocortex subdivision where prime evolutionary advance-
ments in mammalian brains have occurred. While primate learning
skills are not solely accounted for in terms of the volume of the
neocortex relative to total brain volume, it is significant that
the primate neocortex is proportionately larger (46-58%) than it
is in carnivores (40-46%) and rodents (30%) (Harman, 1957).
The complex cognitive processes and advanced learning skills are
accomodated by increased cortical fissuration, increased numbers
of cortical units in the fine structure of the cortex, and the
refinement of subcortical structures which interrelate the thala-
mus and cortex (Norback and Moskowitz, 1963; Rumbaugh, 1970).
There are advances in all these measures from monkeys to apes.

B. What Must Be Learned?

        Table I emphasizes that under natural conditions pri-
mates have a good deal to learn.

                    Table I - Some Learning Chores
                        (adapted from Hall, 1968)

Feature (physical, social)   Learning task

    Home range   Routes to feeding areas, sleeping
                                  places, overlap areas with adja-
                                  cent groups, day-ranging patterns,
                                  seasonal changes, danger areas.

    Food and water   Locations, discrimination of edi-
                                  ble from nonedible, ripe from un-
                                  ripe, and manipulatory techniques.

    Day-activity pat-   Times of resting, times of activi-
    tern   ty, coordination of movement, feed-
                                  ing, and so forth.

    Other animals   Discrimination of predators or
                                  noxious creatures, warning cues of
                                  conspecifics and of other animals.

    Conspecifics   Tolerance distances between groups,
                                  habituation or avoidance or ter-
                                  ritorial display.

    Size and composition   Process of socialization contin-
    of groups   ually involves familiarization
    Sexual reproduction   with one's own, its behavior,
    Individual social devel-   foods, and communication matrix.
    opment
    Group social interac-
    tions

C. Types of Primate Learning Processes

        What are the social learning processes chiefly involved
in these conformities? Although learning processes vary from
species to species, there are some consistencies. Social facilitation and observational learning seem to be most important (Hall
and Goswell, 1964). However, when we study the complex interactional system of a primate group, which comprises a kind of
natural unity, we may suppose that any of all of the defined learning processes may be operating in the adjustments of individuals

                                21

to their social and physical environment (Hall, 1968). Learning processes integrade with one another, constituting a more or less continuous interactional system through which survival habits of feeding, avoidance, dispersal, or aggregation are acquired.

To some extent the infant follows the actions of its mother, "modelling" its actions and the directions they take to the objects to which they relate. However, any animal's behavior may be set or facilitated by the perceived example of another group member. Animals observe each other's behavior, with or without awareness of the reference; later they may behave in a similar manner in a similar situation. Observational learning probably contributes in major proportion to the broader problem of social learning. Kawamura (1959), Hall (1963), Hall and Goswell (1964), Menzel (1966), and Tsumori (1967) have stressed the acquisition of much of primate behavior through observational learning. An animal learns the consequences of another's behavior through direct visual experience and adjusts its own behavior accordingly. The frequency of events occasioning direct and indirect learning will be markedly influenced by ecology, especially vegetation density which affects inter-animal observation, seasonal food shortages occasioning increased rates of travel, increased foraging time and individual and group dispersal, availability and size of sleeping sites occasioning group splitting or congregation,and population density determining the extent and frequency of intra- and inter-group interactions.

Social conflict also seems to play a significant role in primate learning. Berlyne (1960), concerned with the role of conflict in learning, points out that conflict "... is an inescapable accompaniment of the existence of all higher animals, because of the endless diversity of the stimuli that act on them and of the responses that they have the ability to perform" (10). In primate societies there is continual interplay of friendly, sexual, aggressive, and fearful impulses, all of which must be individually balanced. The balancing of these, rather than actual experiences of punishment and reward, help maintain the social framework, and, when the balance is upset, permit relearning and modification by means other than aggression. The significance of social conflict in social learning studies is something that should be investigated experimentally in ways more meaningful than those of the interanimal conditioning attempted to date (Hall, 1968).

Some primate learning also occurs during "instructed" sessions. In some circumstances animals may receive positive or negative reactions to certain behaviors. An infant not only learns what to eat by watching its mother, but also by the mother's watching what it eats. Numerous instances of mothers taking nonedible items from their infant's mouths have been reported. Youngsters also learn what animals and possible dangers must be avoided when a mother, or other adult, normally a male, chases

22

the infant from a dangerous stimulus. Young females who handle
infants roughly are often physically or verbally rebuked by the
infant's mother. On the other hand, should they manage well,
they receive a positive reward by being allowed to retain the
infant. Some measure of primate learning is certainly influenced by positive or negative responses from animals about them.
Such circumstances seem to be less frequent than is observed
among humans, however. As compared to nonhuman primates, a
greater component of human learning occurs as directed instruction.

D. Variables Influencing Learning

     Besides individual traits affecting the learning pro-
cess, other variables, such as age, sex, troop structure, and
kinship relationships, intercede. Summarizing the results of a
number of experiments, Tsumori (1967) notes that until the age
of 6 or 7 Japanese macaques make rapid progress towards learning new behavioral patterns. In older monkeys, however, there
is a decline which Tsumori attributes to a motivational loss.
Besides age, there are gender differences in motivation. Tsumori feels that sex is not a factor in terms of cue-producing
or cue-retaining processes, but it is a factor during the motivational processes supporting them. Japanese tests concerning
the acquisition of new feeding habits suggest that youngsters
are more adaptable and learn to eat new foods prior to becoming
adult. However, Japanese macaques above three years of age
stagnate in their adaptability to new situations (Itani, 1958;
Kawai, 1965; Tsumori, Kawai, and Motoyoshi, 1965).
     Support for the Japanese data comes from my study of
the acquisition of new foods among feral Nilgiri langurs (Poirier, 1968a, 1969b, 1970a, b). Nilgiri langur infants and males
are more apt to accept new foods than females, suggesting that
adult males are less conservative in their behavioral patterns
(and therefore perhaps more adaptable) than adult females. Females seem to be more conservative in their behavior. This may
be adaptive, for an adventurous female not only risks her own
life, but her infant's also.
     Kummer (1971) suggests a selective advantage for be-
havioral conservatism. Less flexible adults form a safety res-
ervoir of previous behavioral variants, which will survive a
new invention for at least ten years. If the new behavior
proves harmful, in the case of food because of parasitic infec-
tion, the adults would survive to reproduce another generation.
In learning and spreading of new behaviors, adult rigidity has
the same function as low mutation rates in evolution. Juveniles
(and in many cases expendable, superfluous males) are the most
obvious candidates for acquiring new behavioral patterns since
they are the most easily replaced investment in terms of food
and experience.

Kinship ties also affect the transmission and learning of new behavioral patterns. Japanese studies show that pathways of habit formation follow pre-established networks of group affinities. In the Koshima macaque group, for example, habit propagation was influenced by kinship. Entire lineages consisting of a mother and her descendants tended to acquire or reject new behavioral patterns as a unit. Between 1951 and 1960 the sons and daughters of one Koshima female acquired an average of 3.6 of the new behaviors invented by the group, whereas descents of another female acquired only 1.6 new habits per individual (Kummer, 1971).

All normal primate learning is essentially social. Where the individual is in temporary isolation learning a task without reference to others of its species, that learning is not normal. The primary reinforcement for all normal primate learning comes from the social context, the group in which the animal is born and nurtured. Even the sensorimotor activities of observing, manipulating, and exploring that are indicative of individual independence receive some facilitation, or inhibition, from the group setting (Hall, 1968). Contrasting group social structures impose differences in learning patterns leading to the formation of individual behaviors and imply that group modification, through whatever process, will alter the socialization process yielding individuals with changed behaviors. The various social interactions which different social structures allow influence the amount and type of social learning possible (see for example, Sugiyama, 1972).

E. Individual Learning vs. Group Tradition

Individual learning is often an experimental focal point, but group learning, or group tradition, may be more important. The group is the locus of knowledge and experience far exceeding that of its individual members. Within the group experience is pooled and the generations linked (Washburn and Hamburg, 1965). Troop traditions (the sum total of individual learning experiences) are more advantageous than individual learning in a number of situations (Kummer, 1971). Tradition is superior to individual learning if the new behavior is difficult to acquire individually in direct interaction with the environment. Troop traditions pool individual experiences. Secondly, environmental experimentation may be dangerous, as with poisonous plants or predators. In this case, troop tradition is the safe way of acquiring adaptive behavioral patterns. Third, some environmental situations, such as drought, are too rare to permit direct experience by every troop member. Therefore, an experienced elder may be the only animal knowing the right response.

Tradition requires a long life expectancy and a leading role for the older animals. (In fact, primate societies may be viewed as gerontocracies.) Tradition is the appropriate vessel

24

for information that is relevant only to a few generations within a limited area. On the other hand, direct individual experience with the environment is appropriate if the information is relevant only to the individual who has the experience and if it is easy to discern.

F. Gender Differences in Rearing--Learning the Maternal Role

We could list a long series of learning experiences, however, I will discuss only the learning of gender roles. There is a direct correlation between the socialization and learning processes of infant males and females and their subsequent adult roles. Goy (1968) and his associates have studied hormonal influences upon the development of sexual differences among rhesus macaques. The high hormonal levels circulating in the blood of newborns suggest that during fetal or neonatal life, hormones act in an inductive way on the undifferentiated brain to organize certain circuits into male and female patterns. Early exposure to such hormones may affect the ease of learning and expression of appropriate behavior patterns later in life, even though the level of sex hormones is very low during the period between infancy and adolescence. Hormones may act to produce behavioral patterns in various ways. For example, hormonal influence at a critical period may affect later sensitivity to certain stimuli, helping account for the varying reactions of males and females to natal coat infants. Hormones may also act by reinforcing some behavioral patterns over others. For example, hugging an infant to the chest may be very pleasurable to a female whereas the large muscle movements and fast actions useful in play-fighting and aggressive behavior may be more pleasurable for the male (Lancaster, 1972).

Sexual differences in behavior may be developed partly by the dynamics of social interaction within the group, by learning role patterns. Even in animal societies social roles are not strictly inherited (Benedict, 1969). Some laboratory studies suggest that animals without social experiences lack marked sexual differences in behavior (Chamove, Harlow, and Mitchell, 1967). In a study on pigtail macaques, there were clear sexual differences in the development of independence from the mother (Jensen, Bobbitt, and Gordon, 1968). Similar findings have been reported for rhesus macaques (Mitchell, 1970). Gender determination is by direct observation; many field workers report that group members pay close attention to a newborn's genitals by peering at, touching, sniffing, or mouthing them. This may represent the first basic step towards classifying the gender of a new group member. The manner in which an individual learns its role, including the male and female role may be heavily influenced by the environment of the movement, as well as the individual's genetic composition (Lancaster 1972).

Early behavioral differences between males and females

25

are manifested in various ways. Jensen et al. (1966) found that a deprived laboratory environment, e.g. where an adult male was missing, affected an infant male pigtail macaque's behavior more adversely than it did a female's. This suggests that in their early development males may be more adversely affected than females by the lack of a father or adult male paternal figure. Nash (1965) has reviewed much of the literature relevant to the role of the human father in early experience. Studies exploring the effects of the paternal relationship on boys and girls separately indicate that the father's absence is more harmful to later behavioral development and role playing of males than females.

A major feature differentiating male and female primates is the amount of aggressive output, males are more aggressive than females. Present information suggests that both the mother and infant show behavioral differences dependent upon the infant's gender. Mothers of male infants are more punishing and rejecting than mothers of females, who tend to be restrictive and protective of the daughter. From the very beginning, male and female infants are treated differently, due perhaps to the fact that male infants behave differently and that the mother reacts to this difference. Studies of the development of laboratory-raised rhesus elucidate some interesting points regarding male aggression. A rhesus mother treats a male infant differently than a female infant; she threatens and punishes her male infant at an earlier age and at more frequent intervals. Female infants are restrained, retrieved, and protected more often than males (Mitchell, 1969; Mitchell and Brandt, 1970). Even brutal isolate-reared laboratory "motherless mothers" are more brutal towards male than female infants. Since exposure to excessive early punishment has been correlated with later hostile behavior (Mitchell, et al., 1967), the infant male's characteristic predisposition toward rougher play and rougher infant-directed activity is subtly supported by its mother's behavior, and through his observations of other mothers with their infants. These findings have also been reported from the provisioned Cayo Santiago rhesus colony (Vessey, 1971). On Cayo Santiago, infants began receiving aggression from their mothers in the second month, with a peak in months 9 to 11. Most aggressive behavior was associated with weaning and involved pushing the infant from the nipple or slapping it. Males received significantly more of this aggressive behavior than females.

Do early differences in maternal behavior affect the infant's socialization and learning of adult roles? Quite clearly, the answer seems to be that it does. The mother's earlier rejection of her male infant forces it into earlier contact with other infant males, usually in the form of peer play group interactions. In most nonhuman primates, young males show a definite preference for rough-and-tumble play and are often found in age-graded play groups which range farther from the mothers as its members age. Females, however, are more often found with the adult females, manifesting an intense interest in newborn infants (Chamove et al., 1967).

Macaque and baboon play groups generally include more juvenile males than females; in hamadryas baboons the ratio is about 8 to 1. While young males play, young females remain with the adult females of the family group. Sociographic analyses show that male juveniles interact in larger groups than females, who mostly associate with only one partner. Preliminary data based on the same methods reveal a similar pattern in human children (Kummer, 1971).

Ransom and Rowell's (1972) study on feral baboons shows that there are consistent differences in the development of the mother-infant relationship and peer interactions as early as 2 or 3 months. By the time of the transitional period to the juvenile stage, sexual differences in play activity, frequency of initiation and withdrawal, and duration and roughness of play bouts, are present. These differences increase with age until, by the time of the next birth, young males have joined relatively permanent peer play groups where they spend much of their time. Young females, however, avoid rough and prolonged peer-group interactions and spend most of their time with the mother subgroup. During the next 4 or 5 years males continue to interact mostly with each other on the group's periphery, and are generally avoided by mothers and other females. In this same period females maintain close proximity to adult females and attendant adult males. The course and timing of gender role learning through experiences with older individuals of both sexes differ markedly.

In a recent study of nursery school children, Knudson (1971) found similar differences in play and aggression among young boys and girls. Boys engage in a higher total frequency of dominance behavior than girls. Secondly, although boys and girls show more physical than verbal dominance behavior, girls engaged in a significantly higher proportion of verbal dominance behavior than boys. A similar gender correlation was found in a study of Nilgiri langurs (Poirier, 1970a, b. c, in prep.). Knudson also found that the frequency of rough-and-tumble play for boys is significantly higher than for girls, that girls tended to rely on adults more than twice as often as boys, that children tended to play in uni-sex groups, and that it was easier to establish dominance rankings for boys than for girls. The latter is also true for most nonhuman primates, e.g., it is usually easier to establish dominance rankings for males than for females.

Other behavioral differences become pronounced early in the life of nonhuman primates. Vessey (1971) found that the most striking qualitative difference between male and female rhesus infants was the occurrence of mounting behavior in males and its absence in females. Among baboons, females are more

27

consistently involved in close associative behaviors, such as grooming, and proximity to other animals, than are males. Males apparently begin the process or peripheralization rather early in life (Nash and Ransom, 1971).

The different socialization and learning processes characteristic of male and female primates is related to their adult roles. The major role which a female must learn is that of being a mother. Field and laboratory studies have consistently shown that females (even by the juvenile stage) are more closely attached to the mother, show more interest in young infants (Spencer-Booth, 1968; Chamove, et al., 1967), and are simply gentler (less aggressive) in their social relationships than are males. Field reports note that few, if any, adult females lack the experience of caring for youngsters prior to themselves giving birth. There is little data suggesting that primiparous females are less effective mothers than multiparous females, and it seems reasonable to conclude that playing a mothering role as a juvenile contributes to the success of the primiparous mother (for example Lancaster's [1972] study of vervet play-mothering). This does not mean that all maternal behavior patterns are inborn, for we know that a total lack of social experience leads to the development of very infantile and aggressive mothers. A laboratory study by Harlow, Dodsworth, and Arling (1966) found that motherless mothers raised in semi-isolation, or females deprived of peer interaction, responded to their first infant with active rejection and hostility. However, they also found that social experience with an infant, no matter how minimal, affected maternal behavior. The same females who rejected their first infant often accepted the second.

Although some basic patterns of maternal behavior may be relatively inborn, learning does play an important part in the development of skill in performing them. Many studies note that young juvenile females are inept in handling infants, but when they reach adulthood they can carry and handle infants with ease and expertise (Jay, 1962; Lancaster, 1972; Struhsaker, 1967). The dynamics of the maternal learning process occur under the mother's watchful eyes. Instances of carelessness, clumsiness, or real abuse are punished. Through a simple conditioning process, juvenile females learn appropriate behavior patterns with their reward being the continued presence of the infant. Laboratory studies support the idea that this early experience may be practice for adult maternal behavior patterns (Seay, 1966).

G. Conclusion

In this section we attempted to outline some of the processes and variables involved in primate learning. Genetic, as well as individual factors, impinge upon the learning process. However, all primates learn, their brains and nervous systems are

28

adapted for learning. The ability to learn is adaptive, and throughout their evolutionary history primates seem to have been programmed for ease of learning. Primate learning involves a number of different mechanisms, observational and conditioned learning seem to play a prime role. As among humans, young animals seem to be more adaptable and learn more easily (are more educable) than older animals. Adult conservatism is adaptive in that it ensures future generations. It is the older animals who are primarily involved in maintaining group traditions, which surpass individual learning in a number of important ways.

Primate social roles are learned social roles. Rather than inheriting their behavioral tendencies, males and females learn them. From very early life males and females are reared differently; mothers and other group members soon discern gender and act and react differently towards males and females. Males are soon forced from their mothers out to the peer group where they mature and become less dependent upon the females. Males learn to be assertive, aggressive individuals who protect the group from external harm. Females, on the other hand, remain with their mothers and other females. They learn to interact with other females, and most importantly to care for the infants. The socialization and learning process of female primates seem to be geared towards producing a healthy, effective mother.

NOTES

1. The situation may be reversed e.g. prolonged immaturity may be a biological response to group life.
2. A recent study of the St. Kitts green monkey does not fully support this (Poirier, in press b).

REFERENCES

Altmann, M.
    1958   Social Integration of the Moose Calf. Animal
                Behavior 6:155-159.

Anthoney, T.
    1968   The Ontogeny of Greeting, Grooming, and Sexual
                Motor Patterns in Captive Baboons (Superspecies
                Papio cynocephalus). Behavior 31(4):358-372.

Beach, A. F.
    1945   Current Concepts of Play in Animals. American
                Nat. 79:523-541.

Benedict, B.
    1969   Role Analyses in Animals and Men. Man 4:203-214.

Bertrand, M.
    1969   The behavioral repertoire of the stumptail maca-
                que. Bibl. Primatol. 11:1-123.

Berlyne, D.
    1960   Conflict, Arousal, and Curiosity. New York:
                McGraw-Hill.

Booth, C.
    1962   Some Observations on Behavior of Ceropithecus
                Monkeys. Ann. N. Y. Acad. Sci. 102(II):479-487.

Brandt, E. and Mitchell, G.
    1971   Parturition in Primates: Behavior Related to
                Birth. In Primate Behavior Vol. II, L.A. Rosen-
                blum, ed. New York: Academic Press, pp. 178-
                223.

Burton, F.
    1972   The Integration of Biology and Behaviour in the
                Socialization of Macaca sylvana in Gibraltar.
                In Primate Socialization, F. E. Poirier, ed. New
                York: Random House, pp. 30-62.

Chalmers, N.
    1968   Group Composition, Ecology and Daily Activities
                of Free Living Mangabeys in Uganda. Folia primat.
                8:247-262.

    1972   Comparative Aspects of Early Infant Development
                in Some Captive Cercopithecines. In Primate Soc-
                ialization, F. E. Poirier, ed. New York: Ran-
                dom House, pp. 63-82.

Chamove, A., Harlow, H. and Mitchell, G.
    1967   Sex Differences in the Infant-Directed Behavior
                of Preadolescent Rhesus Monkeys. Child Dev. 38:
                329-335.

Child, I. L.
    1954   Socialization. In Handbook of Social Psychology,
                Vol. II,G.Lindzey, ed., Cambridge: Addison-
                Wesley Press, pp. 655-692.

Clausen, G. A. (ed.)
    1968   Socialization and Society. Boston: Little Brown.

Collias, N. E.
    1956   Socialization in Sheep and Goats. Ecology 37:4
                228-239.

Crook, J.
    1970   The Socio-ecology of Primates. In Social Be-
                havior in Birds and Mammals. J. Crook, ed.,
                New York: Academic Press, pp. 103-169.

DeVore, I.
    1963   Comparative Ecology and Behavior of Monkeys
                and Apes. In Classification and Human Evolu-
                tion, S. L. Washburn, ed., Chicago: Aldine,
                pp. 301-319.

Diamond, I. and Hall, W.
    1969   Evolution of the Neocortex. Science 164:251-
                262.

Doyle, G., Pelletier, A. and Bekker, T.
    1967   Courtship, mating, and parturition in the Lesser
                Bushbay (Galago senegalensis moholi) under semi-
                natural conditions. Folia primat. 7:169-197.

Erickson, E. H.
    1950   Childhood and Society. New York: Norton.

Freud, S.
    1923   The Ego and the Id. London: Hogarth.

    1930   An Outline of Psychoanalysis. London: Hogarth.

Gartlan, J. S.
    1969   Sexual and Maternal Behavior of the Vervet Mon-
                key, Cercopithecus aethiops. J. of Reproductive
                Fertility, Supplement 6:137-150.

Gilman, J., Gilbert, C.
    1946   The reproductive cycle of the Chocma baboon
                (Papio ursinus) with special reference to the prob-
                lem of menstrual irregularities as assessed by the
                behavior of the sex skin. S. Afr. J. Med. Sci.,
                Bio. Suppl. 11:1-54.

Goslin, D. (ed.)
    1969   Handbook of Socialization Theory and Research.
                Chicago: Rand McNally.

Goswell, M., Gartlin, J.
    1965   Pregnancy, birth and early behavior in the captive
                patas monkey, Erythrocebus patas. Folia primat.
                3:189-200.

31

Goy, R.
    1968   Organizing Effects of Androgen on the Behavior
                of Rhesus Monkeys. In Endocrinology and Human
                Behavior, R. Michael, ed., pp. 12-31.

Graham-Jones, O., Hill, W.
    1962   Pregnancy and parturition in a Bornean orang,
                Proc. Zool. Soc. Lond. 139:503-510.

Hall, K. R. L.
    1963   Observational Learning in Monkeys and Apes.
                Brit. J. Psychol. 54:201-226.

    1968   Social Learning in Monkeys. In Primates: Studies
                in Adaptation and Variability, P. Jay, ed., New
                York: Holt, Rinehart and Winston,pp. 383-398.

Hall, K., Goelkins, E. and Goswell, M.
    1965   Behavior of Patas Monkeys, Erythrocebus patas,
                in Captivity, with Notes on the Natural Habitat.
                Folia primat. 3:22-49.

Hall, K. and DeVore, I.
    1965   Baboon Social Behavior. In Primate Behavior:
                Field Studies of Monkeys and Apes, I. DeVore, ed.,
                New York: Holt, Rinehart and Winston, pp. 425-
                473.

Hall, K. and Goswell, M.
    1964   Aspects of Social Learning in Captive Patas Mon-
                keys. Primates 5(3-4):59-70.

Harlow, H.
    1962   The Development of Affectional Patterns in Infant
                Monkeys. In Determinants of Infant Behavior, B.
                M. Foss, ed., New York: Wiley, pp. 75-97.

    1963   Basic Social Capacity of Primates. In Primate
                Social Behavior, C. F. Southwick, ed., Princeton:
                D. Van Nostrand Company, Inc., pp. 153-161.

    1966   The Primate Socialization Motives. Trans and
                Studies of the College of Physicians of Phila.
                33:4 224-237.

Harlow, H., Harlow, M., Dodsworth, R. and Arling, G.
    1966   Maternal Behavior of Rhesus Monkeys Deprived of
                Mothering and Peer Associations in Infancy. Proc.
                of Amer. Phil. Soc. 110:58-66.

Harlow, H., Harlow, M., and Suomi, S.
    1971   From Thought to Therapy: Lessons from a Pri-
                mate Laboratory. American Scientist 59:5,
                pp. 538-550.

Harman, P.
    1957   Paleoneurologic, Neoneurologic and Ontogenetic
                Aspects of Brain Phylogeny. James Arthur Lec-
                ture on the Evolution of the Human Brain. Am.
                Mus. Nat. Hist., New York.

Hartman, C.
    1928   The period of gestation in the monkey, Macaca
                rhesus, first description of parturition in
                monkeys, size and behavior of the young. J. Mam-
                mal. 9:181.

Hinde, R. and Spencer-Booth, Y.
    1967   The Effect of Social Companions on Mother-Infant
                Relations in Rhesus Monkeys. In Primate Etholo-
                gy, D. Morris, ed., Chicago: Aldine, pp. 267-
                286.

Hopf, S.
    1967   Notes on pregnancy, delivery and infant survival
                in captive squirrel monkeys. Primates 8:323-332.

Imanishi, K.
    1957   Social Behavior in Japanese Monkeys, Macaca fus-
                cata. Psychologia 1:47-54.

    1960   Social Organization of Subhuman Primates in Their
                Natural Habitat. Curr. Anthrop. 1:393-407.

Itani, J.
    1958   On the Acquisition and Propagation of a New Food
                Habit in the Natural Group of the Wild Japanese
                Monkey at Takasakiyama. Primates 1(2):84-98.

    1959   Paternal Care in the Wild Japanese Monkey, Macaca
                fuscata fuscata. Primates 2:61-93.

    1972   A Preliminary Essay on the Relationship between
                Social Organization and Incest Avoidance in Non-
                human Primates. In Primate Socialization, F. E.
                Poirier, ed., New York: Random House, pp. 165-
                171.

Itani, J., Tokuda, K., Furuya, U., Kano, K., and Shin, Y.
    1963   Social Construction of Natural Troops of Japanese

Monkeys in Takasakiyama. Primates 4:2-42.

Jay, P.
        1962   Aspects of Maternal Behavior Among Langurs. Ann.
                    N. Y. Acad. Sci. 102:468-476.

        1965   The Common Langur of North India. In Primate
                    Behavior: Field Studies of Monkeys and Apes, I.
                    DeVore, ed., New York: Holt, Rinehart and Winston,
                    Inc., pp. 197-250.

Jensen, G., Bobbitt, R., and Gordon, B.
        1966   Sex Differences in Social Interaction Between
                    Infant Monkeys and Their Mothers. Recent Adv.
                    in Biol. Psych. 9:283-293.

        1967   The Development of Mutual Avoidance in Mother-
                    Infant Pigtailed Monkeys, Macaca nemestrina. In
                    Social Communication Among Primates, S. A. Alt-
                    mann, ed., Chicago: University of Chicago Press,
                    pp. 43-55.

Jolly, A.
        1966   Lemur Behavior. Chicago: University of Chicago
                    Press.

Kaufman, I. C. and Rosenblum, L.
        1969   The Waning of the Mother-Infant Bond in Two Spe-
                    cies of Macaque. In Determinants of Infant Be-
                    havior IV, B. Foss, ed., Methuen: London, pp.
                    41-59.

Kaufman, J.
        1966   Behavior of Infant Rhesus Monkeys and Their
                    Mothers in a Free Ranging Band. Zoologica 51:17-
                    28.

Kawai, M.
        1958a   On the Rank System in a Natural Group of Japanese
                    Monkeys. Primates 1(2):84-98.

        1958b   On the System of Social Ranks in a Natural Troop
                    of Japanese Monkeys I: Basic and Dependent Rank.
                    Primates 1:111-130.

        1965   Newly Acquired Pre-cultural Behavior of the Nat-
                    ural Troop of Japanese Monkeys on Koshim Islet.
                    Primates 6:1-30.

Kawamura, S.
    1958   Matriarchal Social Ranks in the Minoo-B Troop:
                A Study of the Rank System of Japanese Monkeys.
                Primates 2(2):181-252.

Kawamura, S., and Kawai, M.
    1956   Social Organization of the Natural Group of
                Japanese Macaque, Animal Psychology 6.

    1959   The Process of Subcultural Propagation Among
                Japanese Macaques. Primates 2(1):43-60.

Knudson, M.
    1971   Sex Differences in Dominance Behavior of Young
                Human Primates. Paper Presented to Amer. Anth.
                Assoc., New York City.

Koford, C.
    1963   Rank of Mothers and Sons in Bands of Rhesus
                Monkeys. Science 141:356-357.

Kummer, H.
    1968   Social Organization of Hamadryas Baboons: A
                Field Study. Chicago: U. of Chicago Press.

    1971   Primate Societies. Chicago: Aldine Press.

Lahiri, R. and Southwick, C.
    1966   Parental Care in Macaca sylvana. Folia primat.
                4:257-264.

Lancaster, J.
    1972   Play-Mothering: The Relations Between Juvenile
                Females and Young Infants Among Free-Ranging
                Vervet Monkeys. In Primate Socialization, F. E.
                Poirier, ed., New York: Random House, pp. 83-
                101.

Loizos, C.
    1968   Play Behavior in Higher Primates: A Review. In
                Primate Ethology, D. Morris, ed., Chicago: Aldine,
                pp. 176-219.

Lorenz, K.
    1937   The Companion in the Bird's World. Auk 54:245-
                273.

    1956   Play and Vacuum Activities. In L'Instinct dans
                le compartement des Animaux et de L'Homme, S. Au-
                turi, ed., Paris: Masson et cie.

Mason, W.
    1960   The Effects of Social Restriction on the Behavior of Rhesus Monkeys: I Free Social Behavior. J. Comp. Physiol. Psychol. 53:582-589.

    1961a   ...II Tests of Gregariousness. J. Comp. Physiol. Psychol. 54:287-290.

    1961b   ...III Dominance Tests. J. Comp. Physiol. Psychol. 54:694-699.

    1963   The Effects of Environmental Restriction on the Social Development of Rhesus Monkeys. In Primate Social Behavior, C. F. Southwick, ed., Princeton: D. Van Nostrand, pp. 161-174.

    1965   The Social Development of Monkeys and Apes. In Primate Behavior: Field Studies of Monkeys and Apes, I. DeVore, ed., New York: Holt, Rinehart and Winston, pp. 514-544.

MacRoberts, M.
    1970   The Social Organization of Barbary Apes (Macaca sylvana) on Gibralter. Am. J. Phys. Anth. 33(1): 83-101.

Mead, M.
    1935   Sex and Temperament in Three Primitive Societies. New York: Morrow.

Meier, G.
    1965   Maternal behavior of feral and laboratory-reared monkeys following the surgical delivery of their infants. Nature 206:492-493.

Menzel, E.
    1966   Responsiveness to Objects in Free-Ranging Japanese Monkeys. Behav. 26:130-150.

Mitchell, G.
    1969   Paternalistic Behavior in Primates. Psychol. Bull. 71(6):399-417.

Mitchell, G., Arling, G. L., and Moller, G.
    1967   Long-Term effects of Maternal Punishment on the Behavior of Monkeys. Psycho. Sci. 8:197-198.

Mitchell, G. and Brandt, E.
    1970   Behavioral Differences Related to Experience of Mother and Sex of Infant in the Rhesus Monkey.

Devel. Psych. 3:149.

1972   Paternal Behavior in Primates. In Primate
        Socialization, F. E. Poirier, ed., New
        York: Random House, pp. 173-206.

Morris, D.
    1964   The Response of Animals to a Restricted En-
            vironment. Sym. Zool. Soc. Land. 13:99-118.

Nash, J.
    1965   The Father in Contemporary Culture and Current
            Psychological Literature. Child Dev. 36:261-297.

Nash, L. and Ransom, T.
    1971   Socialization in Baboons at the Gombe Stream
            National Park, Tanzania. Paper Presented at the
            Amer. Anth. Assoc., New York.

Norback, C. and Moskowitz, N.
    1963   The Primate Nervous System: Functional and
            Structural Aspects in Phylogeny. In Evolu-
            tionary and Genetic Biology of Primates, Vol. I.
            J. Buettner-Janusch, ed., New York: Academic
            Press, pp. 131-175.

Petter-Rousseaux, A.
    1964   Reproductive Physiology and Behavior of the Lem-
            uroidea. In Evolutionary and Genetic Biology of
            Primates, Vol. II, J. Buettner-Janusch, ed., New
            York: Academic Press, pp. 91-132.

Poirier, F. E.
    1968   The Nilgiri Langur (Presbytis johnii) Mother-
            Infant Dyad. Primates 9(1):45-68.

    1969a   The Nilgiri Langur Troop: Its Composition, Struc-
            ture, Function and Change. Folia primat 11:20-47.

    1969b   Behavioral Flexibility and Intertroop Variability
            among Nilgiri Langurs of South India. Folia pri-
            mat 11:119-133.

    1970a   Nilgiri Langur Ecology and Social Behavior. In
            Primate Behavior: Developments in Field and Lab-
            oratory Research, Vol. I, L. Rosenblum, ed., New
            York: Academic Press, pp. 251-383.

    1970b   Characteristics of the Nilgiri Langur Dominance
            Structure. Folia primat 12(3):161-187.

1970c   The Nilgiri Langur Communication Matrix. Folia
             primate 13(2-3):92-137.

1971   Socialization Variables. Paper Presented at
             Amer. Anth. Assoc., New York.

1972   Socialization: A Theoretical Perspective. In
             Primate Socialization, F. E. Poirier, ed., New
             York: Random House, pp. 1-28.

in press a   Nilgiri Langur Behavior and Social Organization.

in press b   The Ecology and Social Behavior of the St. Kitts
             Green Monkey (C. aethiops sabaeus). Folia priat.

in prep   Ecology and Social Behavior of the Nilgiri Lan-
             gur. Chandler Publishers.

Ransom, T. and Rowell, T.
    1972   Early Social Development of Feral Baboons. In
              Primate Socialization, F. E. Poirier, ed., New
              York: Random House, pp. 102-144.

Reisen, A.
    1961   Critical Stimulation and Optimum Periods. Paper
              Presented at Amer. Psychol. Assoc., New York.

Rosenblatt, J., Turkewitz, G. and Schneirla, T.
    1961   Early Socialization in Domestic Cats as Based on
              Feeding and Other Relations Between Female and
              Young. In Determinants of Infant Behavior, B.
              Foss, ed., London: Methuen and Co., pp. 51-74.

Rowell, T., Hinde, R. and Spencer-Booth, Y.
    1964   "Aunt"-Infant Interaction in Captive Rhesus Mon-
              keys. An. Beh. 12:219-226.

Rumbaugh, D.
    1970   Learning Skills of Anthropoids. In Primate Be-
              havior: Developments in Field and Laboratory
              Research, Vol. I, L. Rosenblum, ed., New York
              Academic Press, pp. 2-70.

Russell, C. and Russell, W.
    1971   Primate Male Behavior and Its Human Analogues.
              Impact of Science on Society 21(1):63-75.

Sade, D. S.
    1965   Some Aspects of Parent-Offspring and Sibling Re-
              lations in a Group of Rhesus Monkeys with a

Discussion of Grooming. Amer. J. Phys. Anthrop.
23:1-17.

1967   Determinants of Dominance in a Group of Free-
            Ranging Rhesus Monkeys. In Social Communication
            Among Primates, S. Altmann, ed., Chicago: U. of
            Chicago Press, pp. 99-115.

Schultz, A.
    1956   Postembryonic Age Changes. In Primatologia, Vol.
            I, H. Hofer, A. Schultz and D. Starck, eds.,
            Basel: S. Karger, pp. 887-964.

Scott, J. P.
    1945   Group Formation Determined By Social Behavior.
            Sociometry 8:42-52.

    1950   The Social Behavior of Dogs and Wolves. Annals
            N.Y. Acad. Sci. 55:1009-1021.

    1958   Critical Periods in the Development of Social
            Behavior in Puppies. Psycho. Med. 20:42-54.

Scott, J. P. and Marston, M.
    1950   Critical Periods Affecting the Development of
            Normal and Maladjustive Social Behavior of Pup-
            pies. J. Genet. Psychol. 77:25-60.

Seay, B.
    1966   Maternal Behavior in Primiparous and Multipar-
            ous Rhesus Monkeys. Folia primat 4:146-168.

Shimahara, N.
    1970   Enculturation--a Reconsideration. Curr. Anth.
            11:143-154.

Simmel, E. C.
    1970   The Biology of Socialization. In Early Experi-
            ences and the Processes of Socialization, R.
            Hoppe, G. A. Milton, E. C. Simmel,eds., New York:
            Academic Press, pp. 3-7.

Simonds, P. E.
    1965   The Bonnet Macaque in South India. In Primate
            Behavior: Field Studies Of Monkeys and Apes, I.
            DeVore, ed., New York: Holt, Rinehart and Wins-
            ton, pp. 175-197.

    1971   Bonnet Macaque Infant Socialization. Paper Pre-
            sented at Amer. Anth. Assoc., New York.

Sluckin, W.
    1967   Imprinting and Early Learning. Chicago: Al-
                dine Press.

Spencer-Booth, Y.
    1968   The Behavior of Group Companions Towards Rhesus
                Monkey Infants. An. Beh. 16:541-557.

Struhsaker, T. T.
    1967   Behavior of Vervet Monkeys, Cercopithecus aethi-
                ops. U. of Calif. Pub. in Zool. 82:1-74.

Sugiyama, Y.
    1965   Behavioral Development and Social Structure in
                Two Troops of Hanuman Langurs (Presbytis entel-
                lus). Primates 6:213-248.

    1967   Social Organization of Hanuman Langurs. In Social
                Communication Among Primates, S. Altmann, ed.,
                Chicago: U. of Chicago Press, pp. 221-237.

    1971   Social Characteristics and Socialization Among
                Wild Chimpanzees. In Primate Socialization, F.
                E. Poirier, ed., New York: Random House, pp.
                145-163.

Takashita, H.
    1961   On the Delivery Behavior of Squirrel Monkeys and
                a Mona Monkey. Primates 3:59-72.

Tanka, J.
    1965   Social Structure of Nilgiri Langurs. Primates
                6(1):107-122.

Tinklepaugh, O.
    1948   Social Behavior of Animals. In Comparative
                Psychology, F. Moss, ed., New York: Prentice-
                Hall, pp. 366-394.

Tinklepaugh, O. and C. Hartman
    1930   Behavioral Aspects of Parturition in the Monkey.
                J. Comp. Psychol. 11:63-98.

    1932   Behavior and Maternal Care of the Newborn Monkey
                (M. mulatta, M. rhesus). J. Genet. Psych.
                40:257-286.

Tsumori, A.
    1967   Newly Acquired Behavior and Social Interactions
                of Japanese Monkeys. In Social Communication

Among Primates, S. Altmann, ed., Chicago: U. of
Chicago Press, pp. 207-221.

Tsumori, A., M. Kawai, and R. Motoyoshi
    1965   Delayed Response of Wild Japanese Monkeys by the
                Sand-Digging Test (I)--Case of the Koshima
                Troop. Primates 6:195-212.

van Lawick-Goodall, J.
    1967   Mother-Offspring Relationships in Free-Ranging
                Chimpanzees. In Primate Ethology, D. Morris,
                ed., Chicago: Aldine, pp. 287-347.

Vessey, S.
    1971   Social Behavior of Free-Ranging Rhesus Monkeys
                in the First Year. Paper Presented at Amer.
                Anth. Assoc., New York.

Washburn, S. L., and I. DeVore
    1961   The Social Life of Baboons. Sci. Am. 204:62-71.

Washburn, S. L., and D. Hamburg
    1965   The Implications of Primate Research. In
                Primate Behavior: Field Studies of Monkeys and
                Apes, I. DeVore, ed., New York: Holt, Rinehart
                and Winston, pp. 607-623.

Williams, L.
    1967   Breeding Humbelt's Woolly Monkey (Lagethrix
                lagothricha) at Murrayton Woolly Monkey Sanctu-
                ary. Int. Zoo. Yearb. 7:86-89.

LANGUAGE AND SOCIALIZATION:
CHILD CULTURE AND THE ETHNOGRAPHER'S TASK

Jan Brukman
University of Illinois

Introduction

In 1936 Gregory Bateson published his classic work
Naven, an ethnographic study of the Iatmul, a tribal people living on and near the Sepik River in New Guinea. In casting about
for an approach that would help me to organize my thoughts about
the socialization process, learning, language, and culture, I
turned to Bateson and Naven.

In that work Bateson outlined two notions that captured
what we all intuitively take for granted--how it is that cultural
forms are replicated in an orderly fashion across the generations.
At that time, Bateson spoke of the affective components of the
personalities of the Iatmul, as the ethos of that culture. But
at the same time Bateson introduced the idea of the eidos, which
he called the "...standardization of the cognitive aspects of
the personality of...individuals...and its expression in cultural
behavior"...(1958:220 emphasis Bateson"s). The eidos are thus
the shared cognitions of a people, along with the realization of
these cognitions in actual behavior. It is the eidos of a particular culture that cognitive anthropologists have been attempting
to map in recent years. As time has passed however, these cognitive mappings have become increasingly difficult to attain as
we begin to understand the complexity of the task we have set ourselves. The eidos then are our goal, but reaching that goal seems
a possibility which fades further and further into the distance
as we become more aware of the kinds of questions we can legiti-
mately ask and expect to have answered given the current state of
our knowledge.

In the context of this symposium we must ask how it is
that the eidos of particular cultures are transmitted. Where
may we look to discover how, in particular detail, the child is
father to the man in some culture.

When we examine closely cross-cultural findings in this
area we discover very little that has been systematically gathered or analyzed which is of relevance for the problem at hand.
That is to say we do not know in any depth what the potential
learning mechanisms are across all cultures. I take the current
argument between the behavior modificationists on the one hand

43

and the open classroomers on the other to be, in its most crude form, the paradigm for this situation. Let me report, then, about the current status of our knowledge of one crucial part of the socialization process--acquiring language.

Language Learning as Paradigm

Because of the success of linguistic theory over the past decade and a half, much research has been devoted to the study of the correlation and covariation of language with other cultural phenomena. One of the effects of the study of language acquisition has been to broaden the scope of our investigations to include language as a vehicle for the study of socialization in general, not just the particular case of language socialization. At the same time, the conception of language has steadily broadened in its scope, so that today what was traditionally the grammatical--that is, the phonological, syntactic, and semantic levels--has become enmeshed in a much larger net of cultural behavior including what was at one time called the pragmatic (Morris) and what later came to be part of what was called performance (Chomsky). The effect of these two quite far-reaching movements within linguistics and anthropology has been unsettling in terms of once clearly stated research objectives. It is clear that current research is almost desperately being programmed to provide some sort of synthesis between linguistics and anthropology that captures the sense of the importance of our new understanding of the relation between language and culture. One of the crucial aspects of this new understanding lies in our renewed awareness of the relation between language and cognition.

Such able researchers as Basel Bernstein, William Labov, and the members of the Language-Behavior Laboratory at Berkeley are all in quite different ways producing exciting and immensely promising new views of the relations between codes and their situated uses. It seems to me that the kind of results produced by these and other scholars have always been implicit in the work of men like Bateson, as well as Fredric Barth and even Levi-Strauss. Piaget's work is once again being mined by young students for insights into the relation between language and cognition. But what in particular are some of the substantive results of these investigations, especially from a cross-cultural perspective?

Universals of Language Acquisition

In July of 1967 the second draft of a very modest field manual immodestly titled "for the cross-cultural study of the acquisition of communicative competence" was published. The preparation of this manual was undertaken with the direction of

44

Susan Ervin-Tripp, John Gumperz, and Dan I. Slobin. A group of graduate students, all anthropologists, took part in the writing of the manual as well as the initial testing phase.

Data were gathered on a variety of language socialization topics in highland Mexico, Samoa, Kenya, South India, and Oakland, California. Although many facets of this work are as yet unpublished, some general results have emerged which merit attention.

Speaking only for myself, I find in retrospect that the fact that all of the investigators in the initial study were anthropologists affected greatly the kinds of data we found most interesting--this independent of the ostensive reasons for our original research. If we could arbitrarily divide the tasks we set for ourselves into two parts, the first covering the acquisition of strictly grammatical rules (phonological and syntactic systems particularly), and the second covering the total environment in which this acquisition took place (in Hymes' ethnography of speaking sense) then it becomes clear that our interests as anthropologists have tended more toward the latter set of topics rather than the former. This is not to say that we do not have interesting data of the cross-cultural sort which applies to the acquisition of grammatical rules (in the narrow sense); rather, most of our communications from the field in 1967 and 1968 spoke to other matters and with a surprising amount of accord.

For example: It was customary at that period to assume certain things about the social structural features of the language socialization process. In particular, most of the work on the acquisition of language (in English, Russian, and French primarily) had been done in the context of middle class families, with children of psychology professors or psychology professors' graduate students. Prior to this time, what we knew about the acquisition of language by children was derived from diary studies done by linguists or psychologists of their own children. As we are all well aware, primary socialization in such families characteristically takes place within the nuclear family; more so certainly than in lower or working class groups, isolated nuclear households make up the bulk of the domestic units in American, French, and even Russian society. Implicit in this early work on language acquisition then, was that the linguistic input to the child was primarily from adults--the child's parents and particularly, the child's mother.

There were thus two assumptions made about our work in the field which we never thought to question seriously: That mother-child interactions would supply us with the data we needed for studying the linguistic input to the child and the context for that input, and, methodologically, we could gather these data by observing closely mother-child interactions in the daily round of family life.

Of course, we turned out to be naive on both points. In

45

Kenya, and South India, and especially in Samoa, all the investigators quickly discovered somthing they already knew, that primary socialization of the child takes place within a much wider circle of kin and non-kin, and that much of the responsibility for the care of the young child is intrusted to children only slightly older in age than the children to be studied. This meant simply that determining the sources of linguistic input to the child was much more difficult than it had been for American investigators. In all of these non-western societies the boundaries of social interaction are much more open and shifting, and, not surprisingly, the children themselves are more mobile than their American counterparts. At that time I wrote from the field:

> It would falsely simplify the problem to talk about mother-child relationships as a one-of-kind enduring relationship where a group of people, especially co-resident women and the lineage to which they are attached, have certain 'rights' in the child. This is a problem in all extended-household types of societies.

A second example comes from certain untested assumptions about the way in which linguistic development proceeds. Although we were aware that it is largely irrelevant whether a child is corrected in his speech ("Don't say 'I'm not doin' nothin', Johnny") for the progressive development of a fully grammatical linguistic system (he will acquire such a system without instruction), from casual and unexamined knowledge of middle class parents' concern for grammatical "correctness" we believed in general that such metalinguistic tutoring was potentially prevalent in a great variety of cultures.

The evidence we gathered in all cases contradicted this assumption. None of us ever heard such corrections in natural situations, and on closer investigation, when examining adults' beliefs about language, we discovered that the possibility of such correction never entered into beliefs about how language is acquired. What we did discover was that in matters of linguistic etiquette, that is, what kinds of speech were socially appropriate, there was a great deal of correction indeed, as well as overtly stated rules about appropriateness.

Many of our observations about socialization practices fell naturally into the two classes of findings just illustrated. We were first of all continually being struck by the features of social and cultural organization which differed from our received notions about how socialization was accomplished--this is not a startling finding, but its implications are enormous. I shall return to these implications shortly. Secondly, we were also beginning to see that many observations did have a familiar "feel" to them. Thus, although strictly grammatical corrections were never made of a child's speech, rules of

etiquette were continously invoked, and in every particular
culture's case, these corrections had to do with obscene or
'dirty' words.

Now, it is not merely by accident that this concern with
a particular kind of etiquette in every culture we have so far
studied. It seems to me that we have here a concrete reflection
of a very important notion which Burling(1970), among others, has
noted previously. That is to say, it is non-functional, culturally useless, for there to be native grammarians, whose job it
would be to instill the rules of phonology and syntax into each
generation of children. All normal human children are language
learning machines pre-equipped with an apparatus which generates
theories about the linguistic structures that they are exposed
to.[1] Every child, without instruction, continually produces a
variety of schemes (hypotheses, theories) about how something
may be said--an abstract form of grammar, if you will. What no
child can do however, is discover the appropriate interactional
circumstance or circumstances in which something may be said,
just by internally manipulating alternative coding structures.
For this kind of knowledge the child must be exposed to the world
of culturally defined appropriateness, he must be exposed to the
norms of his culture in ways that can be made overt, both by the
investigator and informant. The rules of grammar are out-of-
awareness, but the rules of etiquette can never be.

The difference between these two aspects of verbal behavior and how they are acquired points up an issue in current
research on the relations between language and culture that is
engaging the interests of many cognitive anthropologists. I
mean here the effort to distinguish between formal and substantive universals.[2]

Kinds of Universals

A recent paper by Dan I. Slobin (1971) takes up the issue of formal universals in the ontogenesis of grammar. These
formal universals are of two kinds: general operating principles
and specifically linguistic structural principles. Slobin notes
that there are two kinds of variables: those which have to do
with general cognitive predispositions and those which have to
do with language processing itself. There are two cognitively
based operating principles according to Slobin: (1) New forms
first express old functions and new functions are first expressed by old forms, and (2) The semantic relations which a child
can express and interpret in speech are limited by his level of
cognitive development. Taken together, these proposed operating
principles reflect our knowledge of the way in which cognitive
development seems to progress in children. Although in some
ways obvious, their implications are far-reaching, because they
lead to certain very specific predictions about the unfolding of

47

the stages of children's grammar everywhere. Thus for example, expressive functions will precede referential ones; expressions of direction and location will precede those of time; a non-present time-frame is late to develop; the order of presentation of items at early stages of development is isomorphic with the real time occurrence of events talked about (e.g., the passive form of an utterance is interpreted by children as its active counterpart); and so on.

These universals then, although linguistic, are direct reflections of cognitive development. What is crucial about them Slobin points out, is that, since forms are not completely developed when first used, can it be that the acquisition of linguistic forms influences the acquisition of their functions? That is, can the development of language, at least at this level, affect the development of thought? On the basis of the evidence that we have, we would probably have to give a qualified no, because we now have convincing evidence that the child always knows more than he can say. However, this does not preclude the possibility that at the very latest stages of development, when rules with the least scope of application are learned, and sub-tle nuances of features are added to lexical items, cognition is indeed affected. Here, we are dealing with the little under-stood nature of the interpenetration of semantic information and "real-world knowledge", so to speak; indeed, it seems to me that it is at this time the rules of speech etiquette are beginning to be internalized. To take an example that is probably counter-factual: when a child learns there are asses which are donkeys and asses which are buttocks he learns two things simultaneously: first, high level semantically disjunctive coding rules, and second, that either, neither or both meanings may be acceptable or unacceptable in speech depending on the social context. Note here that the distinction between formal and substantive univer-sals becomes extremely fuzzy.

Co-occurrence Restrictions, Competence, and Performance

Take as an example of this fuzziness the differing kinds of co-occurrence restrictions the child must learn.[3] Somehow the child must come to know that there are classes of verbs which can occur with certain classes of objects only. While one may close, open, shut, bang, hit (and so on) the door, one cannot sleep or tell it (Burling 1970:67). These are grammatical rela-tions which are allowed or prohibited (agent-object relations) to be sure, but these relationships also, at least in English, tell us something about the real-world possibilities for doing things to doors. Such co-occurrence restrictions are, at least intuitively, non-arbitrary in ways that, say, number agreement between nouns and verbs is arbitrary. So there is some inter-action here between the linguistic and non-linguistic environ-

48

ments which the child must successfully negotiate when he is
acquiring his language. We do not know how a child accomplishes
this, nor for that matter do we know how a child comes to know
the appropriate labels which attach to individuals within his
life space. We do not know, that is, in any orderly way, whether
children say things like "I have three brothers, John and Jim and
Alice." If children do say such things, does this mean that they
do not know what a 'brother' is, or do they not know what 'Johns'
and 'Alices' are? What are the questions we could possibly ask
to discover what the case is? But again, we are dealing here
with co-occurrence restrictions. The problem is that we have no
good way of characterizing the difference we know is intuitively
there between "John slept the door" and "I have three brothers,
John and Jim and Alice." Both sentences are in some sense formally anomalous, but at the same time they are anomalous sub-
stantively too, since they say incorrect things about the real
world.

    One of the observations that can be made about all such
deviant (from the adult grammar's point of view) utterances is
that the process which produces such utterances is unknown. Although it is possible to separate the acquisition of language into stages on the basis of formal characteristics--babbling,
holophrastic, two-word utterance and so on--the internal and external mechanisms which generate these structures in children
remain largely uninvestigated. On the purely syntactic level it
is possible always to argue, as Slobin has done, that grammatical
development parallels cognitive maturation, which in turn derives
from the neural and psychomotor development of every normal human child. It seems to me that this view, while perhaps true,
begs the question somewhat, since little is known about the actual physical properties of brain maturation.

    Even more serious is the nature of the learning of
those extralinguistic aspects of the real world, (which are man-
ifold indeed), whose understanding gets coded in language. Here
there is obviously an ongoing process in which a child aligns
his internal and external experiences in such a manner that his
speech production is eventually not significantly different from
that of an adult in either form or content. What is particularly remarkable about this stage (say, from the ages of three to
six or seven) is that our information about anomalous or deviant
utterances is almost wholly anecdotal. The cartoonist Bill
Keane, who draws the one-panel Family Circus, has masterfully
captured many of the anomalies I refer to here. These anomalies
are not of the 'two foots' or 'I hitted it' variety but of a different sort entirely. Thus Keane recognizes that children will
say things that are perfectly grammatical but which do not square
with adult perceptions of time or change or taxonomic categories.
So he has a little boy saying to his mother, "Can I still live
with you when I get big and you're my grandma?"
    The fact that children say such things is not particu-

49

larly newsworthy; we all have such experiences with children at one time or another in our lives. What is remarkable is that we are unable to specify the mechanisms which actually generate these sorts of utterances. While it is true that this has not held back the descriptions of children's abilities of the strictly grammatical sort--we can describe, in some cases quite elegantly, what children can accomplish--we do not have any good way to elicit a corpus of the kind of anomalous material I cited from Keane's work. We can make perfectly reasonable inferences about the semantic "errors" the child may be making, but the crucial point is that we cannot be sure that these errors are not rule-governed in precisely the way that we infer 'I hitted it' is rule-governed. We are stymied because we do not have a sufficiently large corpus of materials from any one child to make inferences that apply to many instances of the same phenomena. But more importantly, we are stymied because we have no good way of getting the child who says these things to be self-conscious about his saying them, and to thereby produce some reasoning about his statements.

As we are all quite aware, many of the generalizations about language that have been proposed in recent years have been based on deep intuitions about the nature of certain kinds of utterances. These intuitions Bever has quite rightly labelled a kind of speech event which takes the form of having intuitions about language (Bever 1971). The problem with studying the ontogenesis of language is that children, as far as I am aware, have no intuitions about language that are useful to the analyst. He must infer from a child's performance what the process or processes are that are generating the forms that he observes. Children, at the states in which their most crucial language learning is going on, are incapable of being self-reflective, of being self-conscious about their linguistic abilities.

But the problem is compounded by an additional factor, which especially confronts those working in exotic cultures. This has to do with the distinction between linguistic performance and linguistic competence. This has remained a critical distinction for generative grammarians, and was once unquestioningly accepted by linguistic anthropologists as well. Increasingly however, sociolinguistic investigations of several varieties have led researchers interested in the sociology and anthropology of language to resist and then finally reject, the distinction as made by the linguists. For Chomsky linguistic competence was among other things, the knowledge of the ideal speaker-hearer in a homogeneous community. Such a model, analogous to the assumption of an airless, gravity-less universe for the operation of Newtonian principles, seems at first sight unexceptionable for a scientific understanding of language. On reflection however, one can discover both historical and theoretical reasons for the linguistic anthropologist's rejection of the linguist's

50

model.

Historically, anthropologists have for the most part
been interested in differences, not similarities. The notion of
the homogeneous community, when seen against the backdrop of
cross-cultural studies, has never been a particularly salient one
for anthropologists. Describing and analyzing the differences
among culturally discrete entities has been anthropology's task,
until quite recently. It has long been felt, if only implicitly, that only after these differences were well understood could
the discipline begin to analyze the similarities across communities. The linguist's optimistic view of the kind of community
which can be considered an independent variable in any calcula-
tions about language goes directly against the grain of the anthropologist's awareness of cultural differences of the most far-
reaching sort. The assumption of homogeneity, without any definition of what that term might imply is now seen as an unacceptable restriction on the kinds of research anthropologists
characteristically engage in.

Theoretically too, the notion of the speaker-in-a-
vacuum has come to seem more and more inadequate as a way of
characterizing language. For linguistically oriented anthropologists, the study of language cannot be separated from its
use, since the structure of language is realized in social
interaction. The question that must be answered is an empirical one: can the structure of language, at whatever level, be
described independently of the knowledge and beliefs about reality which it expresses?

Work with children in widely varying cultural communities suggests that the elimination of the cultural context in
which language is embedded could produce faulty structural descriptions of the abstract sort Chomsky recommended in 1965.
Thus in Samoa, where two speech styles that are clearly marked
phonologically exist in the repertoire of every adult Samoan,
children first acquire the formal phonological system, the one
to which they are least exposed. This style interferes with the
learning of the full adult systems, so that the child over gen-
eralizes in a way that produces a consonantal system unlike that
of an adult. (Kernan 1970) The crux of the matter is that this
process, even at the phonological level, is a product of the
interaction between what one could call linguistic--i.e. "normal" ontogenetic processes--and non-or extralinguistic processes--
the presence of formal and informal styles. A linguist, given
just the raw transcripts of the data might conclude that the
'errors' the children exhibited showed a lack of competence, on
the adult model. An anthropologist who knew something about
linguistics, on the other hand, might conclude that two kinds
of competence were involved, and that the competition between the
phonological rules and the sociolinguistic rules produced the
anomalous phonological systems of the children. So, it is possible that we may be able to speak of rule-governed performance

variables as sociolinguistic competence variables in many speech communities--if only we are clever enough to discover these sorts of variables.

In standard linguistic theory, it is assumed that native speaker-hearers are able to make judgments about the grammaticality of utterances they or others produce. The implicit rules which generate these judgments are the competence of the speaker-hearer. Generally speaking, the "errors" which native speakers make, and which are corrected by the judgmental process are said to be performance errors, which are brought about by such things as memory lapses, external distractions, and so on. These errors are believed in no way to compromise the native speaker's knowledge of his language. What controls an individual's performance is therefore in theory extrinsic to his knowledge of his language.

On the basis of the foregoing example from Samoa (and others), I would argue that on the contrary there are controls on a speaker's performance which are properly linguistic, but which stem from rule systems governing language which are different from but parallel to the kind of rules which govern something like the phonological or syntactic systems.

For example, the eliciting situation may either be intimidating to the child in the context in which it occurs because the child is not able to understand the task (eliciting experiment), or there may be rules of interaction in the culture that prevent the child from performing in the task situation, even though he understands how to do what is required of him. In such cases, the child's strictly grammatical competence is possibly masked by a higher order of variables referable to the social situation in which this grammatical competence is necessarily embedded. This is of course one of the areas that is of particular interest to the linguistic anthropologist, since it is the interaction between linguistic competence in the grammatical sense, and cultural competence in the behavioral sense that he attempts to specify and account for.

Therefore, instead of viewing the cultural setting as a confounding variable we must incorporate the setting into our analysis, understanding as we do the embeddidness of linguistics or verbal behavior in some sociocultural context. The result of enlarging our frame of reference is to play down the idea of strictly linguistic competence and to speak rather in terms of what Hymes has called the speech event within the framework of his ethnography of speaking.

Again, I believe there are good theoretical reasons for doing so not least of which is our inability to determine grammatical competence in the way we have come to understand it from the work of the generative grammarians. We know what we believe the child has accomplished in some descriptive framework--but we cannot know what the child believes it has accomplished.

52

Sociolinguistic Performances and Eidos

Now, it seems to me that what is accumulated by the child as his linguistic competence increases is essentially a greater and greater inventory of ways to express _intentions_. From labelling to the ability to express various _modalities_, the child increasingly controls the semantic relationships needed to function in a social group.

What the child comes to possess therefore are more and more powerful means of realizing its ego-centered ends, _and_ the set of rules for using language in appropriate social contexts in which these ends may be attained. In the simpliest case a child learns quite early to request food only in the presence of someone who can supply it. It seems apparent that what will be first acquired and used at this intersect of the verbal and behavioral are pragmatically based, if from an adult standpoint, global utterances that reflect a basic comprehension of ways to achieve gratification. I want to make it clear however that I mean no more by this than that the young child's behavior is both maturated and goal-oriented in essentially the same way that any animal's behavior is so organized.

It is thus no accident, yet quite noteworthy, that the early records we have been able to compile for children in a cross-cultural context show quite clearly that at the state of one word utterance the child invariably has acquired the ability to differentiate his self from that of others in the environment. It may be trivial that the child knows where his next meal is coming from; however the fact that he can store and recall a label which uniquely identifies where that meal is coming from may not be quite so trivial. That is say, the child's recognition of his primary caretakers--his ability to recognize his mother and father--is essentially no different from any young mammal's ability, yet when the mode such recognition takes is that of labelling we unhesitatingly designate that to be a cultural achievement--if it is self-generated that is, and not taught, as in the recent studies of language acquisition in chimpanzees.

It is clear that one of the constituents of the interaction in which a child must engage, verbally and otherwise, is its essential unpredictability, in any sense of predictable we could make rigorous. From moment to moment, the scene changes for the child. New actors intrude themselves upon its life-space, and familiar actors disappear. There is a potential for continual movement of people and objects in a human environment, and what the child must do is induce from within this potential a strategy which will cope satisfactorily with this situation.

What we have learned from dealing with cultural environments that are often widely divergent is that the feat of discerning order within his environment and _manipulating_ that order must be of some considerable magnitude, since we do not come near to understanding it. I mean that the child's access to data of a behavioral sort (that is, appropriate behavior which is not narrowly grammatical) is haphazard in ways quite similar to the undetermined nature of the linguistic input.

I give as an example of this feat a linguistic routine employed by Koya children as a verbal eliciting device with other Koya children (the Koya are a tribal people of South India). The routine is used among linguistically "sophisticated" (five and six year olds) agemates as well as between older and younger siblings, for example. As a routine it has two variants; in the first, the elder child will name a particular food found in the Koya diet and ask the younger child if he or she will eat it. Here, a rising intonation is used, rather than a question word. The point, it seems, is to run through as many different foods as possible--where duplication occurs the speaker will correct himself--in as rapid a time as possible. The hearer replies 'I will eat (that thing, whatever it is)' as rapidly as he can. One might interpret the interchange as one in which the hearer starts out a gourmet and ends a gourmand. The second variant requires a little more of the interlocutor in the exchange. Here, the listener must be able to define his understanding of the various categories of food. The speaker asks, using a question word, what kind of rice or curry or meat his hearer will eat. A satisfactory reply must be a specific kind of rice, curry or meat. What little evidence I have tends to show that this kind of querying has a cyclic character: rice--curry--meat, rice--curry--meat, and so on. There are no winners in such routines, and they are easily dropped for other activities.

The point is that I have three different recordings of these kinds of routines. Two of them are between a girl who is 18 to 24 months old, and her six year old sister, who acts as the questioner. The third is between a mature young man and woman in a sexual joking encounter. Although the little girl's phonological system is totally unstable, and her ability to imitate one-word utterances is equally unstable, she nonetheless controls what I at least see to be the essential formal elements of the routine I have outlined. The question I pose here, and certainly cannot answer at this time, is how does it come about that this child knows this routine?

It is tempting to say that the concern for food which permeates the marginally subsistent Koya culture--the phrase 'have you eaten?' is used as a greeting form--impresses itself on the consciousness of all Koya, young and old, to such a degree that the set of stimuli from which the child selects is heavily concentrated on the symbolism and actuality of food, and therefore logically the source the child would utilize as semantically meaningful at a very young age. From my point of view this explanation, if it is one, does not represent a very satisfactory state of affairs. On the other hand, it may be the only kind of explanation we will ever be able to offer.

54

I would like to reiterate two things: that this routine is not taught in any sense that I recognize, and that the form the child is able to control is quite degenerate in content from an adult point of view. Yet the fact remains that the control of this routine is not remarked on by adult Koyas.

Note also that the routine, although formally or structurally consisting of the same elements, has radically different meanings in the child-child encounters and adult-adult encounters. Searles' concept of the constitutive nature of the rules for a speech act (Searles 1969) "X counts as y in context z" applies quite well to this sort of interchange. For children, the routine is a speech eliciting game, with no serious or lasting consequences; for sexually mature adults it is an interaction eliciting game which is used as a tactic in a larger encounter that can have very serious consequences indeed.

Let us return to the issue raised earlier in this paper. In the study of child grammars, the distinction between performance and competence as it has been made by generative grammarians was seen to be at best blurred, at worst practically unmaintainable. I proposed instead that we play down the idea of competence in this sense and broaden our frame of reference to concentrate more on the consequences of the child's verbal activity in the context of the speech act--and I see a grammar of a particular child's language based in semantics leading in this direction.

This leads me to say that it does not matter, in terms of the speech event, that the 24 month old child cannot use the Koya system of personal pronoun affixations correctly, or that she cannot use any recognizable pronominal system stably. Whatever reason we want to give for her playing the game, the least we can attribute to her is that the game has meaning. How that meaning is organized in her mind we have no way of knowing, and we may never know. However, we have an external indicator that meaningfulness is being accomplished. Neither the child who takes part in the game, nor adults who may overhear it show surprise at this accomplished act. Her ability to play the game is unquestionable; she follows the rules that constitute the game.

In the same vein, how can we evaluate or decide what it is the child does not know to be appropriate verbal interaction? Let me take another example that indeed occurs in Koya culture, but is no less familiar from American culture. This is a kind of behavior we could talk about as insistent, pestering behavior, but only in terms of its consequences. Here, the child may perhaps cling to its mother, saying over and over again "amma, amma, amma" with an oscillating intonation. The Koya mother is quite likely to respond, in a harried and loud voice never used to other adults "baatadi, baatadi" (what thing, one; what thing, one). The message I believe is clear: a global request does not merit a response when the child is peripheral to the ongoing interaction, and in general such global requests are not honor-

able in all circumstances. These kinds of interchanges I believe
are the locus of the process of socialization of children into
what the rules for participating in speech events are. It is a
learning experience in which no one among the Koya recognizes
that there is a teacher and a pupil. Again using John Searles'
terms, the child is here learning what the regulative rules for
appropriate social interaction are, and not the rules that constitute social interaction per se.

I believe that it is necessary to speak of the child's
ability to play the verbal game correctly (no surprise, irritation, and so on) and the child's inability to make requests
appropriately (with the resultant irritation, bad-mouthing, and
so on), in terms of linguistic competence. But the basic problem remains. For this kind of analysis I believe we need the
resources of the self-aware native actor, and the young child is
neither sufficiently self-aware nor complete enough a participant in the culture to serve us very well in this enterprise.

Summary and Conclusion

I began this discussion by introducing Bateson's concept of eidos as a worthwhile descriptive goal for any particular culture. What are the standardized aspects of the cognitive
structures of individuals in some culture? Explicit in the arguments presented here is the notion that language provides the key.

If the logic of this argument is granted, then it seems
obvious that the process of language socialization (in the broad-
est sense) is critical, since it reveals in an orderly and inten-
tional way the manner in which cognitive development in children
proceeds. However, a serious methodological difficulty intrudes
itself--children are notoriously poor informants about their
accomplishments.

As a consequence, if anthropologists are interested in
how children learn to be members of their cultures, the procedures
that recommend themselves as investigative aids are, first of all,
an earnest attempt to collect data heretofore neglected--child-
ren's talk in natural settings--and secondly, the taking of risks
in the interpretation of these data. Children are after all rational beings whose development is grounded in adult cultures
anthropologists claim to know from the inside, as native actors.

NOTES

1. Here, I can only refer the reader to the vast amount
of research devoted to clarifying the meaning of this assertion
as well as to verifying it. The arguments are clearly stated
in Lenneberg (1967), and Chomsky (1965, 1972), for example.

2. As Chomsky notes: "A theory of substantive universals claims that items of a particular kind in any language must
be drawn from a fixed class of items" (1965: 28). Included here
would be Jacobsen's theory of distinctive features in phonology,
or Berlin and Kay's theory that there is a fixed number of basic
color terms (just eleven, in fact) from which all languages select some subset of terms (Berlin and Kay, 1969). On the other
hand, "...formal universals [of syntax, for example] involve
rather the character of rules that appear in grammars and
the ways in which they can be interconnected" (Chomsky 1965: 29).
By extension to the semantic level of grammar, and in keeping
with the substantive universals proposed for color categories
by Berlin and Kay, the fact that "...the color words of any
language must subdivide the color spectjum into continuous segments..." is a formal universal (Chomsky 1965: 29).
3. Co-occurrence restrictions apply generally to the
linguistic relationships among the constituents of a statement
(Gumperz 1971: 155-157). I have never seen the term used to
refer to the kind of example cited in the text above,that is,
the semantic anomaly. Rather, it has been used in a strict and
technical sense to describe the conditioning of semantically
equivalent alternants in some utterance. Thus, if one uses
"ain't" at the beginning of an utterance, it requires "gonna"
rather than "going to" (the full, 'standard' form) as its complement. Co-occurrence restrictions can be seen to have a
much wider scope of application. One might say, on the analogy
to the stylistic example just given, that certain kinds of co-
occurrence restrictions operate to determine the kind of dress
worn to a diplomatic dinner at the White House. It should be
noted that these restrictions apply to complete sequences,
whether the sequence is a short utterance, or a behavioral
event taking place over a long span of time.

REFERENCES

Bateson, Gregory
        1958   Naven (second edition). Stanford University
                    Press, Stanford.

Bever, T. G.
        1971   Discussion of: Hymes's competence and perfor-
                    mance in linguistic theory, In language acqui-
                    sition: models and methods, R. Huxley and E.
                    Ingram, eds. Academic Press, London and New
                    York.

Berlin, Brent and Paul Kay
        1969   Basic color terms. University of California

Press, Berkeley.

Burling, Robins
      1970   Man's many voices: language in its cultural
                    context. Holt, Rinehart, Winston, New York.

Chomsky, Noam
      1965   Aspects of the theory of syntax. MIT Press,
                    Cambridge.
      1972   Language and mind (enlarged edition). Harcourt,
                    Brace, Jovanovich, Inc., New York.

Gumperz, John
      1971   Language in social groups. Stanford University
                    Press, Stanford.

Kernan, Keith
      1970   The acquisition of phonologically marked speech
                    styles by Samoan children. Unpublished m.s.

Lenneberg, Eric H.
      1967   Biological foundations of language. Wiley, New
                    York.

Searles, John
      1969   Speech acts. Cambridge University Press, London.

Slobin, Dan I.
      1970   Suggested universals in the ontogenesis of
                    grammar. Working Paper No. 32, Language-
                    Behavior Laboratory, U.C., Berkeley.

TOWARD AN EXPERIMENTAL
ANTHROPOLOGY OF THINKING

Michael Cole
The Rockefeller University

Introduction

For the past several years, my colleagues and I have
been engaged in the study of the relation between cultural
institutions and the development of cognitive processes (Gay &
Cole, 1967; Cole, Gay, Glick, & Sharp, 1971). In the course of
this work, we have used a great variety of analytical techniques
borrowed from the academic disciplines of psychology, anthropology, and linguistics. The position that I am going to try to
develop in this paper is that the integration of these techniques
to form an enterprise that I shall speak of as "experimental
anthropology" is necessary if we are going to solve some of the
major unsolved questions of the relation between culture and
cognition.

Let me begin by describing the kind of paradox which
often arises when anthropologists and psychologists discuss the
mental processes of a group of people, each discipline using its
own techniques for collecting data and making inferences.

Among the many papers written by Evans-Pritchard on the
features of Zande culture is one entitled, Sanza, a characteristic feature of Zande language and thought" (1962). In this paper,
Evans-Pritchard describes the way in which the Zande exploit the
potential for ambiguity in speech in order to protect themselves
against their supposedly hostile tribesmen. Evans-Pritchard
gives many examples of Sanza, but one which we can all appreciate
readily is the following:

> A man says in the presence of his wife to his friend,
> "friend, those swallows, how they flit about there."
> He is speaking about the flightiness of his wife and
> in case she should understand the allusion, he covers
> himself by looking up at the swallows as he makes his
> seemingly innocent remark. His friend understands
> what he means and replies, "yes, sir, do not talk to
> me about those swallows, how they come here, sir!"
> (What you say is only too true.) His wife, however,
> also underststnads what he means and says tartly, "yes,
> sir, you leave that she (wife) to take a good she
> (wife), sir, since you married a swallow, sir!"

(Marry someone else if tha is the way you feel about it.) The husband looks surprised and pained that his wife should take umbrage at a harmless remark about swallows. He says to her, "does one get touchy about what is above (swallows), madam?" She replies, ai, sir. Deceiving me is not agreeable to me. You speak about me. You will fall from my tree." The sense of this reply is, "you are a fool to try and deceive me in my presence. It is me you speak about and you are always going at me. I will run away and something will happen to you when you try and follow me." (p. 211)

Evans-Pritchard's formulation for a successful Sanza is as follows: "The great thing...is to keep under cover and to keep open a line of retreat should the sufferer from your malice take offense and try to make trouble." So successful are the Zande in following this practice, and so ubiquitous is the use of Sanza in everyday Zande speech that our renowned Oxonian colleague is led to lament at the end of his article: "It (Sanza) adds greatly to the difficulties of anthropological inquiry. Eventually the anthropologist's sense of security is also undermined, his confidence shaken. He learns the language, can say what he wants to say in it, and can understand what he hears; but then he begins to wonder whether he has really understood...he cannot be sure, and even they (the Zande) cannot be sure, whether the words do have a nuance or someone imagines that they do..." He closes by quoting the Zande proverb, "can one look into a person as one looks into an open-wove basket?" (p. 222)

It is important to mention that while the particular form of ambiguous speech that Evans-Pritchard describes may have special features among the Zande, the use of rhetorical skills as a vehicle for controling one's social environment is a very general feature of both non-literate and literate societies (Albert, 1964, and Labov, 1970).

Now let me describe a different kind of a setting, this time taken from my own work with the Kpelle of Liberia. Two adults are seated at a table. In front of each is a haphazardly arranged pile of ten sticks made of different kinds of wood, of different shapes and sizes. A barrier is placed between the two men and one (whom I shall refer to as the speaker) is told to describe the sticks one at a time to his partner (the listener). One of the sticks is then chosen from a pre-assigned list, laid next to the barrier in front of the speaker, and he describes the stick, after which the listener tries to pick the appropriate stick from his array. This process continues until all ten sticks have been placed by each man. The are then shown the array of ten pairs, errors are described and discussed, and the process repeated.

A set of sticks as I would describe them and as actually described by a Kpelle speaker is listed below in Table 1.

60

Table 1

English description	Kpelle description #1	Kpelle description* #2
thickest straight wood	one of the sticks	one of the sticks
medium straight wood	not a large one	one of the sticks
hook Y	one of the sticks	stick with a fork
	one of the sticks	one of the sticks
thin curved bamboo	piece of bamboo	curved bamboo
thin curved wood	one stick	one of the sticks
thin straight bamboo	one piece of bamboo	small bamboo
long fat bamboo	one of the bamboo	large bamboo
short thorny	one of the thorny	has a thorn
long thorny	one of the thorny	has a thorn
	sticks	

*Note actual order of presentation on Trial 2 was different than Trial 1.

What is striking about this man's performance (and it is representative of the performance of the many traditional Kpelle rice farmers who participated in this study) is that he is failing to include features in his description which, given the nature of the array, must be communicated if the message is to be unambiguously received.

What is the Topic?

I have picked these examples because they can serve as a vehicle for illustrating the ways in which anthropological and psychological approaches to the study of culture and cognition differ.

Consider first the example from Evans-Pritchard. It seems no more than good, common sense to recognize from the data presented that the Zande are subtle and complex thinkers who must consider a host of contingencies when deciding what they are going to say, to whom and how. Assuming equal rhetorical skill among the Kpelle (and there is good evidence that this is so; Bellman, 1969), it seems equally obvious that there must be something wrong with the communication experiment. Perhaps the participants are deliberately shamming, or failing to understand what is expected of them. How could anyone who is an accomplished debator, a user of proverbs and subtle insults, be incompetent in such a simple task?

This style of interpretation has a long and honorable history in anthropology. Starting from the assumption of psychic unity, the anthropologist asserts that all human groups are sufficiently competent to carry out the many complex functions demanded of them by their culture and physical environment. Societies, of course, vary in the kinds of tasks that they pose their members and environments vary in their physical features. The common sense dictum that people will be skillful at tasks they experience often leads to the conclusion that there will be cultural differences in the activities eliciting skilled performance. But these are not differences in "cognitive processes" in the sense that psychologists seem to mean. They are only differences in emphasis.

It may be asked, how could anyone fail to agree? The fact is that able psychologists do fail to agree, both in the interpretation of our two examples, and on the problem of the relation between culture and cognitive processes in general.

I cannot give a detailed account of how these differences arose (for a slightly more expanded account, see Cole et al., 1971, Ch. 1 & 6). The major points seem to be these:

1. Psychologists as a group reject the use of naturally occurring behavior sequences as a source of evidence about learning and thinking processes. The major line of objection can be seen in an example taken from Cole et al., 1971: A man sees black clouds on the horizon and says it is going to rain. Did he make an inference, or did he simply remember the association, black clouds - rain? Complicate the example. Suppose that a man uses instruments to measure wind velocity and barometric pressure. A certain combination of wind velocity and barometric pressure is observed and he says it is going to rain. Did he make an inference? It would seem more likely than in the first case, but it is still possible that he simply remembered this case from an erlier experience. In fact, it is impossible to determine, without specific kinds of prior knowledge about the person and circumstances involved, whether a particular conclusion is a remembered instance from the past, or an example of inference based on present circumstances. Hence, evidence about the "logic of an inference" obtained from anecdotes or naturally occurring instances is always open to alternative interpretation. Just as there are ambiguities when trying to decide what processes are involved in the prediction of rain, there are problems in deciding exactly what people are doing when they use Sanza. Sanza, by its nature is designed to be ambiguous. But the ambiguity of

interpretation for the psychologist is two-fold. We not only need to know what the person "really" meant, we want to know if what he said represented "thinking" or memory. Perhaps people learn a set stock of Sanzas. As children they observe the application of Sanzas by adults and then emulate their elders when the appropriate situation arises. In effect, it might be argued that Sanza requires little more than recall of ambiguous formulae.

2. These kinds of difficulties led psychologists to define thinking as a new combination of previously learned elements, among which problem solving situations have been predominant. Bruner's (1957) definition of cognition as "going beyond the information given" captures the essence of this approach which is shared by psychologists of a wide variety of theoretical persuasions. Such a definition seems to require experimentation in order to make statements about thinking.

3. The dominant pattern of inference in psychology is to use data from experiments as evidence about the psychological processes of individuals and, statistically, about groups. These processes are treated as properties of individuals that are "tapped" by the experimental procedures.

It must be obvious from what I have said so far that I believe there to be a very wide gulf between anthropological and psychological approaches to the study of cognition. The two disciplines do not share the same data base - anthropologists rely for the most part on naturally occurring, mundane events while psychologists rely on experiments. Anthropologists deny the relevance of experiments as artificial, while psychologists avoid natural behavior sequences as ambiguous.

Points of Departure Toward an Experimental Anthropology

In my opinion, the weakest aspect of current experimental psychological research in cross cultural settings is the way that inferences are drawn from "poor performance," instances in which subjects give the wrong answer. This aspect of experimentation is also a fine point of departure for experimental anthropology.

What I am referring to are instances such as the failure of our Kpelle subjects to specify the critical attributes of the sticks they are asked to communicate about. In some contexts (e.g., when middle class American 5 year olds make the same sort of errors in communicating to their peers), such failures are taken as evidence of a failure to take into account the needs of the listener. Further, it may be concluded that prior to a certain age, young children are "egocentric." They cannot "decenter." Similar logic is too often applied to the interpretation of I.Q. tests, Piagetian conservation problems, and a host of other psychological tests of mental development.

63

This practice is as logically indefensible as it is ubiquitous. As one investigator stated recently:

>Experiments in developmental child language can show you what children can do at various ages, but you cannot conclude from them what children cannot do" (Mehler, 1971, p. 154).

I can oly add that this same principle applies generally to comparative research, whether age, culture, or species is the contrast of concern.

The reason, of course, that lack of performance (or a low score) leads to the inference of lack of capacity is that the conclusion so often seems "reasonable." When applied to children in a single culture, the fact that an older child remembers more words, communicates more accurately, and in general behaves more competently is only to be expected. After all, the child has matured! He must have acquired some new cognitive apparatus.

In the same fashion, comparisons involving cultural institutions become plausible. Comparative statements are commonly made by psychologists and some anthropologists, generally in terms of a theory of general cultural advancement as cultures become more westernized. Rarely are the cultural institutions and cultures compared viewed as "different, but equal." Schooling (Greenfield & Bruner, 1966), literacy (Goody & Watt, 1962), and acculturation (Doob, 1960) are all seen as providing people with new cognitive processes, new abilities, and new intellectual tools. It is claimed that without extensive training, the mind is only capable of concrete thought; without writing, analytic thinking is not possible; without new technical challenges, culture and thought are stagnant.

One consequence of such a view is that the "deprived" groups (who lack formal schooling, who have not learned to write, and who lack Western technology) are seen as uniformly lacking in particular, "developed" skills. Another consequence is that the cultural transition to the educated, literate, technological world is often conceived of as causing a transformation in cognitive processes.

It is here that the anthropologist and the psychologist part company in the ways that I have discussed and illustrated above.

My objection to the anthropological treatment of experiments is that justified criticism of the inference drawn from poor performance are combined with unjustified dismissal of culturally-linked differences in performance. Data from psychological experiments, properly treated, are an important source of evidence of the applicability and limits of the doctrine of psychic unity.

Some Illustrative Examples

Even anthropologists noted for their hard-headedness and

acumen have been led to suppose that cultures may differ with respect to the mnemonic skills that they foster in their members. For example, Gregory Bateson's discussion of the cognitive aspects of Iatmul culture emphasizes Iatmul memory skills and relates them directly to central features of the culture (1958, p. 200 ff.). This idea has rather wide currency in the folk lore of anthropologists, but it has received little explicit study (for reviews, see Cole et al., 1971; Cole & Gay, 1972).

A rather extensive series of studies using the techniques of free recall illustrates one procedure that an experimental study of culture and memory can follow.

First, a series of studies was carried out using standard techniques borrowed from contemporary experimental psychology. Subjects were told to remember a list of common nouns consisting of familiar objects: clothing, food, utensils, and tools. They were read the list one item at a time and asked for recall in any order. This procedure was repeated five times for each subject with a single list.

The outcome of these studies was that traditional Kpelle-Liberian farmers recalled relatively few items and failed to learn many new items with repeated presentations of the list. The sequence in which words were recalled conformed to no recognizable pattern of organization. This generalization held even though the experiment was modified to include monetary incentives, different kinds of words, concrete objects, and a variety of other statagems aimed at producing good recall. I might add that an extensive investigation of the items used revealed that they were indeed common and were categorized in the Kpelle language in the way we thought they were.

By contrast, Kpelle who attended high school remembered well, learned rapidly, and manifested a high degree of conceptual organization in the way they recalled the lists.

So far, this story is unusual only in that we seemed to have ruled out some obvious trivial explanations of the relatively poor performance of the Kpelle rice farmers. We still have not accounted for an important fact - in everyday affairs and in certain ritual contexts the Kpelle exhibit normal, and perhaps even very good memory by the standards of any reasonable ethnographer.

Happily, our work continued in search of conditions where experimentally measured Kpelle memory performance would be in line with common observation. We found several such situations. One occurred when we embedded the to-be-recalled list in a Kpelle-style folk story. Asked for the items, our subjects manifested highly organized recall consistent with the story of which it was a part.

In further studies, we were able to trace the difficulty of recall in the standard situation to a difficulty in finding information that was stored, but not effectively retrieved when the instruction to recall was given. Finally, we found still other slightly altered, circumstances that spontaneously produced fine performance in traditional, non-educated people. This occurred, for example, where the objects to be recalled were associated with concrete objects, or when subjects were encouraged to form their own groups during extensive exploration of the objects.

This series of experiments taken as a unit certainly seems to bear out the dictum that people will be able to perform well at tasks they find normal and which they often encounter. As such, it confirms anthropological doctrine. But it does more, I hope. It specifies somewhat more closely than usual what "normal" conditions are. And it turns out that "normal" cannot be simply equated with "encounter often." Some of the experimental situations eliciting fine recall were abnormal in the sense of infrequently encountered. What the successful conditions seem to share with frequently encountered situations is a lot of structure. Where life or the experimental procedures do not structure the memory task, the traditional person has great difficulty. "Normal" in this case, refers to the presence of certain structural features.

Free recall is so named because it permits the subject to repeat back items presented in any order he likes, at any pace. Our current theory of how skilled subjects learn such a task is that they provide structure (via mnemonic devices and rehearsal strategies) which they then use to retrieve stored information. Spontaneous production of such structures in free recall seems to be a learned behavior which is fostered in some cultures (or by some cultural institutions) and not in others.

In summary, this series of studies seems to illustrate the following principles:

1. Cultures differ in the situations that elicit skilled mnemonic performance.

2. Cultures differ in the degree to which members will spontaneously produce structure as a device for enhancing recall of totally unstructured, disconnected material. Free recall is one such task.

3. By pursuing the problem of poor performance - by whom and under what conditions it is manifested - we can tease apart cultural differences in the situations to which skills are applied from cultural differences in the skills fostered in members.

The very tentative nature of these conclusions has to be immediately recognized. To give them greater basis, collaboration of anthropologists and psychologists aimed at exploring natural and contrived situations for the application of mnemonic skills is essential. This is a point to which I shall return.

Let me briefly recount one other example of a research program in which pursuit to the causes of poor performance was instructive. My example concerns inference.

The enduring controversy over the existence or nonexistence of "primitive mind" involved, among other things, an argument over whether the premises or laws of inference differed among "privitive" and "civilized" peoples.

Starting with a device used to assess inferential processes in American children, we set out to study the development of inferential processes among the Kpelle of Liberia. The device we used is pictured in Figure 1.

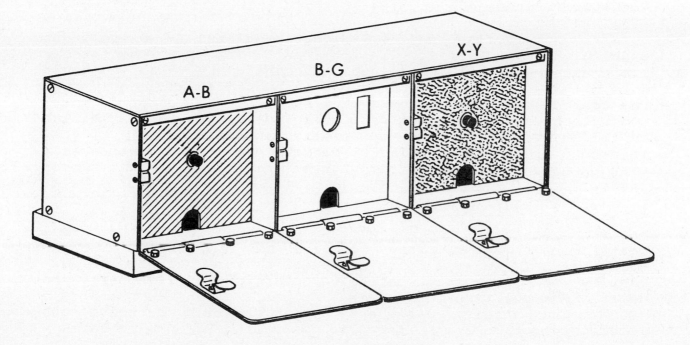

The problem is presented as follows.

First the subject is taught that pushing the button on the left hand panel will yield him a marble. Then he is taught that pushing the button on the right hand panel will yield ball bearing. Then, with the two side panels closed, he is taught that putting a ball bearing in a hole in the center panel will yield him a piece of candy which he can see in a small window in the panel.

Finally, all three panels are opened at once and the subject is instructed to obtain the candy which he can keep and eat.

This problem has the nice feature of specifying the "premises" (the way to get a marble and a ball bearing) from which a solution (get the candy) is to be reached and of ensuring that the subjects know these premises very well before they proceed to make the required inference.

When this problem was first presented to groups of traditional Kpelle (children and young adults), performance was very unimpressive. For example, only 15% of the young adults spontaneously solved the problem and about half reached an incorrect solution.

Another experiment identified the general source of difficulty. When an analogous problem was constructed of match boxes and a small locked chest, even small children were generally proficient performers. This suggests strongly that familiarity with the materials about which one is asked to reason is important if people are going to apply a cognitive skill they have.

One additional study further localized the point in the problem where familiarity was important. Stages of the first two studies were pitted against each other. For example, keys were obtained from our fancy apparatus, one of which could open the locked box. It was shown that subjects who performed poorly did so because they do not deal effectively with the <u>first</u> link in the problem. Once they got started on the right track, the inference proceeded adequately, but the need to initiate a solution on an unfamiliar instrument seems to impede the whole process.

Here again is an instance where following up poor performance has been instructive. It comes as no surprise to the anthropologist that the subject has difficulty with "that foreign contraption." Such findings certainly fit with common observation that some non-technological peoples have considerable difficulty when first encountering various kinds of machinery. But we are in a position to say more. First, we can demonstrate (rather than assert) that the people in question can solve such problems under more familiar circumstances. Second, we have isolated the point in the problem solving processes where difficulties occur; it is not just the presence of the funny device, it is a particular stage in having to work with it that is the stumbling block.

Theoretical Relevance to the Study of Culture and Cognition

I could give other examples of research following the strategy which I like to call experimental anthropology. But I think the major theoretical points can be abstracted from what I have said so far.

Both anthropology and psychology stand to gain from integrated studies of the kind that I am advocating.

For anthropology, a major gain will be in extending the kinds of behavior which are deemed relevant to understanding the intellectual features of a culture. In Bateson's pioneer work, which I mentioned briefly above, he outlines the way in which mnemonic skills must be related to cultural institutions. Speaking of the more general enterprise, he says:

> We may expect to find that cultures differ enormously in the extent to which they promote intellectual activity; though I know of no field work in which any attention has been paid to this phenomenon (1958, p.222).

In Iatmul, Bateson points to the role of naming in ritual and the way that the Iatmul must be good rememberers and fine debators if they are to maintain and improve their social status. He uses features of the debating situation to argue that rote memory is not the chief process involved, but he points out that "it is not possible to say which of the higher processes is chiefly involved" (p. 224). Experimentation of the sort advocated here, promises one way to tell if such "higher processes" are involved and to determine what they are.

Another example can be taken from the work of Thomas Gladwin. Gladwin has long been concerned with an ethnographic account of Micronesian navigation. From his very earliest work (Gladwin & Sarason, 1953), he has also sought to make inferences about the mental processes of his subjects. In that early work with Sarason, before he became professionally concerned with navigation, it was concluded that Micronesians (Trukese) are concrete thinkers. In his first treatment of navigation, influenced by then current psychological theorizing, he concluded that the thought processes of Puluwatan navigators were indeed abstract, but that the "total process goes forward without reference to any explicit principles and without any planning, unless the intention to proceed to a particular island can be considered a plan" (Gladwin, 1964, p. 175). In his most recent work (Gladwin, 1970), he concludes that Puluwatans can plan as part of an overall cognitive process, but that they have not developed "heuristic" thinking. I do not agree with Gladwin's interpretation, even in his later work, and I do not believe that ethnographic work by itself will resolve the difficulties. However, I can think of some ways to test Gladwin's notion within the context of sailing activities. Here again cooperation between anthropologist and psychologist appears necessary.

In each of these cases, a key question is: what kinds of cultural institutions promote what kinds of intellectual activities and processes? To this I would add the question: what is the range of situations to which a given intellectual process can be applied?[1] This latter question, I suggest, lies at the heart of the problem of education in non-industrialized societies and I will return to it presently. Work on answers to both questions could be enormously advanced by the inclusion of properly designed experimental studies.

I believe that psychologists have as much, or more, to gain from a collaboration with anthropologists as do the anthropologists.

Most psychologists believe that the development of cognitive mechanisms depends in some way on interaction between the maturing child and the experiences provided by his environment, although beyond this generality, chaos sets in. At present, we have the anomolous situation where one part of this supposed interaction, the environmentally induced experiences, fails to vary much. It would seem a natural impulse, then, to seek out a wide range of cultural environments in which to study cognition in order to provide variation of experiences. This is an obvious point, but it has consistently run afoul of the problem of relating test performance to psychological process. Most psychologists are aware of the pitfalls of inference working in different cultural seetings, and so conclude that the enterprise is useless (while, I might add, falling victim to some of the same logical problems when comparing children of different ages within their own culture).

A way to obtain the benefits of environmental variation while avoiding the pitfalls of usual cross cultural research is, I believe, for psychologists to explicitly separate two causes of poor performance: 1) the subject cannot do the task (he has not "got the process") and 2) the subject does not do the task (he is not "using the process"). Once this approach is adopted (as it is in the recent work of Flavell, 1970; Flavell & Wohlwill, 1969), search can begin for the situational constraints on performance. I would hope, too, that it would be possible to look to the ethnographer for situations in which a particular kind of cognitive skill is manifested as a guide to the psychologist's search.

Returning to our example of communication performance among Kpelle adults, we can imagine how further research might proceed. Bellman (1971) has documented the way people are very careful about the information they divulge to strangers and Gay (personal communication) has been impressed with the ways in which adults seem to select proverbs for use with special people under specific circumstances. Horton (1967) has emphasized that features of people, not features of objects are of most concern to traditional, sub-Saharan Africans. Might it not be possible to construct analogies of the communication task with people, or proverbs, as the things to be communicated? Certainly, adults cannot often neglect the needs of their listeners. Why do they in our task? When do they not? What can be done to specify the critical features of the situations governing good and poor communication?

Applications for Education

As a final point, I would like to suggest the implications of this analysis of the problem of formal, European-style school among non-technological peoples. So much has been

70

written about the overall problems in cross cultural education that I do not dare to stray afield to comment generally on this problem here. But I do think that some remarks are called for on the specific learning problems which arise even if the child is in school regularly, has enough to eat, has a competent teacher, is trying, and has the support of his parents and the community (ah, Utopia!).

All too often the style of psychological inferences that leads us to conclude that young children lack a process which other children have is carried over in all its essentials to a discussion of the influence of cultural change (particularly the change wrought by the introduction of schooling) on cognition. The more "advanced" culture, and specifically the school as a cultural institution, provides its members with processes that non-members do not have. The dictum that children should be taught to think in school is often taken quite literally, and it is believed that those who are successful are those who have learned the new way of thinking. From what we have been saying, this may or may not be the case. It may also be that schooling operates to broaden the range of situations to which particular ways of learning and problem solving will be applied. The problem is not one of working from a tabula rasa, but of getting children to transfer skills learned in a very different context, and to teach them the appropriateness of particular ways of learning for school-type tasks. Some writers, such as Greenfield and Bruner, have suggested that freeing cognitive process from specific content is a primary outcome of Western-style education.

In our own work, we often find that a little schooling is sufficient to greatly change the way in which certain problems are solved. In some cases, as in the case of memory, it seems to add a new process; but in many others, it seems only to greatly increase the probability that the subject will manifest certain ways of behaving that all subjects have, but which non-educated subjects apply in more restricted, or perhaps just other, contexts. This problem of separating the acquisition of new processes from the transfer of old is a major unsolved problem for future research. It clearly gives some additional meaning to the movement to make available "relevant" material to children from non-technological societies; but now "relevant" takes on a special meaning. It is material that will evoke those ways of learning and thinking that the teacher wants to detach from the habitual objects and to set free in the school.

As a final word, I would like to suggest that we not get carried away with the idea of context-free thinking. It is a dubious goal which, in my experience, seems too often to lead to the creation of men who have learned how to think, but no longer have a meaningful, culturally defined, content to think about.[2]

71

NOTES

1. Terms such as intellectual "activity," "cognitive process," intellectual "skill," have no clearly agreed-upon referents within either anthropology or psychology. I have tried to use terms such as "skill" and "activity" to refer to empirically observable behaviors. Assertions about what psychological process is reflected by a particular activity are theoretical, not empirical statements. One way in which to phrase the theme of this paper is to say that inferences about intellectual process must rest upon evidence about performance from a wide variety of intellectual activities, including evidence of both and experimental and ethnographic observational nature.

2. The preparation of this manuscript has been supported in part by grant # OEG 1695 from the Office of Education and grant # GM 16735 from the National Institute of General Medical Sciences. The ideas presented here have developed during the course of my collaboration with many people, notably J. Gay and J. Glick. For a somewhat different formulation of the role of experimentation in anthropological settings, see Glick, 1969. I would like to thank E. Schegloff, D. Rundus, and J. Lave for their comments on the manuscript.

REFERENCES

Albert, E.

"Rhetoric," logic, and poetics in Burundi: culture patterns of speech behavior. In J. J. Gunperz & D. Hymes (Eds.). The ethnography of communication, American Anthropological Association, Washington, D. C., pp. 35-54.

Bateson, G.
    1958   Naven. Second edition, Stanford: Stanford University Press.

Bellman, B. L.
    1969   Some constitutive factors of secrecy among the Fala Kpelle of Sucrumo, Liberia. Paper delivered at the meeting of the Liberian Research Association, Stanford, California.

Cole, M. and J. Gay
                Culture and memory. American Anthropologist, in press.

Cole, M., J. Gay, J. Glick, and D. Sharp
    1971   The cultural context of learning and thinking. New York: Basic Books.

Doob, L.
    1960   Becoming more civilized. New Haven: Yale
                University Press.

Evans-Pritchard, E.
    1963   Sanza, a characteristic feature of Zande langu-
                age and thought. In Essays in social anthro-
                pology. New York: Free Press of Glencoe, Ch. 9.

Flavell, J. H.
    1970   Developmental studies of mediated memory. In H.
                W. Reese & L. P. Lipsitt (Eds.), Advances in
                child development and behavior, Vol. 5, New York:
                Academic Press.

Flavell, J. H. and J. F. Wohlwill
    1969   Formal and functional aspects of cognitive
                development. In D. Elkind & J. H. Flavell
                (Eds.), Studies in cognitive development:
                Essays in honor of Jean Piaget. New York:
                Oxford University Press, pp. 67-120.

Gay, J. and M. Cole
    1967   The new mathematics and an old culture. New
                York: Holt, Rinehart, & Winston.

Gladwin, T.
    1964   Culture and logical processes. In W. Goodenough
                (Ed.), Explorations in cultural anthropology:
                essays in honor of George Peter Murdock. New
                York: McGraw-Hill.

Gladwin, T.
    1970   East is a big bird. Cambridge: Belknap Press.

Gladwin, T. and S. Sarason
    1953   Truk: Man in paradise. Viking Fund, Publica-
                tions in Anthropology, No. 20. Wenner-Gren
                Foundation for Anthropological Research, Inc.

Glick, J.
    1969   Culture and cognition: some theoretical and
                methodological concerns. Paper presented at the
                American Anthropological Association meetings,
                New Orleans, November.

Goody, J. and I. Watt
    1962   The consequences of literacy. Comparative
                studies in sociology and history, 5, pp. 304-
                345.

73

Greenfield, P. M. and J. S. Bruner
    1966   Culture and cognitive growth, International
                Journal of Psychology, 1, pp. 80-107.

Horton, R.
    1967   African traditional thought and Western science:
                Parts I and II, Africa, 37, pp. 50-71, pp. 155-
                187.

Labov, W.
    1970   The logic of non-standard English. In Language
                and poverty, F. Williams (Ed.). Chicago:
                Markham.

Mehler, J.
    1971   In R. Huxley and E. Ingram (Eds.). Language
                acquisition: models and methods. New York:
                Academic Press, p. 69.

II. RITUALS OF SOCIALIZATION

ITERATIVE ACTIVITY AND BEHAVIORAL PIETY IN PRIVATE PLACES

Otto von Mering
University of Florida

Introduction

For many years, I have been concerned with the problem
of inter-group relations and the formation of a sense of personal and social identity. A particular focus has been the
ethnic dimension of individual and group-ways of experiencing
opposition and conflict, and practicing security patterns,
different and yet the same. (von Mering 1953, 1959, 1961, 1971,
1972a).

For this symposium, I turn my attention to certain
persistent regulative behavioral aspects of intra-group life
which anthropologists have more often studied with reference to
large-scale social structure, culture change and minority-majori-
ty culture conflict. (Spiro 1955; Foster 1960; Barth 1969;
Spicer 1961, 1971). In general terms, I am speaking of ordered
iterative activities which have been observed ubiquitously in
all primary human groups. They are invariably linked with man's
perennial search for shelter, and concern over loss of social
cover. They take place in the majority-minority context of
inter-generation and peer relations; they are repeated on ordinary occasions of everyday; and they pace the seasons of the
year with special anniversary markings. In a large measure,
they are the basis of the formation of personal character and
the transmission and maintenance of specialized or generalized
social response systems throughout the life-cycle.

Ordered, iterative activities range from simple one-
person, task-oriented routines to elaborate multi-person behavior
systems. The organizationally most complex, and individually
most memorable forms of activity, those having overriding social
significance in addition to a problem-solving function, I have
chosen to call behavioral pieties. They are recurring and sequential interpersonal statements, or rather, condensed social
messages of the special mix of cultural myth, conventional legend, and familial tale persisting in a well-defined network of
individual action programs. Both the story told again and again
and the visible behavioral events form an experiential unit,
signifying one of the minimum requirements for continued full
membership in a particular human group. An assemblage of
such learned and transmitted behavior is basic to the process
of socialization and individuation. Hence, a given observed

behavioral piety represents an elementary form of classifying
and counting, and of measuring and equating the social appearance and behavior of the individual in the group.

The present discussion of iterative activities and behavioral pieties will be paradigmatic rather than exhaustive.
Moreover, my consideration of their persistence in the formation
and expression of individual assets and liabilities in social
intercourse is restricted to behavior observed and recorded in
ordinary urban and rural American households.

Background

A general proposition about social learning which has
guided most of my anthropomedical researches, (von Mering 1962,
1969, 1970, 1972b) together with three social science approaches
to myth, ritual and madness are the stimulus for the present inquiry. The proposition is simply stated: In the long history
of man's quest for security (i.e., order and maintenance), and
of the individual search for identity (i.e., growth and development), "socialization is a matter of learning about man-made
structure, [while] individuation is a matter of understanding
processes of human nature. [Hence, what] an individual must
learn and will repress in order to live in his society is not
identical with what he can learn or wishes to forget." (von
Mering 1972) Thus, for every social being the source of both
differentiation and conflict, of progression and change lies in
the experiential opposition of this quest and search.

My wish to examine the nature and function of iterative
behavior in private places in light of this model of personal
identity and security formation became feasible for me upon re-
considering the views of A. M. Hocart on myth, James Bossard on
the family, and Jules Henry on madness. Like Hocart, I went so
to speak, "round the world in search of true myth, the myth
that is bound up with life; I too concluded: we have come home
to find it at our door." (Hocart 1970)

In my studies of 'well' and 'sick' families, I was often struck by the analogy between how much a private family tale
and negatively sanctioned conduct,--oft retold--, can bind an
individual to his lineage, and how much cultural myth,--as a form
of public knowledge--, does link man to deity in the course of
formal ritual procedures. Hocart's cogent observations about
myth and ritual seemed to support this line of reasoning. He
stated:

> The myth which has some relation to the serious
> business of life...is a precedent; but it is more
> than that...it gives the ritual its intention...
> ...Thus the myth is part of the ritual, and the
> ritual part of the myth: the myth describes the
> ritual, and the ritual enacts the myth...The prin-

78

ciple is the same; the myth completes the desired
information of man and God [and Lineage] for the
attainment of plenty.

...The connection between myth and life is...ap-
parent...The myth itself confers life, but it cannot be recited without ritual: The two are insep-
arable. It is necessary to go back to the original
meaning [of myth] a sacred story; a story which
purports to be true, and which research shows more
and more to be true in essentials, however, much
the details may become distorted. (Hocart 1970)

The sociological studies of James Bossard and his associate, Eleanor Boll on family living (Bossard and Boll 1950; Bossard 1953, 1966) corroborates anecdotally Hocart's aphorism
about man's continuous involvement in ritual activity: "The mere
sightseer gains no religious merit;...knowledge, without works
cannot long survive." (Hocart 1970) Bossard and Boll's enthu-
siastic immersion into the study of patterned domesticated behavior led them to apply the term "ritual" too loosely to almost
any form of it.

According to their usage, it is behavior which arises
out of family interaction and is directed toward some specific
end or purpose. Using informants, diaries and autobiographies
of middle and upper class New England and Philadelphia families,
they profusely documented how "family rituals" acquire "rigidity" and an aura of "rightness" as a result of repetition. They
attributed a large assortment of social functions to family ritual. For example, they stressed its importance as a concrete
means of attitude and goal communication, and as a tool for social
participation of the young. They were impressed with family ritual as a practical way of teaching children about social reality
and as an agency for family continuity and control.

Bossard and Boll saw "ritual" rampant in the family
fold; and, focussing on its structural significance and formal
maintenance functions, they largely ignored its relationship
to character formation and psychopathology. Nevertheless, their
non-systematic review of the many kinds of "family rituals" convinced me of the need to rigorously reconsider the integral role
of ordered iterative activity in everyday family processes.

At this juncture, I began to take another reading of
Jules Henry's pioneering first-hand studies of contemporary American families (Henry 1963, 1971). Reflecting back on his earlier
work, it bacame clear that he had, indeed, engaged in a life-
long search for invariable aspects of social interaction in the
formation of personality and individual response; and that this
led him to reexamine the psychologically overdetermined significance of behavioral regularities in 'normal' and ordinarily disturbed families. Moreover, it allowed him to formulate the
transmission and retention of man's many ways of falling from
reason and acting out of reach of sanity in terms of certain

79

attitudinal and expressive behavior "pathways to madness".
Finally, he seemed to have remarkable personal success in systematically reducing to a minimum the problems of naturalistic
observation of family process.

Most instructive for my understanding of the operation
and cumulative impact of ordered iterative activity in the family
have been Henry's observations on the phenomenon of "availability" as a necessary underpinning for all human interaction and
socialization. He said:

...People are made available to others through the
love and determination of those who make themselves
available -- and the process of bringing to life
has to be repeated every day because all the fundamental tasks of existence are repetitious..., and
nobody can become a human being alone.

The cause of humanness is the availability of
another person, for a human being has his being in
the availability of love. I want to make clear
that I am talking about our culture only, for the
self has many forms, depending on the culture. In
our culture one cannot be a self without love. I
distinguish between being a self and being merely
nonvegetable, an entity that can perform the roles
society assigns him. Mere attentive availability,
without persecution and ambiguity, is enough to
generate language and acceptable social behavior
in a child, and in any culture, these alone are
sufficient to make it possible for him to survive.
In our culture, however, we do not think it's
enough if people can merely talk and do what they
are supposed to do. Only love provides the rest -
the rest of what it is to be human.

Some people are available only to their families,
others only to their jobs, still others to boys but
not to girls; some are available to adults but not
to children; some are available in sex but at no
other time and so on. Nobody is available to everyone; everyone, except some psychotic people, is
available at some moments and not at others and
everyone is limited by his personality. In the
course of evolution only those cultures could have
survived in which mothers or their surrogates were
adequately available to infants. Societies must
disappear which place such burdens on people that
there is not enough time for sufficient interaction
with infants to make them human; hence today only
those remain which achieved the proper balance. It
is axiomatic, therefore, that a culture must give
children enough social contact to enable them to
learn to talk and to become socially acceptable.

But beyond this what a culture requires of the individual is unique to each culture. (Henry 1971)
     In the course of his careful observations of human pat-
terns of inaccessibility and availability, Jules Henry succeeded
in documenting best the essential absurdity, even madness of certain iterated forms of seemingly reasonable behavior in the cave
of ordinary domesticity. The probable reasons for this lament-
able reality could be stated in terms of several alternative
reductionist models of human nature. Whatever the essential
reason, the scientific journey into the familial network of ordered activity and behavioral messages has only just begun.[1]

Rubrics of Iterative Behavior

     The systematic analysis of condensed behavioral pieties
in the context of the full range of observable iterative primary
group activity requires a simple operational classification. A
decade of intermittent direct observations of these expressive
behavior events in one, two and three generation households in
Western Pennsylvania, as well as interview-based data on a contemporary communal "family" in Norther New England is the basis
of the following six-cell grid of domesticated behavior rubrics.[2]
Each cell is horizontally ordered according to whether one, two,
three or more individuals have to be available for the behavior
and social message to occur. The cell content of single or
multi-person behavior systems is vertically specified according
to whether their functional or expressive (i.e., message) significance is primary for the group or individual.
     Since all repeated patterned activity can be shown to
be both functional and expressive in some sense, the following
classificatory scheme has been adopted. Iterative behavior,
having functional primacy is defined according to its evidential
focus on instrumental activity. This includes, (a) particular
work or leisure doings, (b) problem-solving in general, or (c)
discharging a special task or acquiring a needed skill. Behavior is deemed to have expressive primacy if the activity communicates to participant and observer alike special codified
sensory and behavioral messages, over and above its instrumental
focus. Such messages may (1) entail a discrete effort at presenting aspects of personal character or features of individual
family style. (2) They may also amount to a lock-step group
enactment, a learning, transmitting and maintaining, a retelling
and re-inventing, so to speak, desired forms of social conduct.
Or, they (3) may make visible and audible a particular shared
(i.e., 'well-remembered' or 'persisting') cultural myth, social
legend or family tale about the necessary 'is's' and 'oughts'
of existence. In certain places and at certain times, all
three ways of expressive message-making may be present in one
complex condensed behavioral piety.

81

This classificatory approach results in a six-cell grid of distinct rubrics of iterative behavior in private places. (See Figure I) According to its functional or expressive primacy, an iterative activity has been termed a Routine, or a Habitual Stance when it has a particular task or interest focus, and is done, or expressed (i.e., presented) by one individual. It may be classed as a Procedure, or Transactional Performance when it involves the organized division and sequencing of labor, or ordering and 'memorializing' of relationships between two people. Lastly, certain domestic behavior patterns are experienced, expressed and recognized as a Program when three or more people engage in a work-oriented sequence of coordinated acts in relation to a particular common practical purpose. Such an iterative undertaking is a Condensed Behavioral Piety when the assemblage of behavior components clearly denotes a memorable sensory and social message interaction.

FIGURE I

RUBRICS OF ITERATIVE BEHAVIOR

	Functional Primacy	Instrumental or Significance	Expressive Primacy	Message or Significance
		Work/leisure/problem solving; task/skill learning		Social conduct learning & character presenting; culture myth & social legend evoking.
RELATIONAL NETWORK	One	Routine		Habitual Stance
OR				
PERSON-SYSTEMS	Dyad	Procedure		Transactional Performance
	Triad or More	Program		Condensed Behavioral or Piety / Iterative Social Message

Some Interpretive Questions

In my research to date, all of these behavior events have been observed or reported to me on visits to households in the early, middle or late phases of the biological family life-cycle. The process of formally allocating particular behavior patterns among the six possible grid positions is based on the rigorous reexamination of the data on a given household with the aid of a series of interpretive questions. Those found useful in my work are presented herewith:

1. When, and where do the various forms of behaving take place?

2. Who, and how many persons are involved in it?

3. How public or private is the event? Who is audience and who participant? (e.g., is it strictly 'en famille,' or does it include relatives, or others as well?)

4. Is it recognized as belonging to a given category of behavior by participant, by audience, or by both?

5. What is the nature of person participation?

6. How rigid or flexible is it in detail?

7. What is its frequency of occurrence?

8. Has it undergone any changes through time? If so, what are they?

9. What is the origin and scope of the patterned behavior?: (a) Was it initiated in this family or passed on? (b) Will it terminate with this family or be passed on? (c) Does it occur in a particular phase of the family's life-cycle? Is it linked to a particular place, day, occasion or season? (d) Is it particular to this family, or if not, how is it related to the nature of the extended kin group, class, ethnic group, and size of the family?

10. What is the purpose or nature of the goal of the event?

11. How well organized, or elaborated into sequential behavior units is the event? How clear or ambiguous is the behavioral message?

12. To what extent is the event symbolic of something? At what level of personal awareness is there recognition that a special social message is being communicated?

13. Is the whole behavior event expressing, i.e., demonstrating, exhibiting, or asserting, something that is or is not, should not be (or cannot be because it is not allowed to be)?

14. Is the entire behavioral event continuing despite having "outlived" its initial function, or message significance?

A Sampling of Iterative Behavior

The potential list of interpretive questions is of course endless. A few illustrations of different rubrics of ordered family behavior is more persuasive of the manner in which this

83

conceptual universe has been mapped.

Ex. #1 (Family A.): Devised an efficient sequence of getting 5 family members in and out of the bathroom in one-half hour every weekday morning. (A Program)

The same family has a solomn Christmas tree decorating and candle-lighting ceremony during which the trials and work of near, distant or dead relatives on the male side of the family are reviewed by father. The eldest son acts as assistant story teller, while mother and only daughter watch the boys (their term of reference) in silence. (A Behavioral Piety)

Ex. #2 (Family J): Before the Jones children could read, Mr. Jones always read to them for an hour every Sunday night. The children are now in their teens but every Sunday night an hour is reserved for reading aloud. The two daughters now take turns reading poetry; the son presents a special current events topic. (A Behavioral Piety)

Ex. #3 (Family S): In preparing for a dinner one of the teen daughters always sets the table, another always makes the salad, and Mrs. Smith prepares the hot food. The food is placed in serving dishes before Mr. Smith who fills and passes out the plates. This is a Sunday affair. Mrs. Smith's parents followed the same pattern; and her two sisters now do likewise in their households. On weekdays, though not on Friday and Saturday night when she prepares food only for her husband while children are on their own, Mrs. S. does the entire evening meal preparation and serving. Her daughters divide the work of cleaning up and dishwashing. (A Program)

Ex. #4 (Family D): At 6:30 AM, Mr. D., a company production manager, is awakened by clock radio and places himself on an invariable behavior sequence: wash-up, face and hands only; underwear next, socks thereafter, then shirt. On his way to auto-timed perc coffee, he picks up tie, puts on shoes, and then puts on pants. He likes everything set up the night before. His spouse commented: "He got assembled that way on workdays when he started at the plant; now it's everyday." (A Habitual Stance)

Ex. #5 (Family S. III): Learning extends to the whole family of Smythe III. Except for weekends, one of the little Smythes is "captain" each week with the task of awakening all of the other Smythes at 6:45. From then until 8:20, the schedule calls for a family meeting, songs, Bible reading, breakfast, and a speedy recorded French lesson (ten minutes) for the head of the family. (A Behavioral Piety)

Ex. #6 (Family G.): Anniversaries of birthdays and deaths are carefully noted on a "master calendar" prominently displayed in the kitchen. "Only mother writes on it; father checks in and we find out what to do," commented the oldest daughter. Planning for and having the annual family reunion on Thanksgiving is a major undertaking, with special assigned tasks for parents and children in the George household. On this and similar patriotic and religious holidays, the Georges are high Episcopalian, the calendar becomes an interactional focus. (An Iterative Social Message). Moreover, on these occasions it is especially noticeable how the husband and wife organize their work as a pair; the older and younger daughter, and the youngest twin sons carefully divide various assigned tasks between them. (A Procedure)

The formal, across-the-table exchange of two unwrapped set of small gifts of sentimental value between Mr. and Mrs. George, during a late dinner without children, and prior to eating a special occasion desert of fruit-out-of-season with real cream, marks their wedding anniversary. They started this after the second child was born and continue to do so. (A Transactional Performance)

Aspects of Iterative Activities and Pieties

The every-day and unique actuality of family-oriented behavior patterns and messages may be analyzed from many vantage points. However, a general statement of the crucial analytical aspects can be made at this stage of my research. This paradigmatic exposition is provisional, and intended to evoke comment and stimulate critique.

A. As such, primary group oriented iterative activity does not generate or reflect all the subjective content of domestic or private life; that is to say, all group feelings, attitudes, values and goals. However, as patterned or structured behavior it is a visible, individual and inter-subjective sign of subtle group process. Taken as a whole, iterative behavior conveys concretely the instrument and message content of the entire group from person to person, and from one generation to the next.

B. Primary group oriented pieties, in the sense of ordered behavior messages, tend to represent a set of finalized status reports on its socio-emotional and normative household. For example, their manifestation in condensed family tale or social legend evolves gradually from experience through time. As iterative social messages, they most often define the content of ideal and normative conduct by "telling it as it is" or ought to be or cannot be.

Such ways of doing and commanding things encompass various preferred individual routines, customary dyadic procedures, or complex group programs. They will take place in all manner of circumstances, but especially in ordinary and recurring domestic situations. They often mark major and minor crises of family life (e.g., illness). They may perdure for the life-cycle of the family of orientation, and beyond into the new procreative household.

C. A particular assemblage of such behavior sequences
tends to be selected and elaborated by one family unit, and,
hence serves to distinguish it from another household. In this
operational sense, there are certain family patterns that bear
the mark of a particular socio-cultural class or ethnic heritage.
Their relative position and durability within the framework of
family life-cycle activities has demonstrable impact on stability
and change in self-perception, reality-testing, and individual
function. Characteristically, (1) some behavior sequences acquire an aura of rigidity and rightness, even sanctity. (2)
Under certain circumstances, they may acquire an out-of-phase
or arresting force on individual development. (3) Others
remain flexible in form, though stable in content in continued
practice; still others (4) have only transitory significance
and legitimacy in relation to different periods of individual
passage through the family life-cycle into adulthood.
D. Some, though not all family-ordered behavior conveys
a body of pragmatic information and material content between
child and adult. That is to say, some behavior becomes a set of
habitual and convenient techniques for social participation and
disengagement. Depending on its saliency, habitualness and
context, some instrumental behavior cluster may also denote a
given family's reliable way for the formation of individual
social identity.
Such behavior sequences amount to iterated socio-
emotional messages which, depending on time and place of
occurrence, focus on one or all of the following components of
social character formation: (1) developing a sense of personal
history and a sense of family time; (2) discovering a sense of
place in society: a sense of the specific and a sense of community; (3) binding the offspring to his involuntary or unwitting
familial inheritance of material and symbolic assets and liabilities; and (4) revitalizing a sense of loyalty and perhaps, a
feeling of 'embeddedness' in the family fold at special occasions
such as anniversaries and reunions.
E. Some familial iterative activities are a primary
medium of transmitting values and attitudes, and of behaviorally
bridging or separating generations. If viewed as processes of
interaction and as behavioral messages of passage, they represent the Family Way of Learning about (i.e., internalizing) and
dealing with psycho-social reality at home and in the outside
world.
In particular, family-ordered pieties can be vehicles for seven crucial tasks of social learning and individuation: (1) Releasing/supporting (stimulating) or inhibiting/
constricting (freezing in) intra-familial transactions. This
refers to all manner of tension, stress, and conflict exchanges.
(2) Building and regulating, actually, standardizing or starv-
ing familial and individual expression of affect (i.e., energy).
(3) Exhibiting and legitimating forms of control and individual

86

power roles of moving with, moving toward, moving away, and moving against another group member. (4) Assorting and cementing working coalitions and symbolic dyads of giving and taking, of seeking and grasping, of yielding and keeping, losing and winning, and of competing and cooperating, hedging or negotiating. (5) Dividing or distributing and simplifying household functioning, or the opposite. That is to say, they are vehicles for defining and organizing leisure and work; and for transferring useful skills from one domestic task to a related one. (6) Presenting and channeling opportunities for (a) naming things and events; for tagging messages as important or unimportant; (b) expressing individual family achievements, i.e., providing for the display of personal character and the family image; (c) arranging for gradations of individual invisibility or protection within the group; and (d) glossing over, explaining away or putting up with inherent ambiguities and ambivalences in intra-familial relations. (7) Demonstrating and exploring problems of inter-individual living, particularly, the human predicaments of living with inequality between un-equals and of enduring inequalities among equals (e.g., coping with problems of 'dues payment,' 'position entitlement,' and 'status validation' within any group).

F. The understanding of the various properties or characteristics of ordered iterative activity and of its effect upon child and family must become an integral part of the longitudinal study of human development, and hence a key focus in the detection of the behavioral sources of social misfunc-tioning and emotional disorders.

G. In sum, family-oriented pieties are to be understood in the following terms: (1) As symbolic of 'the child in man,' and expressive of change and growth in the life-cycle of the individual; (2) As symbolic of the structure of love and the organization of function which denotes group goal structure; (3) As invariant vehicles for learning the ground rules of social existence in a given culture; (4) As elementary forms of itera-tive behavioral and oral messages for (a) coming to terms with the passage of time, for (b) learning to manipulate a personal or group sense of time and, (c) for evoking the sensation of timelessness; i.e., to conjure up the continous present; (5) as the means for concretizing and dramatizing, experiencing and connecting, and reexperiencing intra-familial and individual response systems; (i.e., as the acceptable social medium for experimenting with and ordering the variegated nature of individ-ual membership in the primary group); (6) As an individual and group system-maintaining variable in terms of short-term func-tional adjustment, and as (7) a system-changing variable in terms of long-range human adaptation to the species - given categories of experience of sex and reproduction, food and hunger, health and sickness, and language.

87

Discussion

Interpreting the cultural learning significance of these rubrics of behavior, and gaging their unique impact on individual character formation does, of course, depend on the nature of the conceptual framework which guides our selection of precursor and outcome criteria. For the proper study of iterative activity and piety in the primary group we must, however, take note of several important, invariable points of reference. I will discuss those I found most valuable in my work.

Let me emphasize again that this discussion is limited to what I learned from studying the life styles of nuclear and three-generation households of different American ethnic families. It is granted that the conventions and rules governing the management of interpersonal behavior (which also specify the locus and define the nature and function of privacy) vary from culture to culture. Moreover, the occurrence of "high domestic privacy" appears "indicative of general cultural complexity" (Roberts, 1971); and the nuclear family has become the epitome of the private place in the cultures of the Western world.

Even though the canvas of my observations has been restricted to one cultural category of 'private places,' my conclusions are not necessarily culture-bound for the same reason. The nuclear household as a general type of small group is a high intensity, face-to-face environment for transforming the trivial into the sublime, sham into substance, and the most crucial learning tasks into an ordinary, everyday response. Hence, the nuclear household ranks as one of the best cultural contexts for the study of how and why it is that man becomes a part of all that he has met.

What really matters is why people create and partake in behavioral pieties, not whether they do. What seems to count for individual and group is the interative expression of a shared, special understanding of certain social and personal meanings. What people tend to await and abide by is symbolic, it is the ethical stature and social purpose of the activity.

A behavioral piety as a social message has an essential normative stature when it conveys certain explanatory, albeit incomplete notions on inevitable aspects of being human: (1) when it 'originates,' so to speak, the idea and problem of order and power in human affairs; and (2) when it welds the conception and perception of each, - 'the way they appear' -, into a particular form of expression and experience. The behavior sequence, - the actuality of the performance of a piety itself -, is a belief-charged perceptual message about order when it repeatedly states and validates a particular view of sorting and dividing 'what belongs together, and what does not,' and 'reinvents' a classification of what is performed by naming events 'different

88

or the same.   The identical behavior sequence can also be a
special message about power when it fills a human organizational
vacuum with the investiture and legitimation of one person as
the primary source of responsibility and justice in the group.

The proceedings and happenings, the rules and structure
characterizing a behavioral piety function in the service of cultural learning in still another way. They foster, intensify
and rejuvenate a critical understanding of commitment and obligation, of loyalty and affection in both the individual and the
primary group. While learning to know the rules and behavioral
events, there is also learning to learn a developmental empathy
into the social contractual meanings of the entire transactional
situation. In the course of acquiring such person and group
'understandings', or rather, 'comprehendings' of difference and
similarity amongst people in private places, they become convenient markers in all attempts at adjudicating or reconciling the
central human conflict between commitment to oneself alone, to
one other person, or to the group as a whole. Such comprehendings also become a 'measure' for handling the social problema-
tics of 'deals' and 'collusion,' of compromise and sacrifice
which devotion to personal development and direct gratification,
or dedication to becoming a group number in good standing entails.

As a rule, individual participation in a succession of
development-cycle appropriate, familial behavior pieties becomes
the life-line against congealing into a self-absorbed and self-
indulging secessionist from group and culture. Learning self-
transcending understandings of social contract is, however, a
kind of learning which is predicated on what has already been
learned and remembered from earlier messages of order and power
conveyed by other familial pieties. It is the rare individual,
and rarer still the primary group who fully internalizes and
then routinely acts upon all the messages of self-transcendence
contained in the entire body of behavioral pieties lived through
before reaching maturity.

The crux of the problem of individuation and social development lies in how different people 'overlearn' or 'under-
learn' various combinations of messages of order and power, responsibility and justice on the one hand, and those of commitment
and obligation, of loyalty and affection on the other. Most
fateful for the human group and tragic for the individual are not
the consequences of learning behavioral pieties too well. They
obtain if maturity is reached within a primary group which never
took the time or had the collective energy to assemble, participate and persist in even one behavioral piety.

It is not possible here to detail the cultural and individual ramifications of these developmental problems. It can
only be done well by analyzing the occurrence and significance of
particular iterative behavioral events in terms of the relationship between individual and group time coordinates. This means

making a precise fix on the time period in the activity life span of the primary group, and on the age or developmental period in the individual life-cycle during which the person begins his iterative behavior experiences.

Whether a human being lives out his coming of age, his maturity or late maturity in a particular primary group, and whether this occurs while the group is a young, mature or senescing organization does make a difference in the socialization process. Their impact on the operation of man's perceptual-conceptual apparatus in the particular instance of social learning is especially noteworthy. This is so because every human being tends to teeter between an implicitly reinforced ability to doubt and an explicitly trained incapacity to question the managed behavioral actualities and social messages of his primary group. Hence, he is apt to reject or modify only some interactive activity, and what he does not discard he will genuinely believe as an immutable piety.

If we accept the preceding argument, we can briefly touch on some high-lights of individuation in light of patterns of participating in family-oriented behavioral pieties. Members of a household, whether small or large in size, will engage in such behavior to tell the young and reassure elders that an attainable ideal exists in their everyday lives, even if they intuit or know for a fact 'how tough it is out there in the cold world'. In a developmental sense, family pieties can be the most direct way of saying why it is not from hypocrisy that elders want to relive, and give children a sense of the possible about shaping their own future.

Participating in the shape of some sensible action program during childhood is a matter of becoming what one does as much as it is learning to behold the useful news of the grown-up world, a world about what to expect, to aspire to, and do when one gets to be older. This can be especially useful news because childhood, adolescence and young adulthood in the USA are, in a sense, times of forever becoming and never getting there. Such living is most arduous learning matter!

This is perhaps one of the important reasons why it is punctuated in some households by certain familial occasions which celebrate a feeling of shelter and satisfaction in being a child. It may also be marked by other behavioral events whose openess of structure and content suggest that the future should be treated as intention and flexibility rather than product. Without such occasions, neither the young can acquire nor the old can rely on that irreducible sense of private worth which is needed to endure through natural and man-made failure, sickness and lost opportunity.

The interplay over time of instrumental activity and behavioral piety learning has a crucial bearing on how well an individual becomes and can maintain himself as a social minority of one. It hinges on the conjoint resolution of what it is to be

90

your own Who, and of what it takes to have your own Where. In searching for an answer, some will choose the path of the head-less giant who blithely declaims that he can have in another place a better time of it. Another may follow the lead of the footless ghost who is ready to play it out anyway the other person or group likes. Still another will persist in spinning wheels by confusing the Who with Where he was. Or, in the best circumstances, a person can learn to subordinate his sense of I am where I am to his knowing I am who I am.

In essence, therefore, iterative family-oriented behavior facilitates learning life-long answers to the question of how do things get the way they are so that the individual not only knows where he is, but also who he is. The growing-up person, of course, learns that there always are other people from other families in the same home town. For quite a while though, they are just people to him. This is of course, what everyone is; except that everyone does not really matter to him until he is told, in word and deed, "some are different, just like you are different from them." He only begins to abandon his innocence of other people when he begins to ask himself, "How can I be so different and yet the same?" Family pieties help bring on this change of self in relation to others.

At this point, the growing-up person will find familial behavioral pieties, those he is still a part of, a great source of respite and comfort. They tend to shelter him from the equally perennial question "Why isn't there a place I can go to, some nice quiet spot, where no one will hold it against me that I was begotten where I was by people not of my choosing?"

Restated, iterative behavior sequences often are personally irreversible and pedagogically significant as concrete social messages of seemingly immutable human dilemmas. Again and again, they will tell how people come into their own by coming to terms with what is their own when they are little. Over and over, they can speak about how man goes about taking and keeping, losing and retaking his place and station in the network of adult life.

The persistence of behavioral piety in everyday life is largely a matter of the necessity that gave it birth. In this sense, it can be taken as a sign of the well-being of the primary group. Valuable as its durability may be to the group, however, the implicit slow rate of change often is a greater source of danger to individual growth than the imperfect statements a behavioral piety tends to make on the actualities of living. Indeed, this danger lies in having learned a piety too well, so that belief in fact is easy to suspend. For credence is what the child in man craves and the piety intends to create. It can lull the growing-up person into an unthinking acceptance of all family ways. Thus, when he begins to confuse their antiquity, if not their ambiguity with venerability and maximum utility, his capacity to interpret the here and now with realism

91

and detachment will be seriously impaired.

It may well be, that familial behavioral peities are too well remembered or too readily repressed because they are recognized micro-images of well known 'hero' or 'villain,' 'fool' and 'loser' myths in the Judeo-Christian tradition. Could it be that in every family there must transpire a sometimes tragic sometimes comic, and more often tedious replication of the myths of Oedipus and Job, of Lazarus and Mary Magdalena; the legends of Prometheus, Dionysius and Sisyphus, of Don Quixote and Don Juan and the family tales of magna mater and mater dolorosa, of pater noster, papa maximus or flaccidus? It is the exact duplication of these pathways which prepare us for life?

At this point in my studies I am not prepared to answer such questions. I believe, however, they not only must be, but can be answered with further research.

Conclusion

In the best sense, perhaps, this anthropological essay on culture-learning theory points to the importance of dealing with man's ways of making and undoing himself in the process of growing up by means of the most detailed specification of ordinary variables in his primary life space. The affirmation of the individual human being within the network of his most significant relationships permits us to see him as keenly and closely as possible for what he is. It also subjects ourselves to equally candid and unsparing scrutiny.

A behavioral piety in a private place is a condensed message of a general drift of affairs, and a physical statement of an emotional and volitional condition. It is an example of the union of life and belief, of real acts and magical ways sought by man and woman of all ages, in every era. It mobilizes and reaffirms, as it reflects and clarifies the complexities of human nature and man-made environment. Sometimes, it is a double portrait, painting all the dark on one side and all the light on the other. More often, it is a composite behavioral enactment of the ties that bind human absolutes together.

As teachings of the primary group, the individual will and often must take behavioral pieties seriously. Ordinarily, he can equate them with rudimentary, everyday good sense. Occasionally, he may view them as 'rational action'; that is to say, measures in harmony with the structure of perceived facts, rather than with that of logical inference. When faced, however, with the immensity and variety of contemporary human problems, we may only recall the pieties of our growing up years as mediocre wisdom.

NOTES

1.   It is of considerable interest that the past decade of my intermittent work in this problem area has seen an
enormous resurgence of anthropological interest in the study
of what R. P. Armstrong has recently called The Affecting Presence (Urbana: University of Illinois Press, 1971). This is
closely paralleled by the rapidly expanding behavioral science
literature on all manner of non-verbal communication. (See
Julius Fast, Body Language, N.Y., M. Levins in Assoc. with
Lippincott [1970]; Robert Sommer, Personal Space, Englewood
Cliffs, N. J., Prentice Hall [1969]; Edward T. Hall, Silent
Language, Garden City: Doubleday [1959].)

The comparative ethnography of expressive behavior as
exemplified in games, folktales, riddles, as well as other ver-
bal and non-verbal leisure and work activity is also germane
to my study of iterative activity in private places. (See
John M. Roberts, Expressive Aspects of Technological Develop-
ment, Philosohpy of Social Science 1:207-220 [1971]; John M.
Roberts and Michael L. Forman, Riddles: Expressive Models of
Interrogation, Ethnology 10:509-533 [1971]; Brian Sutton-
Smith and John M. Roberts, The Cross-Cultural and Psychological
Study of Games, pp. 186-212 in Luschen, Gunther [ed.] The Cross-
Cultural Analysis of Sports and Games [1970].)

2.   During 1970-1971 these researches were supported by
a Grant-in-Aid from the Maurice Falk Medical Fund of Pittsburgh,
Pa. My initial studies were carried out with the assistance of
Mrs. Nancy Morey, now of Salt Lake City, Utah.

REFERENCES

Barrabee, Paul and Otto O. von Mering
    1953   Ethnic Variations in Mental Stress. Social
                Problems 1:48-53.

Barth, F. (Ed.)
    1969   Ethnic Groups and Boundaries. Boston: Little
                Brown.

Bossard, J. H. S.
    1953   Parent and Child: Studies in Family Behavior.
    1966   Sociology of Child Development.

Bossard, J. H. S. and Eleanor S. Boll
    1950   Ritual in Family Living, Philadelphia: Univer-
                sity of Pennsylvania Press.

Foster, George M.
    1960   Interpersonal Relations in Peasant Society, Hu-
                man Organization 19:174-184.

Henry, Jules
    1963   Culture Against Man. New York: Random House.
    1971   Pathways to Madness. New York: Random House.

Hocart, Arthur M.
    1970   The Life-giving Myth. London: Methuen.

Roberts, John M. and Thomas Gregor
    1971   Privacy: A Cultural View in Pennock, J. Roland
               and John W. Chapman (Eds.) Privacy. New York:
               Atherton Press pp. 199-225.

Spicer, Edward (Ed.)
    1961   Perspectives in American Indian Culture Change.
               Chicago: University Chicago Press.
    1971   Persistent Cultural Systems. Science 174:795-
               800.

Spiro, Melford E.
    1955   Acculturation of American Ethnic Groups.
               American Anthropologist 57:1240-1252.

von Mering, Otto O.
    1959   Mother-Child Pairs and Forms of Fathering in
               The Significance of the Father. New York City,
               Family Service Association of America pp. 5-30.

von Mering, Otto O.
    1959   Social-Cultural Background of the Aging Individ-
               ual. pp. 279-335 in Birren, J. E. (Ed.) Hand-
               book of Aging and the Individual. Chicago:
               University of Chicago Press.

von Mering, Otto O.
    1961   A Grammer of Human Values. Pittsburgh:
               University of Pittsburgh Press.
    1962   Disease, Healing and Problem Solving. Inter-
               national Journal of Psychiatry 8(2):137-148.
    1969   An Anthropo-medical Profile of Aging: Retire-
               ment from Life into Active Ill Health. Journal
               Geriatric Psychiatry 3(1):61-89.

von Mering, Otto O. and Mirta Mulhare
    1970   Anthropological Perspectives on Socialization.
               Ch. 2, pp. 57-86 in Anthony, E. J., and Therese
               Benedek (Eds.) Parenthood-Its Psychology and
               Psychopathology. Boston: Little, Brown and Co.

von Mering, Otto O.
    1971   Rethinking Ethnic Identity, pp. 30-47 in Peachey,

p. & Mudd, R. (Eds.), Evolving Patterns of Ethnicity in American Life. National Center for Urban Ethnic Affiars. Washington, D.C.

1972a   The Question of Ethnic Identity. CAE Newsletter 3(1):1-5.

1972b   The Diffuse Health Aberration Syndrome: A Bio-Behavioral Study of the Perennial Out-Patient. Psychosomatics (13:293-303).

THE VALIDATION OF ASCRIBED STATUS:
GENTRY CAREERS IN GUATEMALA[1]

G. Alexander Moore Jr.
University of Florida

This is a paper on the salient characteristics of the traditional landed metropolitan elite of Guatemala, and on the social, largely informal, mechanisms whereby some adult men of that elite validate their seemingly ascribed birthright. Not all succeed; but the penalties to the individual aristocrat for failure are such that it is usually his descendants, rather than he himself, who become disadvantaged by being separated from the possession of a distant birthright.

I shall present my data within the context of the traditional gentry's characteristic emphasis on distinguished ancestry and landed estates. Then I shall analyze the social universe of the gentry child and the various pathways by which significant others may induct him, if he is willing, into the role of the successful gentleman.

The Guatemalan traditional elite: a national group viewed in a Latin American perspective. My subject, the Guatemalan landed gentry, reflects the nature of my fieldwork in a municipio or community composed of a central town inhabited by Indain peasants and Ladino merchants and of a series of large estates owned and operated by members of the metropolitan gentry (Moore 1963).

While there are other elites in Guatemala such as those groups that command commercial, industrial, bureaucratic, military, religious and even labor institutions (Lipset 1967), it has been widely recognized that large landowners, who characteristically reside in cities, are a major cultural, political and economic force in Latin America. Yet social scientists have not studied this group in proportion to its importance.

Thus when Wagley identifies ideal patterns which "profoundly influence the behavior of most Latin Americans," he asserts that "most of them are aristocratic patterns and derivative of the gentry." The patterns "include familism, ceremonial and fictive kinship (the compadrazgo system), double standards of sexual morals, emphasis upon social class, a disdain for manual labor, high regard for formal etiquette, an emphasis upon the saints and a love of display in religion (that is, religious processions and festivals)" (1968:3-4). Yet Wagley admits that only Scheele (1956) has written an anthropological study specifically of the metropolitan upper class. However, Scheele concentrates on those Puerto Rican families who were maintaining their prominence by founding or joining U.S. oriented business firms.

Another source, Andrew Whiteford's study of social class in two Latin American cities, offers interesting data on the entrenched upper class of Popayán, a small conservative city in Colombia. The aristocrats of Popayán seem to inherit their wealth and ascribed status effortlessly. Most of the traits of this aristocracy, moreover, can be grouped into two culture complexes; the complex of traits centering on ancestry and the complex of traits centering on landholdings.

Whiteford does not order his description in these categories, but his list of traits he observes is striking. First the upper class has a number of family surnames famous in Colombian history. Their family crests emblazon the doorways of their family mansions, built in the colonial era in a compact residential area around the central plaza. While all upper class families hold cattle estates at some distance from the city, they also generally exercise a profession or hold a political office, visiting their estates mainly as inspectors rather than gentlemen farmers. In the discussion that follows I hope to show that these external traits, the family crest on the colonial mansion, the profession or the local political office, and the cattle estate are all indicative of two common attributes of the Latin American gentry and part of their Iberian heritage. I shall then attempt to show how this heritage weighs upon the Guatemalan gentry.

There are then two central characteristics of the Latin American gentry that I wish to discuss in terms of their cultural origins and present institutional variation: the possession and symbolic valuing of ancestry and land.

To take up ancestry first, the gentry emphasizes both ancestor-oriented lineages and a contradictory lateral extension of kin to include other locally notable families. The emphasis on lineage seems to derive from a strong Iberian tradition whose focus is in North Spain. Douglass's recent study (1969) has illuminated this trait for the Basque country.

Douglass describes a living folk tradition quite different from the Iberian mainstream. Its traits share more with Celtic Ireland described by Arensberg and Kimball (1968) than with Mediterranean Spain. The Basques are settled in scattered homesteads, each of which has title to an indivisible estate, which must be inherited intact and which can only be sold with great difficulty. The house is the seat of the lineage. By the practice of marriage succession the aging farm couple hands the homestead over to a single heir at the time of his marriage when he or she brings in a spouse to fulfill the division of labor and carry on the bloodline. This heir inherits the family seat, retaining and managing any unmarried siblings and the aged

parents under one roof. This, a stem family system, has its
symbolic expression on the floor of the local church. There a
particular funeral plot is the ritual territory of each homestead, upon which each Sunday the mistress of the household
must stand with lighted candles to honor all the house's dead.

The idea distilled from this little tradition into the
Iberian great tradition is the idea of the sacred bloodline and
of the house possessed of an indivisible patrimony in land. The
gentry gave the tradition legal and written form in the creation
of entailed estates, that is landed patrimonies that could not
be divided. During the imperial era the creation of an entail
was the prime goal of the upwardly mobile Spaniard and Creole.
The language of the ceremony of entail lauds the goal:

Let all interested parties know by these presents
that...we (husband and wife) were agreed to make
and constitute an entail on behalf of our eldest
son, considering that possessions divided and
apportioned dwindle and disappear. Whereas if
they are bound together and made indivisible,
they remain and increase, the holder's cousins
and relations may be succoured in their time of
need, houses and families are ennobled and lineages
are rendered illustrious and preserved for posterity,
and those who enjoy the income from such entails are
more inclined to defend and protect the nation and
city in which they reside and to serve their rightful
King and master, in peace as in war, as both divine
and natural law require of them, whereby the Lord Our
Master is served and His Holy Gospel exalted. And
inasmuch as it is both lawful and just to establish
an entail, we most respectfully requested, and received, permission of His Majesty, King Philip.
(Quoted in Chevalier 1963:300)

However, unlike the Basques, the Creole gentry also
emphasizes lateral kinship with local notables. This is so
because the gentry does not alone occupy scattered rural homesteads. Rather their principal residence has usually been urban
and their country houses therefore have only secondary symbolic
values. Thus in their residential patterns and in their marriage
habits they resemble the Mediterranean patriciate, so familiar to
us from the city-state of antiquity.

This Mediterranean pattern has been recently described
by Lisón-Tolosana (1966) for an Aragonese pueblo whose social
organization for many centuries constituted a two class system
of patricians and plebeians.

Patricians were those families possessing lands enough
to employ others (plebeians) to work them. Patrician traits
were centrally located comfortable residences; endogamy to such
an extent that the group of notables had become one large kindred, almost a "deme" in Murdock's terminology; and bilateral

99

inheritance, so that a wife's dowry was an essential part of the landed patrimony of the children of any married patrician couple. Finally political and ritual offices were rotated among the adult patrician householders in a manner agreed upon among themselves.

This aristocratic complex is characteristically urban in the sense that it is associated with dense, nucleated settlement and social stratification. Individual lineages have no interests apart from those of the entire local aristocracy, who are all to some degree kinsmen. The symbols of lineage then are less important than the symbols of social class, particularly those displayed in local religious festivals. Individual residences tend, like political offices, to rotate among the individual married couples of the elite, turning over with the rhythms of marriages and deaths, so that upon marriage the patrician newlyweds set themselves up, not in a traditional family mansion of a particular lineage, but in a dwelling purchased from some other elite family, and recently vacated by death.

It is my contention that the Latin American gentry's emphasis upon ancestry and possession of land represents a blending of these two little traditions: one the stem family of the "Celtic fringe" of North Spain (Arensberg 1963) and the other the Mediterranean folk tradition of compact, nucleated and socially differentiated "cities." However, the behavior of the gentry always manifests a tension between the two traditions. Even during the heyday of the custom of entailing great estates, wealthy houses found ways to pass on inheritances to younger sons. After the abolition of entail through the Hispanic world following the Napoleonic upheavels the tension shifted in the other direction and great houses found ways to favor one heir, usually either the firstborn male, or the most energetic and talented of his siblings, over the others. This selection process has been documented for the grandees of Spain by Malefakis (1970:68) and for the Mexican provincial elite by Hunt (1965).[2]

Thus the Latin American gentry kinship system contains two dimensions. The first is that of their ancestor-oriented lineages, which ideally would resemble a single stem line on a Basque model, but which in fact seldom approximate the ideal. The second is the dimension of lateral and affinal links with the entire established upper class of the city of their residence.

I shall next take up that other prime characteristic of the Latin American gentry, the possession of land, for both in Latin America and in Spain the gentry possess landholdings that are quite different from those of country folk. Everywhere these urban families possess large estates, variously termed latifundia, cortijos, haciendas, fincas, plantations, and so on. It is this trait which distinguishes the aristocracy of Popayán from the more parochial upper class of an Aragonese pueblo.

100

This system of great landholdings has been studied by anthropologists in widely differing contexts. The 1957 symposium on plantation systems in the New World held in San Juan, Puerto Rico (Rubin 1959), has gone quite far in conceptualizing the range and dynamics of this territorial and social form. From the symposium the Latin American estate emerges as an ideal type, divided into three subtypes: the hacienda, the plantation, and the central. Each subtype on the continuum is characterized by ever-increasing rationality in its more intensive use of four resources: land, labor, technology, and capital.

To briefly characterize the three subtypes, first, the hacienda uses old, pre-industrial equipment, markets its product within the region or nation, and very often uses such "archaic" devices as allowing peasants access to land instead of cash payments. While any crop may be produced by any of the three subtypes, cattle has been the favored product of the hacienda, precisely because cattle ranching lends itself to extensive practices and light overseeing. Historically the hacienda has been the landholding favored by the great houses establishing entail, and the characteristic landholding of conservative urban groups generally, such as the Popayán group mentioned above.

Next on the continuum, the plantation specializes in a monocrop in international demand, such as sugar, the classic plantation crop. Consequently often these crops are underwritten by foreign capital from Europe or North America. However, these estates are owned by native aristocrats who find their management more demanding than that of the hacienda.

In the central, however, modern processing technology is given much greater expression. The central's industrial plant is of such capacity that it often absorbs the products of many erstwhile estates, which are reduced to the status of local production units or branch farms. The central also uses advanced techniques such as fertilizing and irrigation, which require very heavy capital investments. Its huge productivity requires rational management and marketing. In short, the central is a complex organization, and the kinship organization we have considered above usually gives way to partnerships and corporations in its management: be they family, joint-stock, or state. The advent of the central poses crucial questions for the traditional land-owning class. In Puerto Rico at least, that class has become a commercial one, more intimately related with the urban corporation than with the landed estate (Scheele, 1956). In Guatemala the question is not yet acute, for the dominant landholding may still be identified as the plantation.

Let me summarize then what I regard as the salient characteristics of the Guatemalan traditional landed elite. They are heirs to two culture patterns, each with its own internal contradictions. One is their emphasis on ancestry, in which they must resolve the tension between growing numbers of aristocratic offspring each generation, and the limited nature of the traditional patrimony. The mechanism of entail and stem family succession is no longer available as an explicit device to preserve great houses and their estates. Today the tension is partly resolved by class endogamy, whereby partners to new marriages each bring the security of an inheritance to pass on to their children. Such a mechanism, however, further dilutes the emphasis on the blood line descended from a single illustrious ancestor. The symbolic focus shifts from a single, often rural, ancestral residence, to several, all located in the capital city.

The gentry's other and closely related culture pattern is that of the hacienda-plantation-central continuum. The old hacienda pattern probably lent itself very well to the colonial stem-family system of entailed estates. The plantation pattern provides, however, the opportunity to expand wealth and to provide for more heirs. The central pattern seems ultimately to transform the old landed elite into a group of corporate managers and perhaps stockholders, as described by Scheele for Puerto Rico. Whether such elites can also maintain endogamy, pride of lineage, and residences sanctified by genealogy, is as yet unknown for they are a phenomenon of this century. Logically, however, with further industrialization such elites can merge with that international group holding industrial and banking fortunes, the haute bourgeoisie or the "jet set." Or as in Cuba, they can be deliberately destroyed to make way for the public corporation.[3]

Gentry Careers: Securing a Birthright. If we next turn to the universe of persons into which the Guatemalan gentry child is born, we can divide them into several categories. First there are kinsmen, who are either peers or elders. Second there are clients, who include household servants, estate workers, and all others in the city dependent on the gentry family for employment or crucial favors.

At birth a child is surrounded by a wide range of biolateral kin who interact with him and his parents. They of course include the members of his own household: usually his parents and his siblings (although it is possible unmarried siblings of his parents may live under the same roof). A child's peers include his siblings and his first cousins, as well, usually, as his second cousins, the children of his parents' first cousins. Interactions among second cousins are quite likely to be selective, depending upon congeniality and mutual business interests of the adults to keep them going. However in very wealthy kindreds, pride of name and shared landed interests may unite many kinsmen related at the third degree or even beyond.

A child's elders include his parents, their siblings and their spouses, and his parents' cousins, his grandparents, their siblings and their cousins, and also his godparents,if they are not already among those persons listed by kinship. In many kindreds, cousin marriage constricts the actual number of persons occupying these roles of older persons.

A child's family clients include the houseservants. All gentry households have at least a cook, and in those of reduced economic means, such as those of newlyweds, the cook has to share nursemaid duties with the mother. With greater affluence, households expand their servantry. A chambermaid joins the cook, followed by a laundress. Sometimes houseboys replace or reinforce the chambermaids, while serving as gardener. Some few households, particularly those inhabited by members of the grandparental generation, retain chauffeurs as well. In less affluent households, the hapless cook-nursemaid partakes of all the tasks which would otherwise be parcelled out among a host of others.

Country clients include all the plantation personnel with the same kinds of houseservants. From the viewpoint of the gentry child the children of plantation workers provide him with an opportunity to find playmates, not quite peers, however, on visits to the country.

City clients, save those employed for occasional household tasks, or those who are rising quite rapidly on the social scale, are not ordinarily welcomed into the gentry household. The gentry child meets them only on visits to his male kinsmens' places of work.

The child born into an urban gentry household of comfortable means passes a sheltered childhood during which he interacts with kinsmen and clients from outside his own household on a fairly regular schedule of reciprocal visits among kinsmen. Indeed, elder kinsmen are likely to demand visits of the entire junior household for dinner or lunches as part of their regular prerogatives. One young couple of my acquaintance, for example, regularly dines with the wife's father on one night a week, and lunches with her maiden maternal aunts on yet another day of the week. In addition her unmarried brother dines at her household on another night of the week.

Weekends at the plantation or at some other country retreat are also almost a monthly occurrence for the household of the child, and unite him with peers, elders, and clients. Birthdays, or saints days as they are called, are ceremonially observed, sometimes almost monthly, and help the child to recognize, by attending parties or paying formal calls, the widest range of his kindred. Thus the intensity and the frequency of contacts reflects the importance genealogically and usually financially of the kinsmen and clients to the child.

In these extra-household events the child is trained in two ideal patterns listed by Wagley as being of great importance for Latin American culture: familism and the high regard for formal etiquette. However, this familistic etiquette is not stiff. On the contrary, the child learns that good

103

behavior embraces a wide variety of forms, but with two constants: elders expect at all times demonstrations of affection and respect, but they also may give the cues for relaxations of strict formality. Thus the child learns that a more formal face must be presented to the public and to clients than to kinsmen. Although he must be personable and polite with kinsmen he also learns the cues which permit relaxed behavior with them. In return the child is assured of attention and numerous material favors from a wide range of powerful elders beyond his parents. He also learns that he must be loving and playful with his own peers. Open competition and aggression among siblings and cousins is strictly forbidden by gentry elders.

When schooling comes it provides the gentry child with social lessons, quite as important as the school lessons, which reinforce those taught in the wider family circle. For the first time, the child meets numerous peers who are outside his kindred, yet, since they too attend a private school, these new acquaintances are among the economically privileged. Young Guatemalan aristocrats attend schools operated either by the Catholic Church or by the foreign colonies of the city. Although some pupils do not belong to the traditional elite, the aristocratic pupil may be friends with them and join them in sports and associations. However, it is difficult because of the familistic nature of most high social life for the well-born schoolchild to sponsor such chums into his kindred's social events, unless of course such children themselves have parents who are actively sponsored by a gentry adult.

When the adolescent aristocrat enters the courtship phase of his life cycle--a phase that may last a decade or longer, the doors of his own and other households are now opened to a wider circle of peers. Indeed, households which have seen nothing of each other since the last courtship period, i.e., their own formation, suddenly come into contact. Some eligible young gentlemen have told me they have received invitations from persons who once knew their parents, but whom they had never met, to attend parties for nubile daughters. The events that open doors are familiar: birthdays, national and religious festivals, weekends in the country at plantation or vacation houses; but the attendance draws upon the youth of the entire urban gentry and such school chums who can pass parental inspection. During these years, adolescents learn the qualities which are thought proper for a prospective spouse. A man looks for physical beauty, an attractive manner or good breeding, and good family reputation and connections in his sweetheart. A girl looks for the same qualities with the qualification that good breeding also includes formal schooling at least through secondary school, and the demonstrated ability to take employment to supplement parental largesse or inherited income.

For the young Guatemalan gentlewoman, marriage marks her assumption of adult status. But for a man, marriage means the demonstration of an adult status he had begun to acquire earlier. When he assumes the responsibility of a household, he must be ready to defray its costs. To do so may require considerable cash expenditure. The consumer demands of the industrial world have reached Guatemala City where they have been adopted by the elite, which is now accustomed to a very expensive life style, including a great deal of foreign travel and imported luxuries. The international industrial market no longer lends itself well to those who enter it with a static agrarian income. The Guatemalan gentleman is faced with the desirability of maximizing his resources if he is to keep his household at the minimal level of comfort demanded by the elite, let alone achieve its maximal display of luxury.

The young householder maintains himself by earnings from a job, from an allowance from his family, and/or if he has already some or all of his patrimony, from income from his holdings. If he marries a wealthy girl he may expect an allowance or an income on her part as well, and such a marriage is certainly a victory in his struggle to maintain himself at the level to which he was born. Some men, indeed, will establish new households by using all three resources: jobs, allowances and inherited income. All three resources, however, depend upon the young man's first having mastered the art of getting favors out of his kinsmen elders and/or their connections. Before the young aristocrat can become a householder, he must first become a client, and for a time at least, approximate the condition of so many people of lowlier station he has known since childhood.

The enterprising young aristocrat, then, has three strategies open to him. First he may concentrate on his urban employment, particularly if this is a professional one, and invest his savings in the purchase of landholdings. Second he may concentrate on managing his family's estate directly, particularly if he has been trained, either in school or as an apprentice, in agriculture. Or finally he may concentrate on the financial and marketing aspects of his family's plantation production, by manipulating partnerships, credits and international coffee sales, all from Guatemala City. Some engage in all three activities, although the latter two more commonly go together. The strategy of making alliances or partnerships with peers is common to all three career patterns.

Some men are very successful in these strategies, to which of course they have to have been staked by their gentry elders. The true measure of success, however, is to amass a fortune "on one's own" by the time one inherits from one's parents. Some such fortunes are quite equal to the inherited ones. Such men then have doubled their patrimony, and are the truly successful aristocrats.

Many others, probably the majority, never concentrate upon any strategy, but remain among the aristocratic underemployed. They are sometimes faced with disaster, dipping into capital to support expensive lifestyles. In such cases, they may lose their mortgaged country estates to the banks that accepted them as security, or they sell out to more enterprising gentry, often to their own siblings.

In other cases the decline is less spectacular, but becomes evident in the next generation. In these cases, the indolent aristocrats live comfortably off their inherited incomes, or at least off allowances from indulgent elders. But in the end their own heirs suffer, for their own inheritances are reduced, unless such an heir is able to concentrate the affections of a number of the members of the older generations of his family, and inherit from them what his father failed to provide. The presence of childless persons in each generation facilitates this possibility. Other such young and disadvantaged aristocrats quietly slip out of the acknowledged elite, often by disappearing into the provinces to join socially "unknown" local elites. Life in such centers, I was told, "empobrece, embrutece, y envilice" or "empoverishes, stupefies, and degenerates" the unfortunate exile. Still others do not educate themselves and make "disastrous" marriages outside of society, which is all the more quick to forget them.

Most young aristocrats do try to take jobs. Their employment is of many sorts. Many have been trained at universities for the professions of law, medicine, engineering or architecture. Some are trained at foreign universities in the agricultural arts, and by that early choice are usually assigned by their kinsmen to manage a rural estate. Many others, however, only having finished secondary school, seek employment in the commercial, financial, or agricultural enterprises of their kinsmen or their kinsmen's friends, to be trained by gentlemen or by experienced clients.

But holding down a job or a profession is only the first step in the successful aristocrat's strategy. He must have learned from observation how to fulfill the role of client. As I have said above, all great families have many persons dependent upon them for their livelihood. The young aristocrat has grown up surrounded by such persons. To launch himself he must fill the role of client himself, getting his father or his father's connections--often other relatives or godfathers--to find him a job. Ideally this would put the young man in a position to make business deals, also through connections. Alliances with elders are common in such deals.

At this point in his career, the young man must display an implicit understanding of the principles of clientage. I have treated the subject at length elsewhere (1973) for I believe that it holds the key to the Guatemalan class system. The major point here, however, is that early in his life cycle the young aristocrat must assume a position roughly equal to that of many less well-born clients, who indeed may be competing with him.

The basic principle of patronage-clientage is personal-

ism, in which the superior responds to the appeals of "friendship". In such a situation, the clever aristocrat is at an advantage over his plebeian competitor, because he has the symbols
of genealogy and of familism to manipulate. The less well-born
do this too, although their credentials are not as highly valued. On one coffee plantation which I know well, a group of in-
terrelated families have come to monopolize all the administrative positions by loose appeals to inheritance. It is interesting to note that the largest branch of them is descended from
the concubine of an earlier planter. They, too, have manipulated kinship.

By his portrayal of the basic patterns listed by Wag-
ley--familism, ceremonial etiquette, dashing virility, and fine
display of charm, particularly at family feasts, the young aristocrat may win favors from well-placed patrons. To solidify his
gains, however, he must also further his patron's interest. In
other words, he must work hard, not manually but at managing
others, particularly lesser clients. Alliances with peers soon
follow, replicating the cooperative play of childhood as partnerships are made with energetic siblings or rich cousins and
affines. During all this time the young aristocrat has to manage
clients as well, in ways not so different from the ways he
learned to treat servants in early childhood, personally but with
the respect prescribed by formal etiquette. When the client is
older, or an implicit competitor, the young man often has to
summon all his tact or delicacy, for the loss of a valuable
client may injure his future prospects.

It is at this point in his life cycle that the importance of a "familistic" marriage is revealed, and class endogamy
is seen to be more than a snobbish custom. The young man who
has married well has married more than an heiress, but a woman
whose kinsmen provide him with potential patrons among her elders
and partners among her peers. If her family is one that is
socially unknown but coming up financially, he may add his genealogy and genealogical connections to their ascent in the agrarian and commercial world of wealth, thus lending respectability
in the always semi-closed, household-centered world of social
life.

The kinship pattern, then, in both its lineal and lateral dimensions, is of utmost importance to the young aristocrat
because it provides the raw materials from which to manufacture,
not only a marriage but also a place in the ladder of patronage
and clientage.

We turn now to the hacienda-plantation-central continuum.
It is the intensification of this pattern toward the full blown
plantation prototype that provides the actual task of the aristocratic career. All three subtypes of estates exist in Guatemala,
but in the region which I know best, the dominant type is the
family-owned plantation that verges on becoming a central. As an
example, I cite Finca Rincón del Bosque, where a primitive nine-

teenth century sugar mill (hacienda type) stands alongside a most modern coffee processing plant. The estate usually sells its raw sugar cane to a central on the coast, but does reserve a small amount to make a low-grade sugar for the local market. In its coffee production the estate had become almost a central, managing and refining the products of two branch estates further down the slope toward the Pacific coast, and also purchasing the coffee of peasant producers over a large region. Moreover, like most centrales the estate is owned, not be a single family, but a partnership between a family on the one hand and a highly successful aristocratic magnate on the other. Patronage has combined with familism to produce this ownership pattern; a partnership rather than a joint stock company.

There can be no question that Guatemalan agriculture has been steadily increasing the production of export commodity crops, if one takes a long range view over the last one hundred years. The conservative old family elite is facing competition for the fruits of agrarian wealth. A group of newly rich agriculturists has arisen since 1945 from the profits of cotton growing in a mechanized and speculative way. This group originated among Army officers who took advantage of state credits first extended by the leftist President Arbenz, who was himself an Army man (Adams 1970). I cannot prove that this group stimulates the gentry to make better use of land, labor and credits. But the fact remains that the gentry is doing just that. The finca cited above, for example, more than tripled its coffee production in the decade following 1954.

The intensification of plantation agriculture is the principal means whereby more wealth can be generated to meet the demands of a demographically expanding and individually enterprising aristocracy. This "ecological" process fits very neatly into the social processes outlined above. Plantation agriculture is being intensified in a number of ways. First the technology of agriculture is being more highly rationalized on existing estates. Gentry managers trained a generation ago in agronomy have been leaders in this effort. Second, the large area of idle land held by many estates is increasingly being brought under cultivation. This can be done by an old estate as part of its internal process of rationalization; but often large tracts of idle land are sold to young aristocrats, often in partnership, who may be investing their own savings or using bank loans. The new owners may enter into a marketing or processing arrangement with the original estate. Smaller and less productive estates belonging to downwardly mobile members of the gentry or to hard-pressed members of local (non-gentry) elites are also often purchased by such well born entrepreneurs.

Financial credits are necessary to intensify the productivity of both old and new estates. Thus many old estates take in additional owners as partners with capital. Access to capital depends upon the patronage of bankers as well as of coffee

exporters, two kinds of persons is a position to expand their
interests in many estates.

Let me briefly present a case history of one estate and
its gentry owners. This is the history of the estate El Rincón
del Bosque's quick passage from an hacienda devoted to sugar cane
to its current blossoming as a central for coffee during the
marked vicissitudes of the lineage that has owned it for the last
three generations.

The estate was purchased from its previous downwardly
mobile gentry owners by Don Manuel Maria Talavera, the founding
ancestor of the lineage, just before the coffee boom of the 1870's
transformed Guatemalan agriculture. Don Manuel Maria had risen
from social unknown origins to political eminence during the long
reign of Guatemala's first dictator Rafael Carrera. He was related by marriage to Don Pataleón Azmitia,[4] destined to make the
greatest coffee fortune in Guatemala by virtue, also, of holding
political office. Both men were newcomers to the traditional
elite. The estate was purchased expressly as the patrimony of
one of the magnate's sons. Another son received another estate,
and the two sons were obliged to contribite equally toward a
fixed income for their maiden sister as long as she lived.

The first heir to the estate, Don Cristóbal Talavera, a
lawyer by training, never practiced his profession. Instead he
dedicated himself to the congenial pursuit of natural history
and the management of his land. His brother proved unfortunate.
Years of political exile left him to face heavy debts and the
loss of his land on his return late in life. Although he made
a marriage with a Frenchwoman and provided his som with medical
training in France, that heir disappeared into the provinces. A
daughter, however, made a "good" marriage with a cousin descended
from the other magnate mentioned above, Don Pantaleón Azmitia.
Of her branch of the family, she alone escaped social obscurity.

Each generation has illustrated the principles of competitive succession to high fortune and the intensification of
plantation agriuclture. The naturalist extended his holdings by
buying property adjacent to his finca and by acquiring a subsidiary finca further down the Pacific slope. He did so by commanding and paying off bank credits secured against his favorable
harvests. Late in life he married the daughter of an immigrant
Spanish merchant, securing another link with the city financial
elite. His brother's decline contrasted dramatically, for at one
point Don Cristóbal was obliged to become his impoverished brother's patron by employing him as manager of his finca. This arrangement ceased when Don Cristóbal placed his own son, a head-
strong lad of sixteen who had finished secondary school, upon the
estate. The two clashed and the boy's uncle left, humiliated
perhaps by his obvious subordination to one of the younger generation.

That generation, composed of the three sones of Don
Cristóbal, also illustrates the process. They inherited early,

having been the sons of an older father. One died; one continued
to manage the estate, and married the wealthy daughter of a
neighboring planter, who was also a kinsman descended from Don
Pantaleón Azmitia, the other illustrious ancestor in our composite genealogy. The third brother lived in the city to manage
urban properties for their partnership (they continued to own
the finca in common). He too married an heiress, but not a
cousin. At the high point of their joint careers the brothers
purchased yet another subsidiary finca, quite a large one, on the
lower Pacific slope.

The depression of the 1930's brought financial distress.
The brothers lost all their urban property and much of their land,
including the finca they had acquired the decade before. With
the decline of the international market for coffee, their estates
became mere haciendas, and the brothers, having lost their urban
residences, retreated to the country and literally lived off the
land. Both were saved by the help of their wives' kindreds. One
brother retreated to his wife's plantation; the other saved El
Rincón by the receipt of a favorable loan from his wife's aunt.
Their marriages thus became vital to them.

After the depression the brothers launched their re-
covery by concluding an alliance with a gentleman who had already
made a fortune in Guatemala City. This man was one of several
heirs to an immense finca neighboring El Rincón. The income
from this, his patrimony, provided him with a secure financial
base, soon augmented by income from a highly successful law
practice. The law firm in turn launched him into lucrative investments in urban real estate and then into banking. When he
made his partnership in El Rincón, he brought capital, both his
own and his bank's, to the Talavera land which under the continued supervision of its longtime manager was soon to flourish.
This man, Don Manuel de la Vega, thus consolidated his fortune
by a return to platation investments at the height of his financial career, incidentally salvaging the financial position of
two peers, old friends. Their partnership is one of those in
which the distinction between patron and client is almost invisible. Still, within the partnership there is no question that
Don Manuel is the richest and most powerful associate.

Ownership of the finca took on its present form at the
death of one of the Talavera brothers, who was succeeded by his
only son. Thus today there are three owners of the finca; Don
Manuel de la Vega with a half interest, Don Rodrigo Talavera with
one fourth and his nephew with one fourth. The nephew, an
engineer educated abroad who has become a prominent utilities
executive, is in the upward phase of his life cycle. He married
an urban heiress, and she has given him numerous children.
Agrarian enterprises do not interest him; he prefers to invest
in city businesses, and rely upon the finca for its dependable
income, to help support his large and expensive household.

Don Rodrigo's three children, prospective heirs to

110

another fourth of the plantation (all of the same generation as
the Talavera nephew), are adults with grown children. One woman
married a wealthy coffee exporter and need not worry about the
patrimony of her sons. Another however married a number of
times out of his class and distinctly belongs to the aristocratic underemployed. Moreover he has become himself a grand-
father without having acquired any fortune of his own to pass on
to his descendants. Yet nonetheless he is certainly the most
charming of men.

This man's brother's career, however, has proved a
spectacular success, having at middle age certainly amassed a
fortune equal or better than his prospective inheritance. Starting as an airlines pilot, he married an heiress from among his
mother's Azmitia relatives. Backed by their capital and political influence he has been an airlines executive, a bank director,
a partner in a coffee exporting house, and part owner of two
other fincas in association with his wife and her brother. Here
the patronage of his father-in-law and the alliances with his
brothers-in-law have joined his energies and organizational
skills. It is interesting to note that he has borrowed a client
from his father's estate to manage one of his fincas. In short
he has been almost the ideal model of the successful gentleman
who by a combination of training, marriage, alliances and hard
work validates his birthright.

The heirs to Don Manuel de la Vega's half interest in
the property are his three children with the same histories: the
well married daughter; the son launched by his father's patronage
into a successful urban career in a profession, banking, and
urban real estate; and finally the charming son who only lightly
occupies one respectable job after another and who has married
outside the courtship circle of his youth. Thus of the six heirs
to El Rincón in this generation only two have already validated
their birthright before inheriting.

When viewed from the perspective of the validation of
gentry birthright the ideal patterns listed by Wagley acquire
dynamic meaning. Familism and ceremonial kinship are seen to be
the stuff from which alliances which validate ones birthright
are made. A disdain for manual labor is the natural prerogative
of those who learn from birth to manage others, but who must
learn to do that well, a trait compatible with an emphasis on
formal etiquette. The double standard of sexual morals is the
reflection of the emphasis on lineage, purity of bloodlines and
the necessity to marry an heiress. (The custom of visiting
prostitutes or of seducing lower class women, turning them into
clients, is one practiced in the company of male peers, and
provides not only a leisurely sport but a means of cultivating
alliances with those of ones own generation.) Finally the
emphasis on the festivals and outward display of Catholicism is
a convenient vehicle, first to tie the wider family together
through the celebration of feasts, and second to dramatize the

111

upper class position in the wider social scale.

To conclude, one can see that all is not effortless in the assumption of a place at the seemingly ascribed summit of Guatemalan society. A young gentleman must validate his ascribed status. If not he risks reducing the patrimony and eventually the status of his own children. The child born into the wealthy household must strive to establish such a household for himself. Some are content to remain idle or underremployed, not aiding their more energetic relatives in the process of getting more out of their estates, by better technical management in the countryside and clever financial and marketing management in the city. Such persons are at a disadvantage, for their relatives compensate themselves well for the job of managing corporate agricultural properties. Unless the indolent aristocrat marries well, then his children are even more disadvantaged as they grow up and seek their place in the aristocratic sunshine.

The social lessons then of the life cycle are learned in the social interactions of early childhood and of schooldays. A child is segregated within the circles of kindred, clients, and then of the economic upper class. To maintain himself he must learn how to gain the personal favor, first of his elders, then of his peers and finally of his own clients.

In sum the young aristocrat must use all the ideal patterns listed by Wagley--familism, ceremonial kinship, formal etiquette, dashing virility, and devout display--at once in an overall pattern according to the rhythms of his own maturation, courtship, and the desires of his relatives. The culture complexes which integrate the ideal pattern are those of first clientage, second familism in it lineal and lateral dimensions and in its class endogamy, and finally the practice of plantation agriculture. This overall pattern has proved most adaptive to the incursions of the modern economy and the international market. Whether the Guatemalan elite can continue to retain its familistic form in the face of the probable evolution of the corporately-owned central estate and the appearance of widespread industrialization remains to be seen.

NOTES

1. The fieldwork upon which this report is based was partly sponsored by a Public Health Service Research Grant MN-10151-01 Attachment to FIMH-17,255-03 of NIMH.
2. It is interesting to note that Hunt documents a local group quite distant from the metropolis and the old tradition of entail, yet in fact each 'house' manages to favor one heir over all the others.
3. A reading of recent reports makes it clear that all of Cuban central agriculture is administered as a single coordinated enterprise by a state agency (Bonachea and Valdés 1972).

4. All names drawn from the region of my fieldwork have been disguised.

REFERENCES

Adams, Richard N.
    1970   Crucifixion by Power: Essays on Guatemalan
                National Social Structure, 1944-1966. Austin:
                University of Texas Press.

Arensberg, Conrad M.
    1963   The Old World Peoples: The Place of European
                Cultures in World Ethnography. Anthropological
                Quarterly 36:75-99 (reprinted as a chapter in
                Culture and Community by C. M. Arensberg and S.
                T. Kimball).

Arensberg, C. M. and Solon T. Kimball
    1968   Family and Community in Ireland. Revised edition.
                Cambridge: Harvard University Press.

Bonachea, Rolans E. and Nelson P. Valdés
    1972   Cuba in Revolution. Garden City: Doubleday-
                Anchor.

Chevalier, Francois
    1963   Land and Society in Colonial Mexico: The Great
                Hacienda. Trans. Alvin Eustis. Berkeley:
                University of California Press.

Douglass, Wm. A.
    1969   Death in Murélaga: Funerary Ritual in a Spanish
                Basque Village. The American Ethnological
                Society Monograph 49. Seattle: The University
                of Washington Press.

Hunt, Robert
    1965   The Developmental Cycle of the Family Business in
                Rural Mexico, Essays in Economic Anthropology.
                Proceedings, American Ethnological Society.
                Seattle: University of Washington Press.

Lipset, Seymour M. and Aldo Solari
    1967   Elites in Latin America. Oxford: Oxford Univer-
                sity Press.

Lisón-Tolosona, Carmelo
    1966   Belmonte de los Caballeros: A Sociological
                Study of a Spanish Town. Oxford: Clarendon

Press.

Malefakis, Edward E.
    1970   Agrarian Reform and Peasant Revolution in Spain.
                New Haven: Yale University Press.

Moore, G. Alexander Jr.
    1963   The Guatemalan Plantation System in Historical
                Perspective. Columbia University Master's
                Essay.
    1973   Life Cycles in Atchalán: The Diverse Careers of
                Certain Guatemalans. New York: Teachers College
                Press.

Rubin, Vera,
    1959   Plantation Systems of the New World. Washington,
                D. C.: Pan American Union.

Scheele, Raymond L.
    1956   The Prominent Families of Puerto Rico, in The
                People of Puerto Rico, ed. Julian H. Steward.
                Urbana: University of Illinois Press.

Wagley, Charles
    1968   The Latin American Tradition. New York:
                Columbia University Press.

Whiteford, Andrew H.
    1964   Two Cities in Latin America: A Comparative
                Description of Social Classes. Garden City:
                Doubleday-Anchor.

EDUCATION IN 'AINA PUMEHANA:
THE HAWAIIAN-AMERICAN STUDENT AS HERO

Alan Howard
University of Hawaii

Introduction

The data on which this paper is based were collected over a three-year period between 1965 and 1968 from a Hawaiian homestead community that I shall refer to by the pseudonym of 'Aina Pumehana.[1] The study was an interdisciplinary effort involving primarily social anthropology and psychology, but including researchers from several other disciplines as well. During the initial phases of research, information was gathered by participant observation and open-ended interviewing. In addition, under the supervision of Dr. Ronald Gallimore, a series of social psychological experiments were carried out in a local school with the goal of clarifying developmental processes lying behind Hawaiian-American character formation. During the second year of field work, we constructed a set of questionnaires for the purpose of gathering systematic data on a representative sample of adults in the community, as a means of clarifying and refining our ethnographic observations.

'Aina Pumehana is located on the Leeward side of Oahu, approximately thirty miles from Honolulu. It is one of several homesteads established under the provisions of the Hawaiian Homestead Act of 1920. In order to acquire a lease on homestead lands, individuals are required to demonstrate that they are 50 percent or more "Hawaiian" (i.e., Polynesian Hawaiian) by genealogical descent. Lessees are entitled to a plot of land ranging between one-fourth to one acre at a cost of $1 per year. They are also eligible for low interest home-building and home-improvement loans. In 1965, when we began our research, 394 lots were occupied in 'Aina Pumehana.

From a socio-economic point of view, 'Aina Pumehana may be characterized as a working class community. The majority of men are employed in semi-skilled or skilled blue-colar occupations, many of them commuting to Honolulu and its environs daily. A substantial minority of women also are employed. Unemployment rates in the community are generally higher than state-wide averages, and median income is comparatively low. The community, in fact, is part of a wider area that has been designated as "economically depressed" according to the standards of the state and federal governments, and over the past few years has been the "target" of several remedial programs, including the Economic

Opportunity Act and Model Cities program.

Although lessees may be married to persons of less than 50 percent ancestry, the community is heavily weighted toward Hawaiian ethnicity and manifests a lifestyle that strongly reflects traditional Hawaiian values. Of paramount importance in the modal lifestyle is an emphasis on affiliative values and a devaluation of behavior oriented toward raising one's prestige vis-a-vis others. Although kinship ranking is important within family groupings, egalitarian pressures are very strong between nonkinsmen, and informal sanctions are brought to bear on those who flaunt their achievements or who seek public recognition. "We are like crabs in a basket," our informants frequently told us, "as soon as one begins to crawl out, the others reach up to pull him back." Generosity and reciprocal exchange are normative values; this results in a disbursal of resources even during times when money is scarce, and is one of the major reasons why few Hawaiian-Americans accumulate material capital. The norm is to invest resources in social capital rather than to conserve. These values are reflected in a high frequency of large scale feasts, in frequent social gatherings and in numerous other group-oriented activities. They are reflected negatively in a low level of concern for such status symbols as ostentatious housing or prestige automobiles. There are an abundance of automobiles in the community but no Cadillacs or Lincolns, in contrast to many Ghetto communities on the mainland. In addition to traditional type feasts, or luaus, the strength of Hawaiian heritage within the community is reflected in a high incidence of adoption (see Howard et al., 1970) and in practices and beliefs related to the treatment of illness (Heighton, 1971). Nevertheless, 'Aina Pumehana is also very much a part of the modern sociopolitical system that is the United States and, more immediately, the State of Hawaii.

Perhaps more than any institution, the schools are purveyors of a contrasting set of values, those associated with middle-class Americana. This is accentuated by the fact that the State of Hawaii has a centralized school system, administered out of Honolulu, and dominated by persons of Caucasian and Japanese-American ancestry. Although 'Aina Pumehana parents continually express a fundamental concern for their children's education, their active participation in formulating school policies has been strongly discouraged by the central administration. The school is therefore very much of an alien institution in the community.

My approach in this paper will be a developmental one, and will focus on the contingencies faced by children as they grow up. Of central concern will be the discontinuities in these contingencies as children move from infancy to the toddler stage and then again as they enter the school system. The viewpoint I shall take involves trying to understand children's behavior in terms of the strategies and tactics they must use to cope with these contingencies. The use of concepts such as "strategies" and "tactics" represents an attempt to overcome the implication, so often present in socialization studies, that children are merely reactors to circumstances, rather than being active participants in the learning process. It is my belief that the view of children as mere respondents to adult manipulations not only distorts the actual situation, but also results in misguided educational programs.

Preschool Socialization Experience

During the ethnographic phase of our research we could not help but be struck by the degree to which young children are socially "present" in 'Aina Pumehana. Even casual visitors to the community remark about the ubiquity of children. As one drives down a homestead street they are playing together in front yards; at luaus and drinking parties children's sporadic shouts of glee, bickerings, and challenges are an inevitable part of the background. Even quite late at night, when their murmers have dissolved into slumber, children are visible, sleeping on a mat in a corner of the room, or possibly in their mother's, father's, "auntie's" or someone else's arms.

We were also impressed by the apparent discontinuity between the indulgence of infants and rather harsh treatment afforded children after they become mobile (beginning at about two or three years old). This type of discontinuity was not unfamiliar to us; it has been described in detail by Ritchie and his associates for the New Zealand Maori (James Ritchie 1956, 1963; Jane Ritchie 1957), and has been a point of discussion among a number of psychologically-oriented field workers in Polynesia (see Levy 1969). The overall pattern may be described as follows: During infancy, youngsters are tended to very closely. Much of their waking time is passed in someone's arms, being cuddled, played with and talked to. At family gatherings it is common practice for an infant to be passed from one to another; taking a baby to hold is perceived as a privilege rather than a responsibility, so that age takes preference. Usually it is the older women who monopolize a child, although over a period of time almost everyone--even teenage boys who may like to come on "tough" at times--is apt to be given an opportunity to indulge in fondling, cooing at and pacifying it. Although men, on the average, spend less time holding and cuddling an infant, the pleasure they display when they do so appears no less intense than the delight shown by women. At no time did we hear any male chide another for giving attention to an infant, nor did we obtain any other evidence that to do so is considered unmasculine. Quite the contrary--some of the hardest drinking, most belligerent men openly showed the greatest tenderness.

An infant is rarely allowed to cry for more than a few
seconds before someone comes to porvide relief. Mothers are
pressured to do so; if a child is left crying other persons present show signs of distress. Speculations are made as to the
cause of the baby's discomfort and other indirect cues are emit-
ted to let the mother know that if she does not attend to the
child's welfare immediately she is likely to be branded negli-
gent. Consistent with this pattern is the practice of demand
feeding. Although a few women reported attempts to establish a
feeding schedule, they were almost invariably given up within a
few days; the cries of a hungry baby were just too much to bear.
Feeding an infant is more than just a means of providing nourishment, however. It has symbolic value in the sense that it provides a public display of nurturance, or concern for the child's
welfare. Food was therefore offered to crying infants even when
it seemed clear to field workers that the child was not hungry,
but distressed for other reasons. There were even some reports
of infants being fed when their distress was more than likely to
be the result of overeating.

A parallel enthusiasm accompanies cleanliness care.
Diapers are changed frequently (an informal count indicated an
average of 24 per day for a small sample of mothers) and sometimes before soiling has occurred. One mother said she removed
unsoiled diapers because the child "sweats and gets sore bottom
if you don't change him." Another mother, when asked why she
was removing an unsoiled diaper from a crying infant, remarked
that a clean diaper might "make him feel better."

This general strategy of constant attention to and an-
ticipation of an infant's needs is not accompanied by a proportionately high interest in maturation. Discussions of maturational indicators are rare, and with the exception of changes
they find amusing or entertaining, most 'Aina Pumehana residents
show little concern with a child's rate of advancement. For
example, many parents do not encourage their children to walk
and at times appear to discourage them from becoming mobile in
order to reduce the possibility of injury. Even those who do
seem to view children's attempts to walk with pride and interest,
and encourage them to the extent that they provide supports or
other forms of assistance for brief periods, do not encourage
walking with the passion characteristic of middle-class Caucas-
ians who see in such accomplishment an indication of personal
achievement. In 'Aina Pumehana to make a display of one's
child's accomplishments would be regarded as a vulgar attempt to
show off. Then, too, indications are that parents are in no
hurry to see their babies become toddlers. Thus the majority of
a sample of 27 mothers, when asked at what age they liked children best, showed a distinct preference for infants around six
months old.

As children become increasingly mobile and verbal, parental indulgence begins to give way to irritation and a lack of

118

tolerance for insistent demands. The birth of a subsequent child is generally sufficient to create a marked shift in this direction, but even though no new infants are born (or adopted) into a household, a distinct change in parental behavior is noticeable as a child matures. Although some writers have referred to this altered parental behavior as "rejection," I regard such a characterization as inappropriate, if not thoroughly inaccurate. A more acceptable view is that the change in parental response is related to an overriding concern for rank and authority within the family. Thus, as long as children are passively dependent, their signals for attention are perceived as an expression of infantile need--as cues to be acted upon by nurturant adults. However, as children become increasingly mobile and verbal, and acquire the capacity for making more insistent and aggressive demands, their attention-seeking behavior is apt to be seen as an attempt to intrude and control. It is therefore an assault on the privileges of rank, for only the senior-ranking individual in an interaction has a right to make demands. By responding harshly parents are therefore socializing their children to respect the privileges of rank.

An additional factor may involve parents' own sensitivities to rejection. While a child is an infant and absolutely dependent upon parental nurturance for gratification of needs, he is unlikely to reject overtures; even if he does the rejection is not perceived as willful. But a child of two or three is capable of quite willfully rebuffing nurturant overtures, and Hawaiian-American parents, most of whom are extremely sensitive to such rebuffs, begin to find the relationship somewhat less attractive and are motivated to disengage from it to some degree. This, at least, is how we have interpreted the frequent remarks that children in the toddler stage "become too independent," or wistfully, "They begin to have a mind of their own."

Once the point of change has been reached, children are no longer the indulged center of attention they were as infants. They are removed to the fringes of the adult world, and much of the attention they receive is in the form of demands ("Go get me a glass of water") or admonishments ("Stop bothering me"). Thus children are faced with their initial strategic challenge--how to regain the indulgent rewards of their previously favored status. Quite naturally they rely on the tactics that paid off so handsomely before. They cry, whine, tug on parental clothing, try to climb into adult laps and otherwise attempt to take central stage in the social arena. These tactics may pay off some of the time during the transition period, and may therefore be perpetuated for a time, but they also draw increasingly harsh punishment.

As the risk of drawing punishment relative to the probability of obtaining rewards increases, children begin to explore now strategies and to seek substitute rewards. The strategy that appears to pay off best under these circumstances is to yield the privilege of initiating interactions to one's parents. This not only has the effect of reducing reactive punishment, it also has the advantage of confining interactions to occasions when parental need are salient.

A frequent parentally initiated interaction (i.e., one not triggered by a child's intrusion or misbehavior) is in the form of demands for service or task performance. Children are asked to fetch something for a parent, to convey messages, to check on the whereabouts of a family member, etc. Parents also begin to assign tasks such as sweeping up, clearing the dinner table, emptying the rubbish and cleaning the yard at an early age; in some cases assignments are made as the chores arise, in others they are regularly scheduled. These demands provide children with an opportunity to gain highly desired parental approval, and most children eagerly respond when called upon. Rewards are likely to come in a muted form compared with earlier indulgences--a smile or playful pat, a joke, or maybe an opportunity to sit on a lap for a few minutes. Rarely is overt praise or lavish attention given. But the degree to which children cherish even these muted displays of affection is obvious from the way that their faces light up in response. In addition to demands, there are times a parent may simply feel like being nurturant, or may wish to publicly demonstrate that he loves his children, but there is little that a child can do to promote such circumstances. The most he can do is tune into his parents' expressive codes, so that he can accurately judge when it might pay off to make himself socially visible and when he is better off to stay out of sight. Some children learn to inhibit completely responses, like crying, that previously brought indulgence but now can be counted on to be ignored at best, severely punished at worst. We noticed, however, that when someone (like a field worker) dispenses unconditional rewards, even the older children tend to disinhibit very rapidly and are all over him with very strong demands for attention. The tactic of coming on strong thus remains, for most Hawaiian-Americans, in reserve, to be called upon when threats of admonishment or punishment are removed.

With the promise of parental rewards drastically reduced, children begin to seek the attention of their siblings and peers. Their relations with older siblings parallel to a certain degree their relations with parents; older siblings have authority over them and have power to reward and punish, though to a lesser degree than parents. They are likely to permit more intrusiveness than parents and continue to reward demands for attention for some time after the latter have withdrawn them. However they are also more likely to be erratic in meting out punishment, sometimes using scoldings or beatings as a means of communicating their social power to the child and their peers. Nevertheless, relations with siblings tend to be much more relaxed than with parents once a child has become fully mobile and verbal. It is

with siblings that children learn the value of such strategies
as joking, i.e., turning a potentially threatening situation
into one of play. If they can induce an angry older sibling to
laugh by giggling, clowning or otherwise projecting cues appropriate to a play context, they are likely to be successful in
reducing the degree of punishment, or even in fending it off
completely. With parents this strategy is not apt to be successful since they are less susceptible to being drawn into games
than children. Thus it seemed to us that Hawaiian-American
children learned to rely on a joking, game-type strategy to cope
with potential threats to a greater degree than middle-class
Causasian children, precisely because their parents relegated
more control to older siblings.

The social ranking inherent in parent-child and sibling
relations recedes into the background with peers, although some
weight is still given to relative age. It is with peers that
the joking strategy comes to full fruition. Serious competitive-
ness, attempts to gain dominance and strong demands for attention
are all likely to be met with indignation or anger, perhaps because social interaction would be nearly impossible should all
the latent cravings for attention be permitted to surface. Joking, or to be more precise, tacitly agreeing not to take anything seriously except the most grievous offenses, thus becomes
the prime social lubricant, beginning in early childhood and
extending through adult life. Reciprocity also has its firmest
roots in peer relations. Although most Hawaiian-American parents stress equal sharing among their children, this is an imposed contingency from the latter's point of view. In relations
with peers, reciprocity assumes a positive strategic value of a
somewhat different order. By willingly sharing what he has with
peers a child learns that he is more likely to obtain a reasonable
distribution of rewards through time, for his peers will more
willingly share what they have with him. In a community in which
parental resources are limited, and parental rewarding sporadic,
such a strategy has a high payoff in terms of overall utility.
Reciprocity also contributes to an egalitarian group atmosphere
and an atmosphere of easy sociability. Thus, even before a child
has reached kindergarten age, he is likely to have learned to
rely on the basic strategies that mark the Hawaiian-American social style.

School: The Struggle for Control

By all the statistical standards customarily used by ed-
ucators--scores on achievement tests, rates of dropping out, etc.
--the children of 'Aina Pumehana are educational failures. To
give just one indicator, in 1966 approximately 70% of the tenth
grade students from 'Aina Pumehana fell below the 25th percentile
on standardized tests of achievement. Not only educators are dis-

turbed by this level of performance; the children's parents are equally concerned, for they value education greatly and have high ambitions for their offspring. But the question I wish to raise is whether the children have in fact failed when one examines their performance from the standpoint of the values and behavioral styles they bring to the schools. My thesis is that far from being failures, from some perspectives they must be regarded as highly successful, for they continually win battles with their teachers for control over their lives, in large part because the strategies and tactics they use are far more effective than those used against them. Indeed, they might be viewed as the most potent soldiers Hawaiian-American culture has in its defense against the onslaught of middle-class Americana.

To begin with, we might point to the issue of language. The language of the community is usually labeled as "pidgin English," although it might more properly be described as a colloquial dialect involving a large number of loan words, primarily from Hawaiian. For years this dialect was considered "substandard" English by educators in Hawaii, and vigorous attempts were made to stamp it out. More recently official attitudes have softened, but most teachers still find it difficult to see the colloquial dialect as anything but substandard English. The dialect is, in fact, a richly developed expressive code, well-suited to interaction based on easy sociability, but it has a simpler grammar and denotative vocabulary than standard English. It also varies phonologically from standard English. The children, of course, must use the local dialect to communicate effectively with their family and friends, so if forced to choose will favor it nearly every time. At least three levels of communicative disturbance are involved when a teacher insists on standard English and on making the local dialect a target of ridicule and derision. At the simple overt level, there is phonological interference between the two speech modalities (Boggs, in press). There is also differential emphasis with regard to codes, the children emphasizing an expressive code, the teachers a denotative code. Finally, at an attitudinal level, the teacher communicates a message of disdain for the children's speech capabilities and by extension, for their cultural values and background. That a majority of the children refuse to adopt standard English as a replacement for the local dialect might be interpreted, therefore, as a strategic victory--as a successful defense of their language, values and cultural lifestyle. From one standpoint, at least, they deserve great credit for resisting a highly financed, technologically potent attempt to brainwash them.

But the battle extends well beyond the mere use of language, which in some respects is more symptomatic than central. The core of the struggle really revolves around the issue of social influence. If teachers are to be successful in patterning children's behavior (i.e., teaching them things), they must be

122

capable of directing the children's attention and providing meaningful rewards for approved performances. This, our observations have led us to believe, most teachers in the schools we studied are unable to do. Their influence strategies are ineffective and self-defeating, so they accuse the students of being inattentive, more interested in playing around than learning, and of being generally unmotivated. To fully appreciate the nature of the conflict, we must expand our description of preschool socialization by addressing the question, "How do Hawaiian-American parents control their children, and what do the children learn as a consequence?" or more directly, "What is the nature of the social influence process that Hawaiian-American children must adapt to within their families?"

Our observations made it clear to us that although parents rely heavily upon punishment of unwanted behavior in order to control their children, the number of areas in which demands are made upon a child is relatively limited, since the child is trained early to seek help from siblings and peers, or to help himself. In fact, then, the frequency of punishment is likely to be low since the number of interactions with parents tends to become increasingly restricted. Rewards are dispensed from time to time, but generally on a noncontingent basis. What seems to be distinct about the meeting out of punishment, in comparison with the middle-class American pattern, is the degree to which it is personalized. That is, children are scolded or "given a licking" for unwarranted intrusions or for failing to comply with parental demands, but almost never for failing to achieve a standard that is impersonally valued. Within this system parental inattentiveness serves as a form of reinforcment in the sense that it signals to the child that his behavior is acceptable. By dispensing rewards on a noncontingent basis, parents communicate to a child that they, and not he, have a right to control the nature of their interactions. It is as though parents realize that if they made rewards contingent they would be opening themselves to manipulation, and in effect yielding some control of the relationship to their children. In light of the value emphasis placed on respect for rank and authority within the family, this would be an undesirable outcome.

Thus Hawaiian-American children, unlike their middle-class Caucasian counterparts, are not trained to respond to parental inattentiveness with attempts to secure a rewarding response. Only when parents signal that they are in a nurturant mood do children orient to them and begin to activate behavioral forms that were previously rewarded. For example, a child imitates the antics of a wrestler on a television to which his parents respond with amusement and joking, perhaps even approving, comments. He is likely to continue until his parents show signs of irritation or otherwise signal him to stop. When this happens, the child's best strategy is to "disappear," to transform himself into a "nonperson" in his parents' social field.

Only in this limited sense do parents provide reinforcements for specific acts of behavior. In order to maximize rewards and minimize punishments, a child must learn to actively engage his parents only when they are in a nurturant mood, to disengage when they show signs of irritation or annoyance, and to remain unobtrusively attentive the rest of the time.

Our experimental data supported this formulation. Following a period of isolation, Hawaiian-American children were less attentive to an experimental task presented to them than a control group who were exposed to a period of warm interaction with the experimenter. This result, which is the opposite of that obtained under similar experimental conditions from middle-class Caucasian children, we hypothesized to be the result of Hawaiian-American children learning to attend to cues more closely when adults have signalled that they are in a nurturant mood (see Howard, in press).

If we shift our perspective to that of the child and the contingencies he must cope with in responding to parents, we arrive at the following formulation:

A. When parents are punitive or critical, a child's best strategy is to withdraw, avoid, or inhibit. Under such circumstances there is little point in being attentive because the additional information provided by parental cues is of little utility; nothing he can do is likely to elicit a rewarding response. As a result, task performance can be expected to decrease when children raised in the mode have been criticized or subjected to disapproval.

B. When parents are in a nurturant mood, it pays the child to be maximally attentive, for scarce rewards are most likely to be obtained under such conditions. The value of rewards obtained is comparatively greater than for middle-class children precisely because they are not as freely dispensed. Therefore task performance can be expected to increase following periods of nurturance and social approval.

C. When parents are paying no attention to a child, his best strategy is to remain unobtrusive, but observant to cues that signal the vicissitudes of parental moods. Should he discover a shift toward nurturance, it may pay to enter their social field; a shift toward anger or sullenness is a cue to withdraw completely. Parental neutrality is therefore associated with an intermediate level of children's attentiveness. We would expect intermediate levels of task performance in the absence of either marked approval or disapproval.

With the promise of parental rewards substantially reduced, a child's best strategy is to turn to siblings and peers for primary interpersonal gratifications. It is the salience of the peer group in this early period that appears to generate an overriding concern for affiliation in the Hawaiian-American subculture. As parents recede into the peripheries of a child's social field, the relative value of pleasing them with achievement or accomplishment diminishes in comparison with the pleasures of peer group sociability. In combination, this leads to a reluctance to make one's self vulnerable by socially engaging persons of unknown disposition, particularly if they are of higher rank or social standing (as teachers are); a higher value being placed on sociability and affiliation than on personal achievement; and a greater concern for social rewards than for living up to "standards of excellence," with correspondingly more value being placed on rewards dispensed by others in comparison with self-rewards. We were not only able to validate these observations by social psychological experiments, but were also able to demonstrate that such learning experiences are related to the salience of Need affiliation as a spur to achieving behavior rather than Need achievement, and a concern for accumulating social capital (i.e., an expanded network of interpersonal commitment) rather than material resources.

How does this type of social learning history affect interaction in classrooms structured on the premise that children must primarily attend and orient to teachers for effective learning to take place? The answer seems to be that a struggle ensues in which teachers wheedle, cajole, threaten and use all the other influence tactics that work so well with middle-class Caucasian children, while the students employ such behavioral forms as tactical passivity, initiation of activity with peers and ignoring teachers' overtures. A summary statement is provided by Gallimore, Boggs, and MacDonald (1968):

Generally, children do not like to pay attention, as a group, to instructions given by the teacher, and they almost never listen closely to instructions the first several times they are given. Nevertheless, teachers spend a great deal of time trying to get the children's attention in order to switch them from one activity to another. Teachers have a number of rituals which they employ for this purpose--such as, switching the lights off until all are quiet and ready to begin another activity, playing "Simon says" with such words as "Put books away," "Be quiet," or suggesting, "Let's see if you can hear the pin drop," and many others. Sometimes children enjoy these games and they are often bored by harangues which are intended to accomplish the same purpose. Either way, when the new activity is supposed to begin, the majority have little conception of what is to be done.

Most of the time children are much more strongly oriented toward other children than they are toward adults. They help one another very readily, copy one another's work, and are very sensitive to being outdone by others. . . .

A frequent result of the lack of attention to the teacher's instructions and positive orientation toward other children is that children attempt to do the assignment by copying. More rarely, they may ask questions of other classmates.

Helping one another does not mean sharing possessions, like pencils. There are frequently bitter arguments about this, and a child will rarely yield a pencil to another, even when commanded to do so. In general, children frequently are very "touchy" toward one another, and brief but bitter fights are not uncommon. Whether helping or fighting, however, children most often act as if adults were not present, and other children were the primary source of all gratification and frustration.

The typical classroom works against the powerful peer-affiliation motive which appears to operate in Hawaiian social groups. To diminish the strength of this motive may be futile, at least if one employs a head-on attack--that is, by punitive means in the early grades. Second, and related, the punitive measures used in the attempt to eliminate attending to peers and to encourage attending to the teacher have the effect of increasing passivity, withdrawal, and avoidance. Hawaiian parents train their children to respond to negative sanctions with respect and obedience, and not with active attempts to alter the parents' response. If an Hawaiian parent scolds his child, the child is likely to go to the bedroom, or outside, and remain there until the incident becomes history. Children of certain other cultural groups are more likely to follow a scolding with an active attempt to obtain parental approval and, in general, to seek praise and verbal approval.

Among Hawaiian youngsters, however, many of the social-influence techniques which are verbal in nature are ineffective since children seem largely indifferent and inattentive to adult talk, unless it is deliberately entertaining or directed at them individually. They do not know what to make of verbal praise; it is at best meaningless to them. Protestations of affection, or the withdrawal of affection, are not understood. A teacher's threat of becoming angry is likely to be ignored unless it means that he will very soon use physical punishment--that is what an adult's anger means to a child, not the withdrawal of affection.

They respond warmly to being touched and held, arm around shoulders, or spoken to eye to eye. They also respond to a firm, individually directed scolding, especially if accompanied by a gruff but affectionate gesture. They are sensitive at times to adult approval and anger. When seeking to make recompense to an adult, the most typical act is to engage in some helpful chore. Unless the adult appreciates the intent of this, the

126

child is likely to feel rebuffed. (pp. 36-38)

Only a part of the children's response can be interpreted as a negative reaction against teachers' attempts to control and influence them. They actively strive to restructure classroom interaction patterns into a system more compatible with their previous experience, although teachers rarely recognize these attempts for what they are and usually label such behavior as disruptive. An insight into this process is provided by Boggs (in press), in a recent paper inquiring into "The Meaning of Questions and Narratives to Hawaiian Children." He points out that Hawaiian-American children strive to turn their relationships with teachers into collective ones when verbal interchanges such as questions and answers are involved. "A collective relationship with an adult," he suggests, "seems to be equivalent to relationships among children, so far as patterns of communication are concerned." He reports that, "the response of children when questioned in class has the effect of shifting dyadic relations to collective ones," and states that, "the reason may be that the child finds protection in collective relationships with adults." Boggs summarizes his findings in the form of a rule: "Other children can be queried, answered and talked to at any time, and so can adults when relating to a group of children."

The implication is that when a teacher is willing to interact with children collectively, and permits children to interact with one another, that verbal exchanges are extensive and rich in content, and that children are attentive to the social interactions around them. Boggs' observations, as well as numerous other observations by our field workers, overwhelmingly support the inference that optimal learning takes place in such a social environment.

Unfortunately, many teachers interpret children's efforts to convert dyadic adult-child interactions into collective ones as a form of classroom disruption.[2] They see the children's behavior as willfully inattentive and undisciplined. If they are "weak" teachers, they often simply give up trying to teach the children anything, in exchange for a modicum of orderliness. If they are "strong" teachers, they may resort to authoritarian strategies that approximate those of the children's parents. In the latter case, students may respond by being overtly obedient but thoroughly disengaged from scholastic activities in the classrooms; they rely on behavioral forms such as tactical passivity and self-removal from the social scene as a means of minimizing expected punishment. There are an intermediate group of teachers who attempt to be authoritarian, but whose teaching strategies and disciplinary techniques are so ineffective that the children do not take them seriously. In their classrooms, children interact with one another at will, and ignore the teacher's threats and overtures to gain attention.

Boggs reports that observations in several classrooms

127

comprised of Hawaiian and part-Hawaiian teen-agers in other parts of the state "suggest that the success of teaching techniques is related to whether or not they take advantage of the behavior patterns which have been described. One observer writes as follows of a teacher, herself part-Hawaiian, who succeeds in eliciting extensive communication from a class of such students:

> There was no direct questioning of individual students and most questions were asked of the entire group. All responses were absolutely voluntary; no one was forced to say anything. Voluntary responses were very good, and often students would blurt out an experience or an answer without being recognized by the teacher. There were instances when students talked continuously without being recognized.

This teacher, Boggs points out, is taking advantage of the children's preference for relating to adults as a group, and is using it creatively (ibid.). However, the proportion of teachers employing such a strategy is appallingly low; it is simply too different from institutionalized teaching concepts to be acceptable to many of them.

Conclusion

From the standpoint of educators, the kinds of behavior exhibited by Hawaiian-American children are, at best, an unfortunate impediment to a sound education. Such a view is based on the premise that children need to learn requisite skills in order to survive in our dominant society, and that unless they learn to orient toward teachers and the tasks required of them, they will not learn properly. However, if one looks at the same situation as an interface between ethnic groups, the Hawaiian-American children we have observed might rightfully be labeled as "heroes," for they are defending the core values of their culture against the onslaughts of an alien group. Even though they cannot verbalize it, their behavior may well be interpreted as a communicative statement to the effect that "it isn't worth it; we will not give up our basic commitments to peers, to affiliation, to our general lifestyle, for what you are offering."

Does this mean that future generations of Hawaiian-American children will be forced to fight for their cultural integrity as the present generation has had to do? Are Hawaiian-American parents going to be continually denied the privilege of seeing their children get a good education? The answer to these questions lie not within the Hawaiian-American community, as so many educators would like us to believe, but within the structure and values of the school system itself. It is the educational system that has created the need for battle; the children have merely responded valiantly. I fear, though, that most of the questions educators are asking in response to current crises are more in the spirit of, "How can we improve our battle techniques?"

128

than in the more appropriate frame of, "How can we avoid the battle?"

There are no inherent impediments in the Hawaiian-American learning style, but until the dominant educational system accepts the validity of divergent values and lifestyles, I can only add my encouragement to the battle being waged by the students in 'Aina Pumehana schools. Until schools change, I can only be sympathetic with the combat cry of "Geeve 'em, bruddah!"

NOTES

1. Research in 'Aina Pumehana was supported by grant number MH 15032 to B. P. Bishop Museum from the National Institute of Mental Health. The support of both institutions is gratefully acknowledged.

2. Gallimore reports, on the basis of systematic classroom observation, a difference in the frequency of "working alone" and "working in groups" between Hawaiian-American and middle-class Caucasian classrooms, but a marked similarity in the frequency of working behavior in contrast with other behavioral categories. Unfortunately many teachers categorize "working in groups" as disruptive behavior and punish it (personal communication).

3. Observations by Edison M. C. Chong, term paper for Anthropology 480(3), December, 1969. (as reported in Boggs, in press)

REFERENCES

Boggs, Stephen T.
　　　　　　　The meaning of questions and narratives to Hawaiian children. To be published (in press) in C. Cazden, D. Hymes and V. John (Eds.), The Functions of Language in the Classroom. New York: Columbia Teachers College Press.

Gallimore, Ronald, Stephen T. Boggs and W. Scott MacDonald
　　1968　　　Education. In R. Gallimore and A Howard (Eds.), Studies in a Hawaiian Community: Na Makamaka O Nanakuli. PAR #1, Bernice P. Bishop Museum, Honolulu, pp. 36-38.

Heighton, Robert H., Jr.
　　1971　　　Hawaiian supernatural and natural strategies for goal attainment. Unpublished doctoral dissertation, University of Hawaii.

Howard, Alan, Robert H. Heighton, Jr., Cathie Jordan and Ronald Gallimore

1970   Traditional and modern adoption patterns in
              Hawaii. In V. Carrol (ed.), Adoption in
              Eastern Oceania. Honolulu: University of
              Hawaii Press.

Levy, Robert I.
    1969   Personality studies in Polynesia and Micronesia:
              stability and change. Social Science Research
              Institute Working Paper #8. University of
              Hawaii.

Ritchie, James E.
    1956   Basic personality in Rakau. Publications in
              Psychology, #8. Wellington, New Zealand,
              Victoria University of Wellington.

Ritchie, James E.
    1963   The making of a Maori. Publications in Psycho-
              logy, #15. Wellington, New Zealand, Victoria
              University of Wellington, A. H. & A. W. Reed.

Ritchie, Jane
    1957   Childhood in Rakau. Publications in Psychology,
              #10. Wellington, New Zealand, Victoria Univer-
              sity of Wellington.

PUPILS, PEERS AND POLITICS[1]

Charles Harrington
Columbia University

Introduction

An individual's ability to survive in a political system is based upon his mastery of the tools and knowledge that will enable him to successfully reap premiums from a less than bountiful crop. Premiums are anything in short supply in a society. They may take the form of material goods, power, status, or safety. Since there are no societies in which all of these are in an unlimited supply, there is always the problem of distribution: Who gets what and who doesn't? Political decisions that affect an individual are made both in and out of formal government processes. While government and its processes are a part of political learning they are not its entirety. An individual must be aware of the variety of modes and channels of supply and demand, or constantly risk missing the opportunity to get more of what there is and/or losing that which he already has. Whether men succeed or fail in this quest for premiums the activities are the product of their socialization.

Political socialization has been studied often outside of anthropology. The present paper points out four shortcomings of the literature. I hope to show the potential richness of anthropological studies which focus on those neglected areas by describing a series of recently completed studies addressed to them. My central thesis in the paper and the studies described here, is that new theoretical approaches (especially those which emphasize the role of peers in socialization) and new methodologies (especially observational ones) are needed in the study of political socialization. I then discuss some of the implications of these findings for further research, particularly research concerned with the role of schools in the process of political socialization.

Of course, socialization centered explanations cannot account for all of politics. Certainly some premiums are not available to whole classes of people because of social structural variables, e.g. caste or class systems. Students of socialization cannot account for the occurrence of such systems, but they can help account for how such systems are maintained. This point is made explicitly by Harrington and Whiting (1972: 469) who argue it is their purpose to explain not only how the content

131

of social role is learned but also how a "society induces its members willingly to accept" such role responsibilities. Students of political socialization can also analyze within culture variation in meeting such requirements. That is, by focusing attention on learning and personality dimensions students of political socialization help us to understand (i.e., predict certain characteristics of) who accepts his lot and who rebels against it. For example Gurr (1970) not only specifies the social conditions which lead to rebellion but within that framework examines personality studies which help account for why within those structural conditions certain men do and others do not rebel.

PREVIOUS WORK

As an anthropologist my conceptualization of politics must be cross culturally useful. Therefore, I define politics broadly as decision-making about the distribution of scarce resources. This leads me to focus more on political process than the content of a particular political system thereby facilitating cross cultural comparisons. Therefore, in this paper, my focus is on the learning of skills for participating in the broadly conceived political process. This is a different emphasis from that of the existing political socialization literature. Largely a product of the fields of political science and psychology, it is mainly limited to western style political systems and how knowledge about government institutions is transmitted to future generations.[2] This gives rise to studies about the age at which one recognizes ones' flag (Lawson 1963), attitudes toward the President (e.g., Sigel 1965), congress (Hess & Torney 1967), etc. Further as Easton (1968) and Sigel (1966) have recently suggested the literature is largely concerned with the learning of knowledge and attitudes which support the existence of these familiar regimes ignoring behavior (like rioting) which does not. (For reviews of the present literature on the study of political socialization see Adler and Harrington 1970; Sigel 1970; Greenberg 1970; and Harrington n.d.a.).

The scope and methods of the literature on political socialization reviewed in these sources is then more limited than those of this paper. Indeed there are four major omissions to which our research with its broader scope is directed. This list of omissions is not meant to be exhaustive but reflects the specific limitations which a definition of politics broader than formal government is designed to correct. Specifically, the existing literature 1) neglects the influence of peers, 2) neglects informal processes within schools, 3) is limited to certain methodologies to the exclusion of others, and 4) neglects anything but white, mainstream Americans as subjects.

132

A. Peers

        The compilation and analysis of empirical research
made by Adler and Harrington (1970), of the present literature
on political socialization show that it examines essentially
three inputs to the child; family, school and peers. Until now,
however, there have been relatively few studies of peer influences. The two major books in the last ten years (Hess and
Torney, 1967; and Easton and Dennis, 1969) focus almost entirely
on family and school effects largely based upon an analysis of
the data gathered in 1962 in a national survey of over 12,000
white elementary school children (grades 2-8) in eight large and
medium-sized American cities. Several types of political attitudes are studied: attachment to the nation, relationship to
institutions and authority figures representing government,
compliance with authority and law, attitudes toward processes of
influence on public policy, and orientations towards elections
and political parties. This is an example of the narrow conceptualization of politics referred to earlier. The analysis
deals with the content of these attitudes, their developmental
patterns, and the agents of their socialization. Hess and Torney
found that the school is the most important agent of political
socialization in the United States. Family influence is seen as
limited largely to generalized attitudes toward authority, and
partisan attachments. The school reinforces the child's emotional attachment to his nation, and teaches him norms of citizen
obedience and conformity. Although the school stresses the
obligation to vote, it tends to de-emphasize other forms of
citizen participation. It pays little attention to political
parties, pressure groups, and political conflict. In this study
the individual characteristics that apparently had the most influence on the learning of the particular political attitudes
and behavior measured were sex, social class, and "intelligence,"
i.e., IQ's (note that it is not only politics which is narrowly
defined!) The definition of politics used by Hess and Torney
makes it difficult to use their findings to help construct a
theory of political socialization within the framwork I have laid
out here with its more general concerns. While we will make use
of some of their findings, e.g., that the ages 9-11 are important
ones, it is possible that these years may be crucial ones in
learning what Hess and Torney call politics but not in the learning of political process as we have defined it. Care must be
taken in using any findings based upon one definition of politics
for research of a different scope.
        Kenneth Langton is virtually alone in emphasizing the
importance of peers as an independent variable. Langton in 1967
studied the influence of the informal school environment -- the
social class "climate" of the peer group and the school on lower
class students political attitudes. The results suggest that
learning in peer groups may be more significant than formal civic

education for political socialization. Specifically, his study of secondary school students in Jamaica, West Indies, showed that the working class students had less positive attitudes toward voting and are less politically cynical and less economically conservative than middle class or upper class students. Lower class students whose classmates are also from the lower class are likely to have political attitudes characteristic of the lower class. But lower class students in heterogeneous class peer groups -- those which include higher class students -- are likely to support higher class norms. Thus, the peer group class environment and the social class climate of the school apparently have a cumulative effect on students' attitudes. Interaction with higher class peers functions to socialize lower class students toward the political orientation of the higher classes. What good it will do them in an educational system described by Comitas (1971) as one designed to prevent movement out of the lower class is unclear.

The possibilities of the contribution of interaction with peers to the learning of political skills and attitudes has not yet been pursued adequately by the political socialization literature, however. After all, even Langton only studies one easy measure, social class of peers, and does not directly examine peer interaction or process, and limits politics to attitude variables about a particular system. With our own emphasis on the learning of skills for participation in politics this is doubly unfortunate. The anthropological literature does indirectly offer some data to complement the political sociali-zation literature. For example, Mayer and Mayer (1970) describe socialization by peers in the youth organization of the Red Xhosa. They describe a system through which children advance in stages, each of which successively places more constraints upon them. Younger children are members of largely local groups in which aggression and sex-play is tolerated if not encouraged. As the child moves through the system he learns rules which in-creasingly control his aggressiveness and inculcate a respect for 'law' until, at circumcision he becomes an adult. In adulthood disputes are settled by law (argument) not by sticks (fighting). What is interesting here about the Xhosa is that the youth organization is free of adult control, yet the peer run sociali-zation devices lead to successful entrance into the role of Xhosa adult. Perhaps one of the reasons the political sociali-zation literature has ignored peers is an assumption following Parsons that peer groups are characterized by "compulsive inde-pendence in relation to certain adult expectations,...which in certain cases is expressed in overt defiance...or a certain recalcitrance to pressure of adult expectations and discipline." (Parsons 1949: 221) Since the political socialization litera-ture is largely concerned with system support learning, such an assumption would not lead to studies of peer effects.

However, whether peer groups are rebellious, insulated

or integrated with or from adult culture, they offer their members opportunity to practice and perfect political skills. For example, among the Xhosa "(the peer group) is a junior forum whose members, in a kind of earliest play, practice the political skills they will need in the real forum later on." (Mayer and Mayer 1970: 174). This kind of peer group learning fits in well with a cognitive developmental view of learning as recently developed by Kohlberg (1969).

> The second group in which the child participates is the peer group. While psychoanalysts have taken the family (the first group) as a critical and unique source of moral role taking (e.g. identification), Piaget (1948) has viewed the peer group as a unique source of role-taking opportunities for the child. According to Piaget, the child's unilateral respect for his parents, and his egocentric confusion of his own perspective with that of his parents, prevents him from engaging in the role-taking based on mutual respect necessary for moral development. While the empirical findings support the notion that peer group participation is correlated with moral development, it does not suggest that such participation plays a critical or unique role for moral development...While peer group participation appears to be stimulating of moral development, its influence seems better conceptualized in terms of providing general role taking opportunities...

Kohlberg is then arguing that peer groups provide an opportunity to practice the behaviors that the culture (or elders) prescribe as desirable. This perspective also provides a hint for some of the dynamics in which each child by trial and error acquires behavioral expectations (making organization of diversity possible, see Wallace 1971). Peer groups also provide an opportunity for what Pettit (1946) argued is a most potent kind of learning: directed practice. For a variety of theoretical and empirical reasons then, I feel that the influence of peers on the learning of political skills has been slighted.

Most of the existing anthropological literature on peer group socialization in the U.S. concerns adolescence or young adulthood (Miller 1958, 1964, Whyte 1955, Liebow 1965, Hannerz 1969). However, in examining peer group learning it is important to keep in mind the studies in developmental psychology recently reviewed by Hartup (1970: 411) which show middle childhood to be the period of "greatest responsiveness to normative influence of peers." We focus here, therefore, on the period 9-11 years as the period in which maximal "political" learning is said to occur (by students of political socialization). Since it overlaps the ages which the general developmental psychology literature spotlights for maximal peer effect on learning the absence of studies of peer effects is all the more startling and the need for study obvious.

B. Pupils

Generally when the political socialization literature examines schools, it only examines part of what actually goes on in them. To Langton and Jennings (1968), school means curriculum. Findings for their white sample showed that the civics curriculum had little effect on students' knowledge, beliefs, attitudes or feelings toward government. To Edgar Litt, school means textbooks. Litt reports on a comparative study of civic education in three American communities with differing socioeconomic characteristics and differing levels of political activity. All of the communities were in the Boston metropolitan area. The data consisted of a content analysis of civic education texts used in the three communities during a five-year period, interviews with community leaders and educational administrators on their views of the community's civic education program, and questionnaires administered to civic education classes (and control groups) in the major high school in each community. The results showed that the textbooks of the two middle-class communities emphasized citizen participation to a greater degree than those used in the working-clas community. Only in the upper-middle class community was there an attempt to transmit a view of politics as a political process involving political action and the use of power as a means for resolving group conflict.

In contrast, focusing on teachers, Hess and Torney find for their measures of political knowledge the school, "the most effective instrument of political socialization in the United States." (see above) But, they can't tell us how or why the school has its effect. Adler and Harrington (1970) argued that what was needed were studies that will focus not on the formal aspects of schooling, but on the informal processes within the schools which will help us understand what the schools accomplish and how. These first two problems obviously are related in that as we focus on the informal processes in schools we will be paying more attention to the peer group relations within the schools themselves.

C. Method

These two omissions are related to a third limitation of the political socialization literature which is its limitation to certain methodologies. The conceptual neatness that separates school, family, and peers in the non-anthropological studies referred to above results in part from their reliance on questionnaire-type methodologies, in which these variables are necessarily neatly distinct.

Methodology interacts with theory be leading us to see the world in a particular way and blinding us to others. In focusing on informal interaction, process and peer effects we

136

will use an observational methodology. A study of a classroom
with 30 students and one teacher should be more sensitive to
Gestalt and more likely to reveal process than pencil and paper
questionnaires about child's knowledge of content variables and
measures of his attitudes. Anthropology obviously contains
methodologies (like participant and systematic observation)
uniquely adapted to such a study. We discuss this further below.
In addition, the validity of data generated from say second or
third graders by paper and pencil techniques is, I feel, subject
to severe question. Can we really put much faith in responses
to such techniques for this age? Why has the field as a whole
opted for large numbers for statistical analysis before doing in
depth studies which might reveal better questions?

D. Subjects

     We come now to the problem of whom to use as subjects.
Since the political socialization literature consists almost
wholly of studies of white mainstream Americans it can be
fairly criticized by asking how much of what is seen is limited
just to that group? Litt, above, showed social class to be an
important variable. Jaros, Hirsch and Fleron's 1968 study of
the political orientations of children living in the impoverished
Appalachian region of Kentucky suggest the answer 'a lot.' They
focus on children's image of the President, political cynicism,
and perceptions of parents' political efficacy. In comparing
their results with the findings of previous research on more
middle-class, urban samples of children, the authors found that
the Kentucky children had markedly less positive views of the
President and expressed more cynical attitudes toward politics
in general. The authors conclude that findings of the child's
view of political authority are probably sub-culture-bound.
     We have, therefore, chosen not to focus our observations
at first on the white middle class group, but in order to help
redress the balance of the literature, to focus on a multi-
ethnic working class ghetto-like area of New York City. (We
focus here not only on theoretical but also on moral grounds:
these students are coming from environments in which their parents have not successfully been able to compete for premiums: we
want to know what, if anything, the schools are doing or might
do to redress that and provide these children with the tools
necessary to political efficacy. If our answer is very little
and much harm besides, which the work of Litt 1965, Adler and Harrington 1970, and Levy 1970 suggest, at least we will know more
about processes which could be changed and would then be in a
position to suggest some alternatives.) There are some studies
of black political socialization. However, they are simply
repetitions of methods referred to above coupled with anthro-
pologically naive comparisons of "black and white" children
neither of which labels is even defined for the reader (see

137

Greenberg 1970, Lyons 1970, Engstrom 1970).

SETTING AND METHOD

The research reported here was done in a neighborhood of New York City. Ethnically the neighborhood is about 45 per cent Black, 45 per cent Spanish speaking (made up of approximately equal numbers of Puerto Ricans and Dominicans, with lesser numbers of Cubans: The Dominicans are the most recent arrivals) and 10 per cent white. The neighborhood is striated into ethnic enclaves, Blacks being in the east, Spanish speaking centered, and the middle class white community segregated to the west. The populations in the various schools served in this neighborhood are variations on the above figures. The whites tend to be even more under-represented because the children often go to private schools.

This area is a meeting point of two transitions. First, it was formerly a Jewish and Irish area which has undergone population changes in the last ten years. Second, people who live there now have moved up and away from areas which they consider much worse, like Harlem, part of Brooklyn, the East Bronx, Puerto Rico and Haiti. Neighborhood, for the rest of this paper, will be artificially defined as the area served by one school under study.

I want to describe now studies we have recently done which, I hope, will serve to show the potential richness of the broader approach to political socialization I have delineated. As there are a number of different studies there are a number of different methodologies to review. The primary methodology of the Schwartz (n.d.) and Lopate (n.d.) studies was participant observation with a lot of time spent in the schools themselves (Schwartz 14 months, Lopate 3 months). The Schwartz study was supplemented by interviews with staff and parents and children; Lopate's by interviews with staff and some video tape analysis. Marraccini's study used a more systematic kind of observation methodology in examining peer effects in playground seetings. He severely limited his observation to a particular dimension, following the work of Whiting et. al, 1966 and Whiting and Whiting 1970. My own time organized around a full teaching schedule brings us to a total of about 26 full time equivalent months spent in the variety of field settings examined.

The studies reported here began intermittent field work in the Spring of 1969 and continued until 1971, with the greatest field activity in the Spring and Summer of 1970. The time span covered for any one setting, e.g. a classroom, ranges from 6 to 40 weeks, with three months the more usual figure. Three months is not a large amount of time by traditional anthropology field-work standards. In a field situation in which physical survival is not a problem and in which the native language(s) are the

138

same as the anthropologists' three months is often equivalent when focusing on a particular problem to 12 months in more traditional settings. Also, while the length of time we have spent studying one field situation is short by anthropological standards, it is long when compared with previous work in education, even in anthropology and education. Observation studies in education are often conditioned by a study of Withall's (1955) who showed that the time spent observing a classroom is non-productive after a period of two hours. He argued that you see nothing new in extending your observation time beyond this. Some recent work in anthropology and education has followed this trend (e.g. Leacock 1968). We do not find Withall's findings compelling. All the time spans he studied were too short to discover the dynamics we are after. His work was oriented to the evaluation of teachers; not to the ethnographic descriptions of the dynamics of classroom life. Indeed, such a methodology may be counter productive to such a goal.

We have often noted in our research in a classroom that it is possible to get a quick and clear grasp of what is going on, then for two or three weeks see the 'same thing over and over,' then in the fourth week on to have the initial patterning or structure prove inadequate as an analytic tool. It is almost as if we get down to another level which does not necessarily invalidate the initial structure hypothesized without which that structure seems superficial and incomplete. It is not that by staying longer that you discover that schools are really not authoritarian or rigid as others have described them (Leacock, 1968, Levy, 1970, and specifically for politics Adler and Harrington, 1970: 189-191) but rather that by staying longer it is possible to observe patterns of student responses to those structures; and then the interplay, or lack of it, between students and the structures provided by the school. Goffman (1961) might have called this 'the underlife of the institution.' Be assured that the underlife is not discovered in one hour of observation, yet it is precisely this which we must discover if we are going to follow Langton's lead and study the informal civic learning in the school.

In addition to the data produced by the methods already outlined we have an analysis of the textbooks likely to be used in the classrooms in this district. The methodology for that study is summarized when the data are presented below and fully described in Harrington and Adler (1971), and Harrington (n.d.b.).

FINDINGS

I shall have space here only to briefly summarize major findings. Full publication of these and other studies will occur elsewhere. The findings will be examined within four categories: pupils, peers, pupils and ritual, and finally textbooks.

A. Pupils

By pupils we mean the children as they behave in school
(arbitrarily distinguishing this from 'peers' or children interacting outside of school). Our concern in this first category is
with how children structure their behavior in the school. I have
argued elsewhere that any study of socialization has two components: the delineation (ethnography) of the specific culture
or role set as it exists, and then the study of how it is learned.
Frances Schwartz undertook the ethnographic description of the
child's culture with an emphasis on his peer group relationships
(as opposed to his home life). She takes as a given that school
requires children to respond to institutional requirements and
that these vary within the school itself. On the basis of her
observation she distinguished three settings within the school
which vary in the degree of adult control and the 'type of student activity.' The first she labels "instructional time" (in
class when a teacher is giving a particular lesson); the second,
"lunch time" when children structure their own activities, and
have to do so without adult supervision; and the third "non-
instructional" classroom time when children can talk among themselves less competitively than would be possible in setting two,
presumably because of the protection potential offered by the
presence of an adult.
    Schwartz found that a good deal of pupil time in class-
room was spent reacting against the teachers and the school.
Yet she also observed dynamic processes among the students,
shifting interactions between groups, tightening and loosening
of boundaries in response to school situations and peer generated
action patterns. She found "in learning time, alliances are
networks of communication or identification against the teacher
and the children. At lunch, self created rules lay groundworks
for group formations which maintain lines of political interests
and meet needs for protections of members. Finally, in classroom (non-instructional time) the process is less bounded, more
around interests and less around alliance and protection."
    "In these settings, the activity range is wide and
variable. It alters from hierarchies to dyads, from conflicts
to conferences and from secrecy to exploration. Each of these
elements of behavior has a function in relation to classroom
and lunchroom pressures. The informal systems provide the
under-current of the formal schooling." (Schwartz n.d.)
    The presence or absence of varying degrees of control
and pressure in each setting define the lines of alliances and
determine group dynamics, according to Schwartz. In addition
she distinguishes the three classrooms she studied. The first,
an intellectually gifted class (IGC), the second a middle
ability class, the third a lower ability (ability is defined in

140

New York City schools for classification purposes as reading
test scores) group. While the patterns for school settings
above run throughout all three classrooms, each class is different in the content of its interactions, and these too are seen
as largely peer generated. For example, in the IGC classroom
'instructional time' students share an intellectual life with
the teacher and a separate social life with their peers, while
in the middle ability class students compete with one another
academically as well as physically, and in the lower ability
class students' play reflects their outcast position and simultaneously effectively blocks all academic efforts. In lunchroom
in the IGC class students still plan secretly, the middle ability
students still fight, and the lower ability class' students
continue dyadic and separate activities. In classroom non-
instructional time the IGC class' students unity in the face of
academic pressures dissolves into 'tough' behavior, while the
middle ability class' students set up their own school by teaching themselves, and the lower class' students interactions drift
into reflections about life outside school.

Schwartz' study, therefore, documents some of the complexity and pervasiveness of peer group efforts which increase
our determination to examine their consequences for political
learning.

B.   Peers

Schwartz reports a good deal of aggression in some of
her settings and emphasizes the amount of time that pupils spend
reacting against school structures. Marraccini (n.d.) examines
the forms of social organization that would be manifested by kids
in the absence of any immediate adult supervision. Focusing on
a playground not attached to the school, he follows our definition
of politics by focusing on three swings. As the swings fit our
definition of a scarce resource (there being more than three
children in the playground most times) he systematically observed
how children made decisions about how those swings were allocated.
What he found was something quite remarkable:

> ...in times of great demands kids act not to maximize
> possession of a swing but rather to maximize access to
> a swing.

Those who read Schwartz' paper will be surprised at the
low frequencies of conflict and aggression in Marraccini's data.
He argues that there are rules which are understood by the children which they can activate to get swings without resorting to
violence. Indeed, it is on the playground that we have seen the
most amount of practice of political skills designed to foster
political efficacy. I.e., it is in the peer group that the kids
are able to learn and practice political skills. The further
albeit impressionistic finding that Schwartz and Marraccini feel

that violence is less common here than in the school led us into a more rigorous study now beginning which observes the same children in various 'educational' settings including schools, family and peers. It may be that school generated frustration is an important contribution to aggressive behavior in school.

C. Pupils and ritual

In another study, Carol Lopate focuses on pupil-staff interaction and approaches the problem in a somewhat different way than Schwartz. Discrepancies in the behaviors she observed and what people said they were doing led her to analyze her materials from the perspective provided for ritual events by Gluckman (1962) and Turner (1969), and talk about the separation of myth and reality. She observed a school teetering on the brink of organizational disaster sending parents a letter on how wonderful this school is for their children. She observed assemblies to observe "Spanish-American Heritage Day" whose main behavior for the children was waiting for the program to begin. Under the myth of "Spanish heritage" kids may learn (in Henry's 1957 terms) to be docile.

Lopate's findings are not unique. Teachers are often observed doing one thing while saying another. I was once taken proudly by a principal to observe a bilingual junior high classroom which was part of an experimental program planned in response to community pressures to get instruction in Spanish in a neighborhood which was 50 per cent Spanish speaking. This classroom (one of only four in a school of 3,000 students) was described by the principal as we approached. "It signaled a new age of understanding and communication among peoples." "It provided students with the tools necessary to communicate effectively with their peers, teachers" etc., and "would make it possible for them to learn in Spanish, what they have previously not been able to learn in English." We arrived at the door of the classroom. The teacher emerged. The principal explained our desire to observe. She said, "I'm sorry you can't come in today. I'm not speaking to them. They were so bad yesterday that I am punishing them." So much for the manifest curriculum.

Equally interesting is the suggestion implicit in some of Lopate's material that the teachers themselves are socialized by the school experience. These materials show a teacher who has learned the passivity (docility) lessons well.

> ...although...Miss Mera was concerned that her students understood the rules she might be giving them (say in spelling), when it came to directives from outside the classroom she kept herself in a passive position...(e.g.) when one day Miss Mera got a directive to take her class to a new room for snacks, she showed much the same passivity: not asking why, and not explaining to the students, she simply led them to a new room. Then when

142

the directive appeared to have been a mistake, she
waited patiently for new orders while her children
waited, somewhat less acquiescently, behind her.
(Lopate, n.d.)

Even Lopate's 'Mr. Schwartz' who often threatens rebellion is
only observed to move to open rebellion on one occasion, and
that on the trip to the beach safely isolated from the school
environment and the principal.

After a lesson on individual rights, what is learned
when an entire class of third graders is marched to the girls'
and boys' rooms at the same time? As to justice, watch a boy
accused by a monitor immediately sanctioned by a teacher with
no due process, or watch one boy be punished by a teacher for
something several others had done earlier without punishment.
Adler and Harrington (1970) argued that children learned potent
lessons from this "latent" curriculum. Specifically Adler and
Harrington (1970) suggested children learned that punishment
was capricious, not judicious; accusation was often equivalent
to conviction; and that in the allocation of premiums in the
school some are privileged and some are not. Lopate's data
illustrate each of these phenomena.

Miss Mera has been giving a Spanish grammar lesson.
The room has reached a state of excitement because of
the competition for correct answers. There has been
some talking out of turn, mostly humorous, which until
now Miss Mera has ignored.

She now says, "I'm going to give a verb. You say
whether it's singular or plural." And she adds that
whoever talks out of turn will have to leave the room,
"because we have a lot of work to do." Then she asks
"el singular de papel;" "el plural de automovil;" and
"el plural de calles."

While Miss Mera is asking Aracelis, Elena says
something. "Out," says Miss Mera, "lo siento." Elena
says, "No! No! The protest goes back and forth several
times between the teacher and Elena, and Elena ends up
staying.

Five minutes later Miss Mera is giving more singulars
and plurals. Now Aracelis talks out of turn, and Miss
Mera says "Get out Aracelis." "But you let Elena stay!"
says Aracelis. Mis Mera responds to this by saying
"Both!" and tells them it will be for five minutes.
Once they are out of the room, she continues with the
lesson.

This is an interesting case because when the ideal (equality)
was presented the teacher acknowledged its legitimacy but did
it in a way which illustrated the negative side of equality
("Both!") rather than its protective feature.

Lopate described the rituals of waiting in assemblies,
waiting for the program to begin, and the ceremonies marking

143

entrance into the school. Not only do kids learn status definitions (who can make whom wait -- time = scarce resource), throughout her paper she is arguing that the children are bing led to
accept symbolic definitions of real life situations over their
objective reality. The school is successful, family style, they
are happy, they are learning to be bi-lingual, etc. From these
ethnographic descriptions, in terms of the kinds of learning that
go on in such settings, we would predict two types of learning:
one a content learning to cope with relatively authoritarian
regimes and to respond (overtly) with appropriate docility and
civility; the other, learning a positively charged symbolic
presentation of a reality to legitimate behaviors of such regimes which otherwise might not be acceptable. These are lessons
useful to society. The practical experience the child gains in
school prepares him for certain kinds of relationships and
political realities. However, the reality of the child's life
in the ghetto and the skills he needs to function there become
separated from the view of the world provided him by the positively charged symbolic representations of the school about life.
At the same time the practice he gets in his peer group in
acquiring scarce resources may complement the other learning
and prepare him for other social relationships.

D.   Textbooks

        As anthropologists we can learn or infer much about
political behavior for adults from this area from recent work
by Valentine (1972), Hannerz (1969), Harrington (1971), Leibow
(1965) and Lewis (1965). However, the reality of this political
life is not featured in the curriculum of the school. We argued
above that the symbolic representation of political reality
becomes more and more remote from the actual political behaviors
of the child, until they take on a purely formal, ritualized air
in comparison to his actual life style. This is clearly seen in
the study of textbooks. In a study that drew on school districts
from the entire state of New York, Norman Adler and I did a content analysis of the political socialization implications of
grade school textbooks (Harrington and Adler 1971). One of our
sample districts encompassed the materials used in the schools
in the studies reported here.[3]
        A content analysis (see Holsti 1969) of these materials
was carried out in order to gauge what children were being told
about government in order to compare it with the rest of what
they learned about politics. We limited our coding to materials
relating to American government. Government can be broken down
into three components, authority, regime, and community, following Easton's (1965) systems theory which provides an oft used
means for viewing the inter-relationship of diverse threads in
the fabric of political life. An authority, according to Easton,
is a member of the system in whom the primary responsibility is

144

lodged for taking care of the daily routines of a political system. Elected representatives, other public officials such as civil servants, qualify in our system. Regime refers to the underlying goals that the members of the system pursue, the norms or rules of the game through which they conduct their political business, and the formal and informal structures or authority that arrange who is to do what in the system. It is clear from Marraccini's work that the national regime and the regime of the playground are distinct. Easton defines community (he calls it political community) as that aspect of a political system we can identify as a collection of persons who desire a division of political labor.

Harrington (n.d.b.)[4] found that every class is not receiving books with similar attitude orientations to political authorities. Younger grades (2,4) receive a more positively charged view than higher grades (6, 8). Apparently younger children are not to be "trusted" with the more balanced views of authorities to be found in older children's texts. There is also class bias in the preparation of children for a place in the democratic system that seems to hold up, if not everywhere, at least frequently. There is a tendency for the grade effects to be limited to middle class districts, i.e. working class older grades texts resemble the younger grade texts of both social classes. Images of political leaders as malevolent are seldom found in second grade books, but they are seldom found in any working class texts, either. Second grade texts rarely see the political system as not accountable; but working class texts do not, either. How real a view of politics is this? Harrington and Adler (1971) felt it was merely a symbolic and idealized notion of "the good citizen." Textbook materials seem to aim at depriving the lower social class child as he ages of the benefits of perspectives that will make him a realistic observer and participant in the political system, while more often making those materials available to older children in middle class districts.

Turning to the text materials specifically used in our school we find our materials to reflect an exaggeration of the above patterns. Focusing on the image presented in the text materials about political authorities we found that the 2, 4, 6th grade children in our working class multi-ethnic ghetto are told that authorities are never malevolent, always approachable and almost always accountable.

Table 1

Descriptions of Portrayals of Authorities
in Textbooks Analyzed

Image of Authority

		Neutral		
Malevolent	0%	35%	65%	Benevolent
				(n* = 40)

Relationship of Authority to Constituents

Distant	5%	0%	95%	Approachable
				(n = 21)
Not accountable	8%	15%	77%	Accountable
				(n = 13)

*n = # of units containing material relating to this dimension
out of a total possible number of 396 units.

In addition, Table 2 shows that children in this district are
told that we live in a pluralistic society where politics are
overwhelmingly consensual not conflict oriented. They also are
told that the stress must be placed upon majority rule not
minority rights. In fact, our school (which is itself 90%
minority) gets less material than any other public school
district in the state (studied by Harrington and Adler 1971)
dealing with the rights of minorities in American democracy.

Table 2

Depictions of Nation, Politics and Democracy
in Textbooks Analyzed

Picture of Nation Presented

		Neutral	
Pluralistic	51%	12%	36% Monolithic
			(n* = 33)

Picture of Politics

Conflict	24%	12%	65% Consensual
			(n = 17)

In Discussing Democracy Stress is on:

Majority rule	50%	33%	17% Minority Rights
			(n = 6)

*n = # of units containing material relating to this dimension
out of a total possible number of 396 units.

Clearly the textbook content serves to combine the two lessons
outlined above: i.e., be docile and believe in the symbolic
idealized picture of politics. It is not likely to train the
child to the nitty gritty of political life. It will come as no
surprise to those who see schools as primarily concerned with
the status quo, i.e., as conservative institutions, that these
ghetto children are being excluded from knowledge which could
help them more successfully compete for premiums in the political
process. Given the place of these students though in the quest
for premiums in the large society, how does the never-never land
described by the school cognitively survive comparisons by the
child with the totality of his existence? Our work is progress-
ing on the point, I offer the following discussion.

DISCUSSION

A. Behavior practice

        Levy (1970) has argued that the ghetto school teaches

skills (i.e., waiting) that are in fact those most used in lower
class life (e.g., welfare lines). I think our analysis can go a
little further. Schools are often said to need to train students
to conform as well as create. I have argued elsewhere that the
undemocratic features of schools may be important for a society
to maintain itself; if the society over-anticipates a need to
resort to undemocratic acts to control citizens it would be
important to build a sense of legitimacy for such measures into
its people. Consider the 1968 Democratic convention, the violence in the street, the police brutality, and the frequent
comment that a "police state" existed, both on the convention
floor and in downtwon Chicago. Assuming that police-state
methods were used in Chicago, how is it that 71 percent of the
American people approved of these tactics, as measured by a poll
following the disorders? For a more recent event consider the
mass arrests in Washington in the spring of 1971. It is important to understand that these are not isolates. The political
science literature has consistently found a remarkably high
number of people in this country who don't understand the Bill
of Rights, don't approve of individual items in the Bill of
Rights, or don't understand or approve of the basic civil liber-
ties that the Bill of Rights seeks to guarantee (see, for example,
Remmers 1963). Adler and Harrington (1970) suggested that there
was in our society an underlying penchant, if you will, for
authoritarian regimes, or at least a tolerance of them. That a
large percentage of our population seems to feel a need for
authoritarian methods at certain times seems beyond question.
It is clear that support for authoritarianism has certain
functions for the society. Support for such a regime is probably adaptive in what Wallace (1961) would call a conservative
society threatened by a revolutionary or revitalization movement, in the examples given, the "New Left." Reactionary
measures to control such a movement are a natural response of
a conservative society. Therefore, it is to be expected that
a conservative society will build into its citizens a certain
tolerance for reactionary or authoritarian responses to social
crises in case they are needed.

        The acceptance of authoritarianism must come from some-
where. Studies of classroom behavior offer one explanation.
Adler and Harrington (1970) offered the hypothesis that this
undemocratic pattern of our schools is not a random or haphazard
phenomenon but is in reality functional; that is, it is important
for a conservative state to train its citizens to accept authoritarian regimes in case they are needed to maintain order. Since
the schools are fulfilling that function, they are supported;
and society resists attempts to change schools or to give students power. We must start thinking not only about how undemocratic the schools are, but also about some of the functions
that the organization of the school might have in the larger
society.

B. Symbols and ritual

We turn now to where there is a conflict: between the
symbols, ideals and myths of the school and the political reality of the child's life. Burdieu and Passeron (1970) argue that
curriculum is symbolic violence, a device by which the literate
class perpetuates itself in power. Our anthrpological research
has reinforced for us that the school is an important source of
political learning, but in a different sense from Hess and
Torney's original finding. They argued on the basis of content
learning. We have focused, using anthropological methods
rather than questionnaires, on what political skills, beliefs
and values the child learns in a school setting which will enable him to compete politically in the larger society. Our
findings, tentative as they are, suggest that schools may be
accomplishing much more than even Hess and Torney suggested.

Edelman (1967) argues that much of politics is symbolic.
The art of ruling is the art of calling upon the right symbols
and ritual observances to legitimize a range of activities (for
example, the Department of Defense, Vietnamization). Schools
may, therefore, be effectively training children to respond to
symbolic ritual in granting legitimacy and to pay less attention
to actual behavior. The New Yorker recently argued that

The President's trip to China shows that television
coverage opens up what is virtually a new field of
action to men in power. With television, a President
can draw eyes away from the piecemeal, day to day
unfolding of policy and focus them on complex, powerful, symbolic events that he can manipulate more
easily than he can the work itself. It allows him
to act directly on the country's imagination, like
a high priest. (New Yorker, Notes and Comment, 3/
25/72: 29).   (emphasis added)

What is new is not the use of symbols and ritual by those in
power, simply the use of television to facilitate it.

At one level, the differences between the manifest and
latent occurrences in school would seem to be a powerful impetus for changing the curriculum so that these differences would
disappear yet they are masked by legitimizing symbols. But if
Edelman is right and I think he is, these differences actually
appear in the larger society as well. Therefore, schools may
actually be doing a very good job of training children to respond to symbolic ritual legitimizing cues in granting legitimacy and to pay less attention to actual behaviors. We need
to find out.

But how is it that schools can get away with only
these aspects of political learning in a democracy and not
teach about political process, or skills leading to effective
political action? Two answers suggest themselves.

1) Undoubtedly a large part of the problem derives from

149

a curriculum that centers its attention on turning out "good citizens" while defining "good citizens" as those who are obedient to established legal authority, who conform to the rules and laws of the community without questioning the derivation of those laws or their purpose, and those who do not "make trouble." Indeed, Hess and Torney found that "teachers of young children place particular stress upon compliance, deemphasizing all other political topics...Concern with compliance is characteristic of teachers of all grades (up to eighth grade)." This is reflected in children's perceptions of democracy. A study of sixth graders found that to children, democracy means such things as "helping the class," "being kind and friendly," "not fighting or cheating," "obeying teachers and school laws," and "trying to be quiet."

This resembles a Platonic notion of politics that views the good society as one filled with harmony and views as evil the factionalism, competition, and shifting power base of politics as we know it. Everyone is familiar with the notion of politics as a "dirty business." Indeed, in study after study, groups throughout society rank the practitioners of politics at the lower end of respected and desirable occupations. They do this while ranking those who profit from the fruits of politics (i.e., Supreme Court justices, U.S. senators, and policemen) at the top of the scale. Plato chose to treat the search for competitive advantage in the distribution of the fruits of power (material goods, deference, safety) among the various groups in society as "symptoms of an unhealthy society." His science of politics contained in it what Wolin (1960) has referred to as a major paradox: it was sworn to an eternal hostility to the very subject it pretended to study.

So it is with political education in the schools today. In the search for a foundation that would support the multiple contradictions present in society a dangerous political art is fostered: "the art of ruling becomes the art of imposition." Political education stresses those things in society that produce rules of behavior such as "The Law," or some authority to be venerated such as "The President." Most curriculum is concerned with the promulgation of abstract notions of governance in combination with a sense of respect on the part of students for authorities. The teachers responsible for civics education in school maintain the attitude that the most important goals of such training are the development of knowledge of government institutions and the cultivating of favorable attitudes toward democratic institutions and processes. Far less emphasis is placed on teaching skills for democratic participation.

2) Peer group learning itself may make the school structure possible! Paul Bohannan, writing about Tiv politics calls our attention to "extra processual events" which work for flexibility in an excessively rigid structure. The "revolt" or counteracting aspect of the event structure reported above by

Schwartz' study is brought into play to regain elasticity.
(Bohannan 1958:11) Bohannan calls these counter actions "extra
processual" because while they are outside the formal structure
they help maintain it. Recently, Graham Watson (1970) has presented data concerning schools in South Africa which can be used
to illustrate this framework. There, the rigid system of aparth-
eid symbolically classified people as white, colored or black
which classification (done at entrance to school) determines the
life style from that point on. The system is absolutely rigid;
it is made more viable by extra-processual events. That is, in
reality, some movement is possible from one group to the other.
Specifically, Watson describes a white school in a neighborhood
changing its racial balance to colored. In order to protect the
school budget the principal accepts as white large numbers of
children he 'knows' to be colored. As the official classification is the only important thing, he effectively makes coloreds
into whites for budget reasons. This extra-processual process
has the effect of making it possible for upwardly mobile coloreds
to move (by generations) into the economically privileged class,
helping to perpetuate the formally rigid system.

Perhaps our peer generated learning provides what the
school will not formally provide, and thereby helps perpetuate
that structure by providing the opportunity to learn political
skills essential to operating in the larger society as well as
those necessary to "make out" in the formal rigidity of the
school itself! This, however, means that it is important that
we study peer groupings from various social classes and ethnic
groups in order to describe the kinds of structures they provide for learning, and second, that we just spend more time
studying how such learning can be used in school settings. For
example, we are now embarking on a study which will replace
swings as a scarce resource with 'teacher time' in certain open
classroom situations. Will the findings parallel those of
Marraccini for playgounds, or will setting influence not only
the behaviors but the rules by which the behaviors are generated
(regime)?

Concluding Remarks

One of the limitations of the participant observation
methodologies used here is that while it is useful in delineating
structures and process, it is not as useful in demonstrating that
what seems to be learned in a classroom actually is. For this
we need other kinds of data and it is at this point that the interaction of the fields of psychology and anthropology can be
most useful. That is, armed with anthropological descriptions of
setting, use psychological measures of outcomes to test learning
assumptions. For example, take a recent luncheon debate between
a political scientist and myself. We were focusing on the disparity I have described above between the reality of the ghetto

child's life and the idealized picture of politics offered to
him. The political scientist argued this was a good thing,
giving the child incentive to change the system and make it
more nearly approximate the ideal. I argued that if the picture of politics presented was so idealized that the child
perceived it to be a sham, he could become alienated from the
political process and not act. Further, I argue here that the
ghetto child was getting no training in school which would increase his efficacy even if he wanted to act. Obviously, an
empirical study could be done to ascertain how children in
fact responded to the apparent conflict perceived by the researcher.

Smith and Gumpert (in press) have recently completed
an experimental study which is helpful in answering this question from the perspective of social psychology. Distinguishing
as variable the status a person occupies in a society, a person's assessment of how the status squares with his perceived
competence, and a measure of satisfaction-dissatisfaction, they
found that

> ...having relatively low status in an organization
> or in the society at large may or may not result in
> dissatisfaction, depending upon whether the low sta-
> tus person believes his relative status (in terms of
> outcomes) is in line with his relative competence
> levels.
>
> Trust in those who control the system (i.e., poli-
> tical authorities) is a critical factor in the cer-
> tainty with which a person evaluates his relative
> competences, and in whether the dissatisfaction as-
> sociated with having poorer outcomes than his rela-
> tive competence would imply is accompanied by ex-
> pectations of mobility. We have presented evidence
> that at least where people do trust the impartiality
> of the system, dissatisfaction and mobility expecta-
> tions are associated.
>
> (However) where persons did not trust (authorities)
> they were likely to be dissatisfied without necessar-
> ily expecting mobility.

Since lower status black respondents were more likely to see the
social system as biased against them this study strongly suggests
a negative outcome from the disparity between ideal and real de-
picted above.

We need to move toward a day in which anthropological
methodologies and psychological techniques will not be thought
of as alternatives but as equally useful at different points in
the study of socialization. However, we must emphasize that the
individual studies reported there have not been through that
full process: that we are dealing with working papers and research in progress. These studies do not pretend to be final
answers: they are published instead to raise questions; questions

we feel are important but for too long have not been asked. As research continues, and others begin to replicate our findings, we hope to be better able to describe how education for political behavior occurs. We argued four ommissions in the present literature. This paper has not adequately filled any one of them, but it has begun to suggest ways to do so.

One final point. Our focus has been rather narrowly on political socialization. In doing so we have raised many issues discussed by educators. I have chosen not to take up those debates here, but we are aware of the existence of debate in the field of education as to how schools, classrooms, teaching, should be structured and that the variables we are discussing are relevant to that debate. Our purpose here, and in the field of anthropology and education in general, is to cautiously provide an ever deepening empirical and theoretical base so that policy can more reasonably be made on the basis of empirical research and not polemic. And, when we do become involved with policy it will be, as applied anthropology has often demonstrated, in limited projects of limited goals. The remaking of American education is not going to be accomplished overnight. Anthropologists, of all researchers, should be acutely aware of that, avoid the lure for sensationalism that belongs to the journalist, and continue without prejudging the answers to try to unravel the problem which is American education.

NOTES

1. I would like to express my gratitude to my colleagues in the anthropology and education program at Teachers College-Columbia University, especially William Dalton, Carol Lopate, Ernest Marraccini, and Frances Schwartz, for their careful criticism of the manuscript. In addition,Lambros Comitas, Peter Gumpert, Joan Vincent, and Mary Williams offered comments which improved the final product. Thanks go to Norman Adler for his collaboration on the textbook study, and to the New York State Commission on the Quality, Cost and Financing of Elementary and Secondary Education in New York State for supporting it. The other studies (Schwartz, Lopate,Marraccini) reported here, and the writing of this report, were supported entirely as the Anthropology and Education Project, Charles Harrington Principal Investigator, by the Center for Urban Studies and Programs of Teachers College-Columbia University, Lambros Comitas, Director.

2. Work directly related to political socialization in non-Western political systems is largely limited to some speculations by Levine (1960, 1963); but see Wilson 1970, and Harrington (n.d.a.), chapter 7.

3. Note that our analysis would not include the special summer textbooks used in the classes of Lopate's study.

4. For technical reasons Harrington (n.d.b.) omits the materials used in the district reported here from its analysis, and is limited to three white middle class and three white

working class districts.

REFERENCES

Adler, Norman and Charles Harrington
    1970   The learning of political behavior. Chicago,
                Scott-Foresman.

Bohannan, Paul
    1958   Extra-processual events in Tiv political
                instituitions. American Anthropologist 60:
                1-12.

Burdieu, P. and J. C. Passeron
    1970   La Reproduction. Paris, Edition Minuit.

Comitas, Lambros
    1971   Reflections in curriculum and education in the
                British Caribbean. Mineo. Paper presented to
                the Colloquium in Philosophy and the Social
                Sciences, Teachers College-Columbia University.

Easton, David and Jack Dennis
    1969   Children in the political system. New York,
                McGraw Hill.
    1967   The child's acquisition of regime norms:
                political efficacy. American Political Science
                Review 61: 25-38.

Easton, David
    1965   A systems analysis of political life. New York,
                John Wiley and Sons, Inc.
    1968   The theoretical relevance of political sociali-
                zation. Canadian Journal of Political Science
                1: 125-146.

Edelman, Murray
    1967   The symbolic uses of politics. Urbana, Univ.
                of Illinois Press.

Engstrom, Richard L.
    1970   Race and compliance: differential political
                socialization. Polity 3: 100-111.

Gluckman, Max
    1962   Custom and conflict. Oxford.

Greenberg, Edward
    1970   Children and government: a comparison across
                racial lines. Midwest Journal of Political

              Science XIV: 249-275.

1971   Consensus and dissent: trends in political
               socialization research. In E. Greenberg, ed.,
               Political socialization, 1970.

Goffman, Erving
    1961   Asylums. New York, Doubleday.

Gurr, Ted Robert
    1970   Why men rebel. Princeton, Princeton University
               Press.

Hannerz, Ulf
    1969   Soulside. New York, Columbia University Press.

Harrington, Charles and Norman Adler
    1971   Political socialization implications of grade
               school social studies textbooks in New York
               State. New York State commission on the quality,
               cost, and financing of elementary and secondary
               education in New York State. Mimeo.

Harrington, Charles
    n.d.   (a) Political socialization. New York, Free
               Press. (forthcoming)
    n.d.   (b) Textbooks and political socialization: a
               content analysis. In press.
    1971   Review of Ulf Hannerz' Soulside. T. C. Record,
               72: 471-473.

Harrington, Charles and John Whiting
    1972   Socialization process and personality. In
               F.L.K. Hsu, ed., Psychological anthropology.
               Cambridge, Schenkman Publications.

Hartup, W. W.
    1969   Peer interaction and social organization. In
               D. A. Goslin, ed., Handbook of socialization
               theory and research. Chicago, Rand McNally.

Henry, Jules
    1957   Attitude organization in elementary school
               classrooms. American Journal of Orthopsychiatry
               27: 117-133.
    1963   Culture against man. New York, Random House.

Hess, Robert D. and David Easton
    1960   The child's changing image of the president.
               Public Opinion Quarterly 24: 632-644.

Hess, Robert D. and Judith Torney
     1967   The development of political attitudes in
                   children. Chicago, Aldine.

Holsti, Ole R.
     1969   Content analysis for the social sciences and
                   humanities. Reading, Mass., Addison-Wesley.

Jaros, Dean, Herbert Hirsch and Frederick Fleron
     1968   The malevolent leader: political socialization
                   in an American sub-culture. American Political
                   Science Review 62: 564-575.

Jennings, M. Kent and R. G. Niemi
     1968   Patterns of political learning. Harvard
                   Education Review 38: 443-467.

Kohlberg, Lawrence
     1969   Stage and sequence: the cognitive developmental
                   approach to socialization. In D. A. Goslin, ed.,
                   Handbook of socialization theory and research.
                   Chicago, Rand McNally.

Langton, Kenneth
     1967   Peer group and school and the political social-
                   ization process. American Political Science
                   Review 61: 751-758.

Lawson, Edwin D.
     1963   Development of patriotism in children. Journal
                   of Psychology 55: 279-286.

Leacock, Eleanor
     1968   Teaching and learning in city schools. New York,
                   Basic Books.

LeVine, Robert
     1960   The internalization of political values in
                   stateless societies. Human Organization 19:
                   51-58.
     1963   Political socialization and culture change. In
                   C. Geertz, ed., Old societies and new states.
                   New York, Free Press.

Levy, Gerald
     1970   Ghetto school. New York, Pegasus.

Lewis, Oscar
     1965   La Vida. New York, Random House.

Liebow, Eliot
1965   Tally's corner. Boston, Little Brown.

Litt, Edgar
1965   Education and political enlightenment in
America. Annals of the American Academy of
Political and Social Science 361: 32-39.
1963   Civic education, community norms, and political
indoctrination. American Sociological Review
28: 69-75.

Lopate, Carol
n.d.   Structure, hierarchy and political learning.
Manuscript. To be published in a volume of
occasional papers by Teachers College Press.

Lyons, Schley
1970   The political socialization of ghetto children:
efficacy and cynicism. Journal of Politics 32:
288-305.

Marraccini, Ernest
n.d.   Swinging in New York. Manuscript. To be
published in a volume of occasional papers by
Teachers College Press.

Mayer, Philip and Iona
1970   Socialization by peers: the youth organization
of the Reh Xhosa. In P. Mayer, ed., Socialization: the approach from social anthropology.
London, Tavistock.

Miller, Walter A.
1958   Lower class culture as a generating milieu of
gang delinquency. In M. Wolfgang, L. Savitz,
and N. Johnson, eds., The sociology of crime
and delinquency. New York, Wiley.
1964   The corner gang boys get married. Transaction
1: 10-12.

Parsons, Talcott
1949   Essays in sociological theory, pure and applied.
Glencoe, Free Press.

Pettit, George A.
1946   Primitive education in North America. University
of California Publications. American Archaeology
and Ethnology 43: 1-182.

Remmers, H. H.
    1963   Anti-democratic attitudes in American schools.
                Evanston, Northwestern University Press.

Schwartz, Frances
    n.d.   Peer group interaction: patterns and dynamics
                in one city school. Manuscript. To be published
                in a volume of occasional papers by Teachers
                College Press.

Sigel, Roberta
    1965   An exploration into some aspects of political
                socialization: school children's reactions to
                the death of a president. In M. Wolenstein and
                G. Liman, eds., Children and the death of a
                president. New York, Doubleday.
    1966   Political socialization: some reflections on
                current approaches and conceptualizations.
                Mimeo.
    1970   Learning about politics. New York, Random House.

Smith, W. P. and Peter Gumpert
    in press Life satisfaction, mobility and ideology: a
                social comparison approach. Journal of Applied
                Social Psychology.

Turner, Victor
    1969   The ritual process. Chicago, Aldine.

Valentine, Charles
    1972   Black studies and anthropology: scholarly and
                political interests in Afro-American culture.
                McCaleb Module in Anthropology, Addison-Wesley.

Wallace, Anthony F. C.
    1971   Culture and personality (second edition). New
                York, Random House.

Watson, Graham
    1970   Passing for white. London, Tavistock.

Whyte, William F.
    1955   Street corner society. Chicago, University of
                Chicago Press.

Wilson, Richard W.
    1970   Learning to be Chinese: the political social-
                ization of children in Taiwan. Cambridge, MIT
                Press.

Withall, J.
    1955   Assessment of the socio-emotional climates
                experienced by a group of seventh graders as
                they moved from class to class. In A. P.
                Coladarci, ed., Educational psychology. New
                York, Dryden.

Wolin, Sheldon
    1960   Politics and vision. Boston, Little-Brown.

III.   SOCIAL CHANGE AND EDUCATIONAL STRATEGIES

CULTURAL PLURALISM,
POLITICAL POWER, AND ETHNIC STUDIES[1]

Murray L. Wax

University of Kansas

Since the emergence of separatist and nationalist movements among the Blacks, Chicanos, and American Indians, fresh
attention has been given to notions of pluralism, especially in
educational contexts. In justifying their demands for courses
or programs or schools in Black Studies, Indian Studies, and the
like, spokesmen for these ethnic-racial groups will refer to
distinctive values, orientations toward life, and styles of
interaction, as for example to "soul food," "Black thought," or
to American Indian attitudes toward nature or modes of relating
to fellow human beings. Clearly, what is being referred to by
these nationalistic spokesmen are characteristics of what they
perceive to be distinctive cultures or subcultures, and they
themselves speak of "Black culture" or "Indian culture." On
the other hand, these proponents of Black, Indian, and Chicano
studies seldom use the phrase "cultural pluralism," perhaps
because they are aware of its considerable history in debates
about the status of the White immigrants to North America during
the late 19th and early 20th century.[2] Many of these spokesmen
declare emphatically that the immigrant experience has nothing
to do with the contemporary situation of their own people.
Nevertheless, the phrase "cultural pluralism" does seem to me to
denote the nature of their demands within the educational context, and I shall from time to time employ it within this essay,
as proves convenient.

Against these demands for programs of ethnic studies,
there has been levelled a variety of significant criticisms.
For simplicity, permit me to focus upon the Indian case; much
of what I have been observing here can be transposed into the
other cases. The criticisms offered of programs of Indian
studies in universities (or of special programs or schools for
Indian children in the lower grades) assume two forms: first,
that if there is a distinctive Indian culture, then it is so
irrelevant to modern North America that, were it to be taught
in the schools, then it would prepare children only to live
within an isolated reservation enclave; second, that whatever
once was unique to a rich Indian culture has been lost, so that

all that is left which purports now to be Indian culture is instead merely "a culture of poverty" -- or, in other words, a degenerated or "degraded" culture deriving from oppression. The myths, rituals, customs which once composed a rich and integrated culture have been replaced by an aggregate of hueristic devices for maintaining existence under conditions of oppression and semi-starvation.[3]

Both of these criticisms are wrong, and I wish to expose the nature of their limitations in order to resolve important theoretical and educational issues. First, I would like to inquire whether the terms "culture" and "cultural " (as in "cultural pluralism") assist or obfuscate our efforts.

Among the Indian peoples with whom I am personally familiar there are certainly traits that have the strongest linkages to aboriginal Indian cultures. On the most obvious level, many of the Oglala Sioux that I know are speakers of Lakota; many of the Cherokee of northeastern Oklahoma are speakers of their native language. And, while a scholar could adopt the counter-Whorfian attitude that language is a technical instrument having nothing to do with anything else in a culture, I think it equally easy to argue that if something as complex as language has survived, then this constitutes prima facie evidence that other aspects of culture likewise have been surviving. It is of course true that these languages have changed, and in the cases of Sioux and Cherokee it is true in particular that the most elevated and philosophical vocabularies have fallen into disuse; nonetheless one cannot evade the fact of some kind of linguistic persistence and therefore of some kind of cultural persistence. I can put the case even more forcibly: When Rosalie H. Wax first became involved with Indian groups, she quickly noticed that whether these were Indians at the Chicago Indian Center, or at a University of Colorado Workshop for Indian college students, or at the Pine Ridge Reservation they all manifested some common patterns of social interaction. Together with Robert K. Thomas she described and analyzed these patterns of interaction in an essay titled "American Indians and White People," and this essay has been found valuable by scores of persons who have had to live or work among Indian peoples. Not only has this essay been several times anthologized, but it has also been less formally duplicated for all kinds of workshops which brought together Indians and nonIndians. I judge it quite safe to say that this would not have happened unless she were describing a social reality.

On the other hand, even the most naive observer of Indian peoples must grant the enormous amount of change that has occurred during the past several centuries.[4] Particularly is this evident in material technology, where the hunting and gathering peoples of the Great Plains have been transformed into users of automobiles, television, portable radios, and coin laundries. The Oglala Sioux still annually perform a Sun Dance at the Pine Ridge Reservation, but no living Sioux could have experienced what it was like to be a horse nomad on the Plains, living off the bison herds and sheltering himself within a tipi. And, it is not only that there have been changes for the Sioux people as a whole. Equally important is the loss of homogeneity.

Where the Sioux of the 18th and 19th century practiced a common set of rituals and shared a common store of mythology, today this small cluster of people includes participants in a number of the North American religious denominations: Roman Catholic, Episcopalian, Methodist, Pentecostal (Holy Roller), Church of the Latterday Saints (Mormon), as well as Native American Church. In addition, some Sioux still practice a variety of cults, such as yuwipi or wanblee, whose shamanistic origins are very old. Likewise, the Sioux are remarkably diverse in levels of formal education, or in types of occupation, or in styles of living. Given this heterogeneity, for an observer to attempt to describe something as being "contemporary Sioux culture" becomes a difficult task. What makes this difficult task even harder is the fact that large numbers of Sioux children are spending substantial amounts of their young lives in boarding schools operated by the federal government or mission churches. Children within those schools may learn many things but they do not learn what their ancestors learned on the Great Plains. Nonetheless, the people who are processed by these schools tend to leave with a very strong feeling that they are Sioux (and Indian), even if in terms of specific cultural traits there is very little that they share with their ancestors.

Given this heterogeneity, it would seem evident that in contemporary North America, being an Indian is a social and political identity and not a cultural identity. It is a matter of how an individual identifies himself and is identified by others, and of who he associates with and in what types of interaction, and for what interests. Identity as an Indian is not a matter of the possession of particular cultural traits. Among contemporary Indian spokesmen and leaders are many persons competent in the technology and apparatus of modern industrial society; there is no one fixated at the material culture of Black Hawk or Geronimo. Just as a person can be identified as a Jew in modern North America and yet not be able to speak Yiddish or Hebrew, nor have any but a superficial acquaintance with the Torah, (or sacred law), so can one be an Indian without knowledge of traditional Indian languages or familiarity with traditional Indian customs and rituals. But, if one grants both of these instances, then it follows that the phrase "cultural pluralism" was as dubious in the immigrant case as it is now in the case of the contemporary militant ethnic-racial groups. What is at stake is a form of social and political pluralism.[5]

Of course, I am not denying that features such as skin coloration, physiognomy, body posture, or accented English may serve as stigmata that classify a person as a depressed subcaste within North America. Indians, Negroes, Puerto Ricans and Mexican-Americans have suffered and continue to suffer severe discrimination; so too did (and sometimes still do) Jews, and other ethnic minorities of Europe and the Middle East. In personal contacts with WASPS, certain cultural (or linguistic or paralinguistic) traits became (or remain) markers for treatment as inferiors. But to make a long argument short, I would comment merely that we deal here not with cultures but with symbols of relative power and status.

This is not to deny that for immigrants or modern ethnics "culture" as history or tradition, may have a strong symbolic meaning. In their advocacy of programs of Native American Studies, militant Indian leaders have urged the inclusion of courses in native languages which otherwise are in the process of disappearance. A dispassionate observer may endorse their program while still forecasting that, just as the Scandinavian Lutheran Churches in the U. S. have had to shift the language of their communion to English, despite the feelings of older parishioners that only the Scandinavian mother tongue was suitable as a language in which to address God, so too will North American Indians see the further erosion of many of their native languages.[6] But, if despite the loss of their languages, Scandinavians remain a distinct ethnic bloc, how much more likely it will be that Indians will likewise remain a noticeable bloc within North American society!

In making the foregoing argument, I am challenging the use of the plural concept, "cultures" in relationship to the ethnic-racial minorities of modern North America, and I am suggesting that we recall the relevant intellectual history. For Edward B. Tylor, there was but a single human culture which was equivalent to civilization. About the world, the anthropologist perceived traits of this (universal human) culture in the process of diffusion, or occasionally of invention. Tylor took this concept of culture (or civilization) from the German historians. Those scholars had become conscious of the achievements, not only of the societies of Classical Greece and Rome, but also of India, Egypt, and China; and some historian saw in these societies the distinctive, if transient, manifestations of the spirit of mankind. For some of these scholars each civilization became a stage in the evolution of mankind and human reason.

While anthropologists well know that Franz Boas was a product of the natural science regime of German universities, he was certainly also influenced by that larger intellectual climate, and especially so influenced were such of his students as Alfred Kroeber, Robert H. Lowie, and Paul Radin. These men transferred to the North American continent this comparative vision of human civilization, and in order to make evident their respect for the achievements and values of the Indian peoples, they transformed the term "culture" from the singular to plural. So, each American Indian people was viewed as bearing a distinct culture,

166

and each culture was viewed as having an existence that went from birth to death. While the elements of a particular Indian culture -- the cultural traits -- might have been assembled from a variety of sources (as Tylor had argued) nonetheless, each such culture had an integrity and a unity. To the mature Ruth Benedict a culture had the unity of a pottery vessel -- a cup-- and like such a vessel it could only be whole or shattered. A better simile for the attitudes of Boas and his students was that of evolutionary biology, so that cultures were like species that had evolved but would in time become extinct. It appeared to these scholars, that the set of aboriginal American Indian cultures were like fragile biological specimens whose environment had suddenly become hostile so that they were in the process of becoming extinct. They saw the task of anthropology as an obligation to the science of the future -- namely to preserve in the archives the records of these specimens of the human spirit. The cups were being shattered, the species were dying, but like the civilizations of ancient Greece, Rome, India, and Egypt the record of thier contributions to human life would be preserved -- not in stone but in the pages of monographs.[7]

Since their time, ethnohistorical researches have forced us to re-examine their assumptions about Indian cultures. It is now well established that the Indian societies of North America had been engaged in processes of cultural change for generations, and that they had responded positively and creatively to the opportunities afforded by European contact and trade. What Boas and his pupils were encountering were not the last pure specimens of aboriginal Indian cultures, but rather a set of peoples who had during the 18th and 19th centuries worked out a variety of adaptations to their biological and social environments and who were now striving -- against fearful and even lethal odds -- to create new adaptations. Those whose grandchildren survived are still Indians, or Native Americans, but they no longer practice exactly the same ways of their ancestors. This is not strange, considering that very few of us, whether White, Black, Indian, or whatever, practice the exact ways of life of our ancestors. The anthropological error did not lay so much in employing the concepts of pattern and culture as heuristic abstractions. Rather it lay in equating the existence of a people to the persistence of specific cultural traits and to the accompanying notion that if and when a particular people stops practicing some of the customs of its ancestors, that particular people thereupon becomes extinct or non-existent and is no longer able to function as a social or political entity.

Whether Indian or nonIndian, those who conceive of Indian cultures in this statically pluralistic fashion and therefore as becoming extinct (or degenerating into culture of poverty) are neglecting that which was central to Tylor's vision of culture, namely the place of technology. Those Europeans who established in the Americas what they called "New England" were

able to do so only because they incorporated into the basis of
their agricultural existence the maize-beans-squash complex that
had been developed by the Indians. The history of the nonIndian
peoples of North America would be entirely different were it not
for such Indian inventions which were integrated into their
fabric of life. Conversely, that which for most North Americans
was the sterotype of Indianness -- the Navajo with his sheep or
the mounted Indian chasing the buffalo -- both these represent
adaptations of European technology by Indian peoples. If we can
grant these manifestly simple arguments, then we can see that
preserving the plural form of the term "culture" in relationship
to the ethnic-racial minorities of North America serves more to
obfuscate educational policy than to assist it.

Once we discard the misleading conceptualization of
"culture" in relationship to special educational programs of
ethnic-racial minorities, we are able to plan in a more creative
fashion. On the one hand, we are able to reassert the patent
educational truth that the educator and the curriculum should
begin with what the child already knows and build on his skills
and competencies, rather than analyzing what he does not know
in relationship to some idealized version of the middleclass
child. Thus, if the child enters school speaking Lakota or
Cherokee, this is a facility which should be built upon rather
than condemned as either a deficiency or a vice which if encouraged might lead him to spend the rest of his life in a
reservation enclave. Equally important everyone involved can
take a fresh look at programs of ethnic studies. For the issues
here (and I am not the first to say this) is not that of fitting
the Indian student to return to an outmoded or deteriorated
reservation environment, but that of helping the student to find
himself by giving him a notion of who he is and what his ancestors have been. Especially for ethnic-racial groups like Indians,
Blacks and Chicanos who have been the target of sustained rhetoric which has declared their inferiority relevant to the White
Protestant, a program of ethnic studies is of great value in
helping to redress the balance and assist all parties to a more
accurate and moral perception of history. Ethnic Studies programs also symbolize a respect by the educator of the skills
which the child brings to the school from his home and community.

Insofar as we as anthropologists or other social-
scientists are involved in programs of Indian or other ethnic
studies, we should therefore be among the first to deny the
simplistic assumption that to be Indian is to be a hunter-and-
gatherer wandering about with feathers in his hair. Correspondingly, we may at appropriate times have to deny the mythology
of the special relationship between Indians and nature, inasmuch
as the internal combustion engine delivers pollutants to the
atmosphere, whether it is located in an urban or a reservation
environment.

To assert the notion of socio-political pluralism is to

deny the ideology of Indian assimilation as it has been set forth ever since the major European invasions of what they saw as The New World. Missionaries, government officials and reformers believed or hoped that either the Indians would either be assimilated into the fabric of European civilized and Christian life, or would become extinct. In North America during the 19th century, missionaries thought that once the Indians were converted to Christianity, taught to speak English, and provided the basic schooling, they would merge into the White population. Some of them did in fact so disappear, as one can find in many social gatherings, where individuals who look and act as mainstream Americans will tell you that their grandmother was a niece of Chief Crazy Horse. But it is also true that one can find leaders of contemporary Indian organizations who are as educated and sophisticated as their fellow North Americans and who yet think of themselves and are thought of by others as fully Indian.

Of course, there is another and extremely important dimension to this discussion, and that is power, both political and economic (cf. Yetman & Steele, eds. 1971). For the significant characteristic of the enclaved Indian peoples of the late 19th century was their loss of political independence and of their economic resources and their subordination in both respects to organized White or nonIndian interest groups. And, it has been well argued, especially by critics of the past decade, that the distressing fate of the Indian peoples lay not in their lack of integration with nonIndian (White) peoples but rather in the extent and quality of their integration. Just as, in the case of the Negro in the Deep South of the past century, his difficulties lay not with a lack of integration into that society but rather in the very nature of his integration into the political and economic life of the times as a depressed and exploited caste.

Accordingly, what is significant about programs of Indian Studies or ethnic studies is not merely the ideological content of these programs, but that they represent a transfer into the hands of spokesmen for these groups of a certain quantum of funds and power. White idealists are sometimes sorely troubled when they observe that the ethnic-racial minority in question has been more concerned about how to distribute the patronage represented by these programs--the jobs, the contracts, and the perquisites--then about performing services for the clientele constituted by their students, whether of their own ethnicity or otherwise.[8] But, of course, this activity confirms the theme of this essay that the real issue is not culture, or cultural pluralism, but social pluralism and associated political power.

To summarize. Contemporary American Indian groups are culturally heterogeneous: some continue the native language or display other traits which have the most direct linkages to the aboriginal culture; while others seem to have blended wholly into one or another version of "mainstream North America" (whether middle, working, or lower class). Despite their cultural heterogeneity, Indians have been organizing to advance their aggregate political interests, whether in rural or urban areas, on tribal, regional, or national bases. Sitins, court cases, polemical books, journals, essays and even newsreels or movies, are part of the armamentarium of these native American political groups. Yet, while Indians have been organizing and acting in these fashions, anthropologists and even Indian leaders themselves have continued to talk as if the distinctive feature of Indians was a common culture, either of a tribal or even a continental character.

The present paper attempts to cope with this cognitive dissonance by suggesting that it is more appropriate to conceive of Indianness as a socio-political rather than cultural identity. I do not intend to deny the persistence or significance of Indian cultural traits, but only to point out that in contemporary North America, it is the socio-political membership and activity that is decisive. Particularly in the educational context, it is misleading both to Indian and non-Indian students to portray Indianness as if it were a matter of preserving the traits of an aboriginal and static culture.[9]

NOTES

1. Revised slightly from initial presentation at the annual meetings of the American Ethnological Society, April 17, 1972, Montreal, Quebec. The audience discussion was helpful to me in clarifying my ideas and preparing this revision. In particular, Kathryn T. Molohon directed my attention to the writings of Frederik Barth on ethnic boundaries (1969); while Joan Cassell suggested that portions of this type of analysis were applicable to the contemporary women's rights movement -- a theme which I do not here develop but hope that she will.

Some readers may be interested to follow the linkage of the critique of "culture" in this essay with the more extensive discussion in my "Myth and Interrelationship in Social Science" (1969).

2. Gordon (1961:277) reminds us that the first use of the phrase "cultural pluralism" was by the philosopher, Horace M. Kallen, in 1924 when he was explaining the position concerning American multiple-group life that he had developed in essays published during the previous decade. Subsequently, the position, but not the phrase, was developed further by Robert E. Park as he attempted to comprehend his experiences -- both as a newspaper reporter in metropolitan areas, as secretary to Booker T. Washington, and as a graduate student in Germany. Park argued (1939 and elsewhere) that it was possible for people to be organized together either as ecological communities or as cultural societies. As ecological communities, they would be integrated in terms of symbiosis and division of labor, and so would minimize common features and emphasize diversity; while as

cultural societies, they would be integrated by a moral consensus. Clearly, the ecological community rests upon "cultural pluralism."

3. While this position with regard to American Indians is a generally popular one among the laiety, it has found only a few academic exponents, most notably Bernard James. The more general position regarding "a culture of poverty" was of course advanced by Oscar Lewis, and there is by now a rich polemical literature (cf. Leacock, ed. 1971).

Rosalie Wax has remarked to me upon the similarity between Lewis' "culture of poverty" and the theory of cultural degeneration which had so many exponents in the early and mid-nineteenth century. In 1810, for example Samuel Stanhope Smith characterized primitive peoples as "the generative offshoot of an original higher civilization, the product of 'idle' and 'restless spirits' who spurned 'the restraints and subordinations of civil society" (Stocking 1968:71).

4. While ethnohistorians as diverse as Eggan, Leacock, Lurie, and Spicer have emphasized the developmental changes among native American peoples, other authors have continued to present the myth of the unchanging traditional Indian (for a review of this myth see M. Wax 1968). The loss of traditional Indian homogeneity is a point particularly developed by Spicer (1962: Parts III & IV).

5. Singham (1971:103, 106) distinguishes between "the social pluralism of a modern society like America" and "the cultural pluralism of traditional societies:"

Whereas in the culturally plural traditional society the very concept of the nation is at stake, in modern societies which are socially plural all groups are accorded legitimacy by the society and allowed to participate, despite their retention of primary group loyalties that may be ethnic or religious (1971:106-107). The distinction drawn by Gordon (1964: chap. 6) between "cultural pluralism" and "structural pluralism" is also worth noting.

6. Among large and enclaved Indian groups such as the Navajo Nation, the native language may continue to flourish. Likewise, native languages may be maintained in specifically religious contexts, as perhaps in the case of the Long House religion among the Iroquois. Yet, many other Indian languages are being eroded, without the group involved being likely to disappear as a social unit.

Robert Breuning reports that among the Hopi, the more conservative parents wish the school to teach English exclusively; it is only the less traditional who fear the loss of Hopi and wish there to be instruction in that language within the schools.

Of course, this discussion does not obviate the fact that a common domestic language (such as Spanish for Mexican-

Americans, Puerto Ricans, and Native Spanish-Americans) can be an important instrumentality for social solidarity and a badge of personal identity. Nevertheless, it has been my experience on a number of occasions to encounter professionals who speak but little Spanish but yet identify strongly with the cause of their people (Chicanos, Puerto Ricans) and even become public spokesmen.

7. Solon Kimball reminds me that these American anthropologists were mostly or often employed by museums and that much of their fieldwork was devoted to obtaining museum specimens. Thus, they tended to view native peoples in a vocabulary derived from the museological perspective, as entities whose remains ought to be preserved and enshrined.

Barth's comment (1969:9) is appropriate: "Practically all anthropological reasoning rests on the premise that cultural variation is discontinuous: that there are aggregates of people who essentially share a common culture, and interconnected differences that distinguish each such culture from all others. Since culture is nothing but a way to describe human behaviour, it would follow that there are discrete groups of people, i.e. ethnic units, to correspond to each culture."

Note here the idealistic expectations of anthropologists and liberal friends of Indians concerning the Rough Rock Demonstration School, and note also the attempt by these parties to suppress the unfavorable evaluations of this school, a controversy reported in "Skirmish at Rock Rock" (1970) a set of articles in School Review, 79:57-140.

9. Barth (1969:11) notes critically that in characterizing ethnic groups "the sharing of a common culture is generally given central importance. In my view much can be gained by regarding this very important feature as an implication of result, rather than a primary and definitional characteristic of ethnic group organization."

REFERENCES

Barth, Frederick
    1969   Introduction. Pp. 9-38 in: Ethnic Groups and
                Boundaries, edited by Frederik Barth. Boston:
                Little Brown.

Erickson, Donald A. and Henrietta Schwartz
    1969   Community School at Rough Rock. Document PB
                184571. Springfield, Va.: U. S. Department of
                Commerce.

Gordon, Milton M.
    1961   Assimilation in America: Theory and reality.
                Daedalus, 90:263-285; reprinted Bobbs-Merrill
                S-407.

1964   Assimilation in American Life. New York:
Oxford University Press.

Kallen, Horace M.
1924   Culture and Democracy in the United States.
New York: Boni & Liveright.

Leacock, Eleanor, B. ed.
1971   The Culture of Poverty: A Critique. New York:
Simon & Schuster, Clarion Book 20846.

Park, Robert Ezra
1939   Symbiosis and socialization: a frame of
reference for the study of society. American
Journal of Sociology, 45:1-25). Reprinted in:
Human Communities: The City and Human Ecology,
ed. Everett C. Hughes, et al., New York: Free
Press, 1952.

Singham, A. W.
1971   The political socialization of minority groups.
Pp. 102-116 in (Yetman & Steele, eds. 1971)

Spicer, Edward H.
1962   Cycles of Conquest: The Impact of Spain, Mexico
and the United States on the Indians of the
Southwest, 1533-1960. Tucson: University of
Arizona Press.

Stocking, George W., Jr.
1968   Race, Culture, and Evolution: Essays in the
History of Anthropology. New York: Free Press.

Wax, Murray L.
1968   The White Man's burdensome 'business:' a review
essay on change and constancy of literature on
the American Indians. Social Problems 16:106-
113.
1969   Myth and Interrelationship in Social Science:
Illustrated Through Anthropology and Sociology.
Pp. 77-102 in: Interdisciplinary Relationships
in the Social Sciences, ed. Muzafer Sherif and
Carolyn W. Sherif. Chicago: Aldine.

Wax, Rosalie H. and Robert K. Thomas
1961   American Indians and White People. Phylon, 22:
305-317. Reprinted in: Native Americans Today:
Sociological Perspectives, ed. Howard M. Bahr,
et al. New York: Harper and Row, 1972.

Yetman, Norman R. and C. Hoy Steele, Editors
    1971   Majority and Minority: the Dynamics of Racial
              and Ethnic Relations. Boston: Allyn & Bacon.

MINORITY EDUCATION AND THE
TRANSFORMATION OF CONSCIOUSNESS

Norman A. Chance

University of Connecticut

Reflecting back on the past fifteen years of study among northern Eskimos and Indians in Alaska and Canada, I have become increasing struck by the fact that most educational and research literature concerned with these people largely disregards their highly oppressed and de-humanizing economic and social condition. Among other statistics, they have one of the highest mortality rates and lowest economic standard of living of any minority group in North America, (Federal Field Committee for Development Planning in Alaska 1968; Hawthorn 1966). Northern natives are clearly on the periphery of society, but like most minority populations, they are not on the periphery by choice. They are kept there through discrimination of varying kinds including economic exploitation, racism and sexism.[1]

In another sense, these people are not really as "marginal" to the broader society as they are dependent on it. They are alienated from active participation in and the receiving of the benefits of that society. This poses a very fundamental question: "Can highly alienated racially distinct people overcome their dependency by involving themselves in the very structure responsible for their dependency?"

Implicit in the question are two hypotheses and recommendations for action: (1) Alienated people are marginal to society. The educator and other allied development personnel must therefore "assist" them to enter the society. This is in many respects an "empty consciousness" theory in which the members of an alienated population are not perceived as having a cultural history. (2) Alienated people are exploited within the society. They, together with the educator, must heighten their awareness of this relationship, i.e., de-mythologize their social reality, and take action to reduce the exploitation.

In the first instance, alienated people are perceived as objects to be integrated into the society. In the second, they develop their own sense of history and their own role as social activists.[2]

I suggest that much of the educational effort in northern North America promotes a kind of cultural inarticulateness or what the Brazilian educator Paulo Freire calls a "culture of silence" in that the minority member learns how others make history, but his education does not enable him to develop or express a sense of his own history. As a result, he becomes dependent, and therefore silent.[3]

If this analysis is correct, it soon becomes clear that issues of educational reform for minority populations like the American Indian are not simply those of increased facilities or improved quality of existing program--two commonly supported recommendations. Of far greater importance is the question of how minority populations increase their level of social awareness or consciousness--such that they perceive themselves as capable of engaging in transforming action toward new and more humanizing social institutions.

Levels of Critical Consciousness

Three levels of consciousness may be delineated: The first is characterized by a "culture of silence" in which the minority members are seen as an object by others. They have little consciousness of themselves except in a dependent relationship to those in a more dominant economic, social and political position. Recognizing this dependence tests the limits of their "self-other" perception. The concept of themselves as subject, as social activists, as a maker of their own history, is lacking. At this level, they remain inarticulate, even in the face of extreme economic hardship or social conflict.[4]

In the second or transitional level of consciousness, the people become aware of the dichotomy between themselves as object and subject. They not only realize that they are alienated from the dominant sector of society, and as such are largely powerless, but that this alienation has deep societal roots. Reflecting on this new consciousness, they then begin to take action to remove the alienation. This action commonly promotes a backlash or reaction which then increases their understanding of the contradiction between the ideal reality they have been taught and the social reality they meet in practice. This is the crucial point at which they can attempt to de-mystify the social world they previously accepted.

At the third transforming level of consciousness, the people not only denounce de-humanizing social institutions and cultural practices, but they undertake to formulate new humanizing institutions and values. Here the role of the educator working in conjunction with, rather than over, the student is of major importance in stimulating learning geared to transforming action.

In Northern Canada and Alaska, from where I draw my experience, thousands of Eskimos and Indians in rural and urban settings are still trapped in an over-whelming culture of silence (Chance 1970; 180-194; Governor's Commission of Cross-

Cultural Education 1970). However, a second level of consciousness is emerging among many young native leaders in schools,
government positions, and in native organizations such as the
Alaska Federation of Natives (Policy Planning Statement; Point
Barrow 1970; Alaska Federation of Natives 1967). Significantly,
some of these young people are making the decision to leave their
jobs in government, industry, and allied occupations, to return
to their own communities where they can assume positions as local
leaders and organizers.

The third level of critical consciousness, one which
serves as a catalyst for transforming society in a more humanizing direction, is also beginning to appear among northern natives,
although as yet only rarely (c.f. Chance, forthcoming). Examples
of these new transforming activities include plans to establish
new community-wide corporations where all village members are
able to participate in and control the given industrial enterprise,
e.g. frozen fish plants, and efforts to exert greater community
control over schools at the primary and secondary level for humanizing ends. Similar kinds of efforts are now being discussed
in conjunction with the recently passed Alaska Land Claims Bill
and dissemination of funds resulting from it.[5]

Theory and Practice of Authentic Education

One of the dominant characteristics of our contemporary
world is the relentless movement of minority and third world populations away from a culture of silence toward a more critical
level of consciousness geared to de-mystifying the socio-economic
structure of society that has reinforced their dependency.

When these groups focus on the process of education, application of this critical awareness immediately draws attention
to the relationship of school to the economic structure of society. Education is economic access. With only minimal education, minority populations are locked into a poverty cycle that
ensures their exclusion from effective involvement in the country's local, regional and national development. Today, most
minority members are well aware of this fact and frequently organize around goals directed toward increased funding and better
quality school programs.

In Alaska, for example, (total native population of 55,
000), in 1970, of the 77 State operated schools located in primarily native populated villages, only six offered work beyond
the 8th grade. In the 73 BIA schools, only four offered 9th
grade courses and only two, 10th grade courses. The Alaska Federation of Natives, like many similar minority-based political
organizations, is actively pressing for more and improved secondary schools for native youth. Significantly, however, while
numerous state and federal agencies have undertaken planning
for regional high schools, none of these efforts have as yet

177

materialized in the opening of such a school (Alaska Department of Education 1970; Governor's Commission of Cross-Cultural Education 1970).

This concerted effort of the Alaska Federation of Natives to improve educational facilities is illustrative of the action taken at the second or transitional level of consciousness where the given group recognized the extent to which they have been excluded by the larger society and begin to take action to reduce this alienation. Not surprisingly, these efforts usually bring about very limited improvement at best.

As stated earlier, the crucial point in the transformation of consciousness is when the minority group members, working together, begin to understand the basic contradictions underlying the ideal reality they have been taught in school and the social reality they meet in practice. This occurs when, for example, they realize that the existing educational system allows for individual mobility without disturbing the class structure, or when they realize that education for most minority members prepares them to fit a niche in society rather than participate in and exert control over their own community and its development. Among the decision making leaders are those who control educational process and, although they increasingly encourage innovative reforms that more effectively serve the existing socio-economic system, they seldom support the kind of participation that leads to reduction in power of their own and their associates privileged position.

The innovative reform movement in education has as yet hardly reached out (or down) to the type of schools populated by most minority group members (Alaska State Commission for Human Rights 1969). But assuming that it eventually will, and it has to some extent already, the implications for exerting control over minority populations who are striving to achieve a transforming consciousness, are considerable. The polarizations in our society are, of course, reflected in innovative reform movements. They include issues such as structure vs. non-structure, competition vs. cooperation, efficiency vs. participation, means vs. ends, secrecy vs. openness, individuality vs. conformity. A core issue is certainly the latter dichotomy.

Few would deny that most of our schools place great emphasis on conformity. As counter to this tendency is the middle class parents support of recent educational efforts to re-emphasize the importance of "individuality" in learning--a dominant American value going back through our whole history. The major constraint on this freedom is the necessity of preventing one man's freedom from becoming another man's bondage.

Minority groups, oppressed by existing educational programs and desiring a slice of the innovative educational pie, should note well, however, that freedom is commonly defined in terms of the particular individual.

The educator, Stephen Mann (1972) states the issue thusly:

> The conformity in our schools...is achieved not through the collectivization of experience... but rather through the rigid isolation of individuals from each other. The most prominant 'pedagogical' tools in use in schools are as much devices for keeping people apart as they are devices to insure learning. Consider the array of practices relating to the proposition that cooperation is cheating. Consider the thrust of 'individualized instruction' which reaches its culmination in the private relationship between the student and a varied-response computer set-up designed to bring the student at his own pace to the farthest point he can reach among a narrowly delineated performance continum. Consider the standard pattern of classroom discourse in which a teacher has mini-conversations with a long string of individual students while simultaneously doing everything in his power to keep the kids from talking to one another. Consider the overwhelming isolating emphasis upon competition.

Mann makes the point very clearly: School conformity is achieved through the separation rather than through the collectivization of experience.[6] At initial glance, how ironic that the isolation of individuals from each other is a major strategy for assuring conformity--and we are taught to call it "freedom" or "individuality." It becomes less ironic when we begin to realize that collective effort and experience can be a major catalyst for individuality. It is less ironic because we suddenly have a flash of insight that the issue is not individuality vs. conformity. Truly authentic education is a process that takes into account conformity and individuality as a continuing collective interdependent and dialectial relationship.

Why then do we have educational systems that so often polarize modes of learning in terms of either conformity or individuality? And while middle class academics may stop with this question, minority groups with a more critical level of consciousness, may go on to the further question: Why is it that education for poor and oppressed populations tends to place greatest emphasis on conformity; whereas education for upper and middle class populations increasingly encourage individuality? When issues such as these are being raised, it quickly becomes clear to both lower and middle class groups that authentic education cannot take place in isolation from other fundamental social processes.

This takes us to a new level of awareness: Not only are many students separated from each other, but the learning process in schools is largely separated from the learning process in communities. The strategy is called "divide and rule." The counter-strategy is called "praxis"—that is, a combination of reflective thought based on increased critical consciousness and action; the continuous testing of theory through practice.

De-Mythologizing Educational Process

When one steps back and looks deeply at the philosophical and theoretical underpinnings of our educational efforts, whether they be undertaken among minority populations or in society at large, one realizes that the issues are not only economic, social and political. At the heart of the matter are divergent images of the people concerned.

It is the underlying purpose of education to assist the people to serve the institutions they have created? Or is it to assist them to review or create new institutions to serve them? Put most simply, are the people dependent or autonomous? The answer, of course, is both. Recognizing the importance of cultural influences, I think most would agree, nevertheless, the social groups are not simply willing to exist. The history of human development suggests that people desire to be more than what they are now. And furthermore, that they have the capability of transforming their existing world in a direction that they deem important. In the words of Freire, man "can undertake to change what he has already determined."[7] Social groups do this by means of their praxis, a testing of theory through practice-- which is what true learning is all about. However, this praxis promotes a kind of backlash. The knowledge gained through theory and practice eventually becomes patterned such that it turns back on the people and "overdetermines" them. It conditions them and defines their cognitive meanings and actions--what many anthropologists refer to as culture.

Formal education, as an important aspect of socialization, tends to reinforce this "overdetermination." Yet education does have an inherent ambivalence. Along with the passing on of existing knowledge, (a kind of static praxis strongly emphasized in primary and secondary education), there is the search for new knowledge. The former process tends to overdetermine; the latter brings out in individuals and groups that which is least determined.

If we look at education from this perspective, we can see that it is never neutral. It is either conditioning or deconditioning, adaptive or transformative, it promotes pacification or liberation. Psychological learning theorists have provided us with considerable insight into the conditioning and deconditioning process. A set of qualities unique to homo sapiens is the capability of knowing what conditions them, their ability to reflect on what they know, and their ability to perceive their perceptions. Only given these attributes can they engage in the deconditioning process of first asking questions about their conditioning; and second, question the conditions themselves. As an anthropologist, I would call this latter process an act of "cultural subversion" of the overdetermining qualities inherent in human socialization.

It is at this point that the educator faces a crucial question. Essentially, there are two opinions: One can choose either an "adaptive" or a "critical" pedagogical approach. The former is associated with what Freire calls the "banking method" of education; the latter with a "problem" approach. In the banking method, the student is the depository, the teacher is the depositor. The more students store up deposits of knowledge, the less likely they are to develope critical skills. The more students adapt to existing "reality," the less likely they are to engage in transforming those features of society they feel are in need of change.

The problem approach, in contrast, challenges students from the beginning to look critically at the "reality" which they are studying. Again this involves a combination of theory and practice, reflection and action.[8]

How do people develop this critical approach to education? They begin by looking critically at their own life situation. They stand back and look at themselves in relation to the external world and ask: "How much are we an object of someone else's history or life pattern? How much are we a subject of our own history, a self-determining group?"

If the group's self-perception is largely one in which they see themselves as an object, they should ask the further question: "How much is this due to internal psychological factors contained within us, and how much to our perception of the external social reality?" If people do not look critically at the external social reality, yet consider themselves as objects of someone else, that group is bound to focus critically on their internal qualities.

Where do anthropologists make their contribution to authentic education and social transformation? By following the same process. By making certain they do not fall into the trap of idealism taken by so many middle class college students that we are all going to enter a highly individualized "Consciousness III" envisioned in Reich's book, The Greening of America.[9] Rather the issue is whether such students and their teachers are going to join with far more oppressed populations in undertaking to transform education and the society at large.

Seeking a type of Consciousness III without developing a broader economic and political awareness leading to action is simply self-seeking individualism. At the same time, politicalization without developing a sense of humanity is manipulation. The goal is to combine the political and the human dimension into one inter-dependent process. And the place to begin is by looking critically at the social reality which we presently perceive.[10]

NOTES

1. However, it is important to remember that while marginal, they still consider themselves to be a part of the larger society, and are so perceived by others. Otherwise, they would be viewed as a more severe threat; as radical blacks and Puerto Ricans are so perceived by many today.

2. Herein lies a crucial contribution of the radical cultural anthropologist--to work with minority populations in developing a greater awareness of their own history and capability as social activists.

3. In a study of educational reform undertaken in Alaska in 1971, I met with community members in a small village outside Bethel. In response to a question concerning possible innovations, the village leaders indicated they would like to have their children learn more of Eskimo history and culture. However, they felt this would have to be offered after school hours "since the teachers would not approve of such a plan being part of the curriculum." Official educational policy is now encouraging such subject matter in the curriculum. The point is that the dependency felt by these and many other minority people discourage them from speaking out; hence, their characterization as having a 'culture of silence.'

4. Or they turn their conflict and resulting aggression inward. The high rate of suicide among American Indian minority populations provides a well-known example.

5. To the extent that these efforts are initially successful, they will seriously threaten existing economic and educational institutions. New strategies to cope with the mounting externally induced pressures will then have to be developed.

6. I would like to acknowledge special appreciation to Steve Mann for many of the ideas he has contributed to this section of the article.

7. Many of the ideas and concepts in this section of the paper have been drawn from the stimulating work of Paulo Freire (1970).

8. This, in turn, requires a solution of the teacher-student conflict, such that members of both groups become teachers and students. Authority or status as a dominant factor in the relationship must be replaced by trust--for without trust there is little effective communication, and without communication there is no true education.

9. In recognizing the trap of idealizing consciousness, i.e. seeing it as an end in itself, one must also be aware of the opposite trap of overemphasizing the objective conditions such that the role of consciousness is relegated to an inferior or non-existant position. Psychologically oriented anthropolo-

182

gists are particularly prone to the former. Anti-dialectical (or mechanical) materialists characterize the latter. For a particularly insightful discussion of this issue, see Eleanor Leacock, (1972)

        10. I would like to express appreciation to Jacquetta H. Burnett, Nancy F. Chance, Paulo Freire, and Brooke G. Schoepf for their comments on various sections of the article.

REFERENCES

Alaska Department of Education
    1970   Source Book on Alaska. Juneau.

Alaska Federation of Natives
    1967   Proposal for Support of the Alaska Federation of Natives Program to Develop the Ability of Eskimos, Indians and Aleuts to Participate Constructively and Live Rewardingly in Alaska. Anchorage.

Alaska Rural School Project
    1966   Interim Report.

Alaska State Commission for Human Rights
    1969   Study of William E. Beltz School, Nome, Alaska. Anchorage.

Chance, Norman A.
    1970   Directed Change and Northern Peoples In G. Rogers, Change in Alaska. Seattle.

Chance, Norman A.
    n.d.   Modernization and Educational Reform in Native Alaska In Rethinking Modernization: Anthropological Perspectives, ed. by John Poggie, Jr. and Robert Lynch, Greenwood Press (forthcoming).

Federal Field Committee for Development Planning in Alaska
    1968   Alaska Natives and the Land, U. S. Government Printing Office, Washington.

Freire, Paulo
    1970   Pedagogy of the Oppressed. New York, Herter and Herter.

Governor's Commission on Cross-Cultural Education
    1970   Time for Change in the Education of Alaska Natives. Juneau.

Hawthorn, H. B. (ed.)

1966 A Survey of the Contemporary Indians of Canada. Ottawa.

Leacock, Eleanor
  1972 Introduction *In* F. Engels, Origin of the Family, Private Property and the State. New York, International Publishers.

SCHOOL REORGANIZATION AND LEARNING:

AN APPROACH TO ASSESSING THE DIRECTION OF
SCHOOL CHANGE

Rosalie Cohen
Temple University

Introduction

During the past two decades, schools have undergone widespread and sometimes radical changes. In addition, the rate of change in them has been so rapid that it is possible to observe those activities which influence it within the professional lifetimes of the observers, themselves. Despite this unusual opportunity, most education research has been less concerned with broad themes in educational change than with more temporal concerns. The foci for change in the schools continue to be varied and distributed: but if one could identify the character of the decision makers for the school, if their intents had been made more or less explicit (as in legislation), if one could identify the bases on which their decisions are likely to be made, one could predict the general directions of change, all else remaining constant.

This paper argues that during the past two decades a system of national decision making has developed in which the gross characteristics of the decision making units can be identified, and that their decisions are limited in part by federal legislation binding on all states and all school districts. The bases on which their decisions are made may be found in national educational data, and in the identification of priorities, target populations, and objectives. Although variety is intended to exist, it is provided for within a knowable framework of legitimate possibilities, and the kinds of changes in schooling may be predicted to be responsive to knowable kinds of variables. The argument is presented in three parts: Two decades of school reorganization; the developing services orientation of the school; and some resulting influences on the congnitive expectations in the school.

The scope of this paper could not include the consideration of more than a few large scale themes in educational change, and its primary concern is with compulsory age schooling in public systems. It presents the point of view that the direction of change in the performance expectations of the

185

school is leading toward the production of increasing numbers of service personnel--qualitatively different kinds of pupils than their parents were. This paper does not suggest, of course, that the themes which are presented are all pervasive or dogmatically determined. It does suggest, however, that the increase in one kind of valued setting over another reflects a set of developing themes, the causes and effects of which are both theoretically interesting and empirically researchable.

Two Decades of School Reorganization

Many important changes in schools during the past two decades have been rational, widespread and rapid. Although the most important changes have been financial and organizational, they are intended to stimulate equally planful reforms in all aspects of legitimate formal schooling.[1] A major influence in this direction has been a new reorganization of educational decision makers for the schools.

Just two decades ago, schooling organizations assumed a powerful and rational new partner in educational decision making...the federal government. The purposes and intents of federal decision makers have determined the direction of innovation in school organization; and their efforts have been responsible to a large degree for the breadth and rate of school change. Although Section 422 of the Amendments to the Elementary and Secondary Education Act of 1965 forbids federal control of curriculum, instruction, personnel and materials,[2] executive mandates and related federal legislation have had a potent influence on school change.

The interest of the federal government in education is not new, of course. Even before the federal Constitution was ratified, the Congress of the Confederation, in 1785[3] began the practice of contributing public lands in the states and territories for school sites, as an incentive to the spread of local education. An Act of Congress created the Office of Education on March 2, 1867,[4] and in 1874, it became a part of the Department of the Interior.[5] Its statutory responsibilities were to collect statistics on the progress of education, to diffuse information on the organization and management of schools and school systems and methods of teaching, and to aid in the establishment and maintenance of education throughout the country.[6] The Office of Education became a part of the Federal Security Agency in 1939,[7] an agency of government which was created to consolidate the efforts of the Office of Education (transferred from the Department of Labor), the Public Health Service (transferred from the Department of the Treasury), the National Youth Commission (transferred from the Works Progress Administration), and the Social Security Board. The Office of Education became a constituent agency of the Department of Health, Education and Welfare in 1953,[8] when a similar reorgan-

ization of governmental activities combined the previously
separate agencies of Health, Education and Welfare, abolishing
the Federal Security Agency and subsuming its functions. The
organizational antecedents listed above, along with those duties
historically assigned to Health and Welfare agencies, became the
basic units of the newly formed cabinet post. Today, Office of
Education functions include all of those of earlier plans or
organizations; its statements of purpose incorporate those of
the earliest legislation along with the new and, in each reorganization, its newer functions are drawn from its most recent
collaborations.

        Such governmental associations have historically in-
fluenced both the curriculum and the organization of schools.
The occupational relevance of the curriculum as a matter of
national policy e.g. arose from the joint efforts of the Office
of Education and the U.S. Employment Service under the powerful
House of Representatives Committee on Education and Labor;[9] and
the health curriculum and innoculation programs emerged from the
joint efforts of the educational and public health agencies.[10]
The newer Health and Welfare linkage with the Office of Education
has prompted more recent acts and executive orders which require
the Office of Education to be responsible for the education of
economically disadvantaged students, Spanish-surname students,
rural youth, the blind, the deaf, the handicapped, and the
emotionally disturbed and retarded (DHEW 1972). Through its ten
regional offices, the more than 100 educational program activities of the Office of Education now affect nearly all of the
nation's more than 21,000 public and non-public school districts
and 2,500 colleges and universities (DHEW 1971b, 1972b). This
broadly based approach to educational innovation, greatly
expands the capacity of federal activities to produce pervasive
organizational changes.

        This broad approach to school innovation is also
responsible for an increased rate of change in the schools.
Reasons for this phenomenon are several. First, because the
Department of Health, Education and Welfare is an office of
the executive branch of government, its policy recommendations
have the character of mandates.[11] Second, its data collection
and program development efforts are national in scope, and
school district "output" has come to be measured against national
averages, rather than local ones or selectively biased ones.
Many school modifications did, in fact, emerge from comparative
school district data feed-back, even when they were not mandated
and the replacement of local school problems of national scope
impelled modifications in programming and school organization
even when they were of limited salience within the local context
(NCERD 1969). Third, the multi-faceted approach which is possible for the federal office creates multiple foci for change,
which, when combined, produce a mutually reinforcing stream of
innovation. For example, when a program is developed for schools,

when instructional materials are developed for the program, when
teachers are trained for the program, when administrative
policies are geared to accomodate the program, when supportive
school personnel are made available to staff the program, and
when program participants are assured of employment opportunities when they complete the program, the forces toward the
acceptance of the program by a school or school district are
greatly enhanced. This range of activities is possible mainly
because it is directed by a complex agency of national scope.
This agency does, in fact, provide incentives to schools to
include new programs in their repertoires, funds for higher
educational training of professionals to staff the programs,
funds for the development of materials and library resources to
support them, incentives to do research and development within
them, and support for a network of Research and Development
Centers and Regional Educational Laboratories to disseminate the
innovations which they and others develop. Federal concern has
thus made possible a multi-pronged approach to educational
innovation which has greatly accelerated the rate of change in
the schools (NCERD 1969:Chap. V).

Federal concern for education has also created the
impetus for a massive reorganization of schooling agencies. A
classic example has been the financial and organizational
changes which resulted from the executive mandate and related
federal legislation to "equalize educational opportunity."[12] A
review of these efforts appears below.

In the collection of comparative school districts data
on a national scale, vast disparities appeared among school
districts in their capacity to finance their educational objectives.[13] The economic "marginality" of school districts was
thus viewed as a measure of their failure to fully develop the
"human capital"[14] within their borders.[15] Vast disparities did,
in fact, appear among the states when their fiscal capacity to
provide educational services were studied in this way. For
instance, in 1965, cost per pupil for education ranged from $200
per child in Mississippi to $750 per pupil in New York (DHEW
1966). Even more marked differences appeared within states when
expenditures for rural and urban areas were compared. Within
school districts, differential allocations and differential
distributions of pupils had produced similar kinds of statistics:
and similar discrepancies appeared when public and non-public
schools were compared (DHEW 1971a).

Since public schools had been financed by revenue funds,
a study of their fiscal capacity revealed some reasons for these
differences. As late as 1971, for instance, the revenue capacities of local government varied from $343 per capita to less
than $100 per capita; fiscal efforts by local governments ranged
from 46% above the national average of 40% below it; tax rates
varied from 8 mills to 14 mills; and the range of market values
upon which school revenues were based, even within a state (e.g.

Florida), might be as great as 10 to 1 (DHEW 1971a).

These data provided the grounds on which rational efforts toward the massive reorganization of schooling enterprises were based. During the past two decades, widely distributed efforts to broaden and equalize the financial bases for school support were attempted. When the California Supreme Court ruled recently that property taxes alone (traditional sources of school support) provided inequitable schooling,[16] other sources of tax revenue for education had long before been tested and found inadequate, school district boundaries had been redesigned to consolidate or stratify tax bases and voucher plans had been tested[17] (DHEW 1971a). Despite these efforts, the 1971 Report of the National Educational Finance Project reported that, at writing, 80% of the 18,000 public school districts still did not have sufficient enrollments to provide even minimally adequate programs and services without excessive costs, and that incentives and directives toward the consolidation of inefficient school districts and the stratification of densely populated school districts had not produced the desired effect. The legislative intent was confirmed i.e. that efforts be directed toward the equalization of education among children, the equalization of expenses among school districts and the distribution of the tax burden fairly (DHEW 1971a).

Although the above efforts to equalize education involved equalizing only the fiscal capacities of school districts, it set into motion a massive reorganization of educational decision makers. Subsequent developments reflect a shift from the control of local decision makers to the state,[18] (DHEW 1972a) and from state regions to inter-state regions (NCERD 1969:Chap. II). Public and non-public schools within each area have been coordinated to some degree,[19] along with a variety of alternate settings in which supervised educational activities may be carried on with public sanction and public funds.[20]

In addition, still greater modifications are considered probable. For instance, the Presidents' Commission on School Finance has recommended several plans to accomplish the objective of providing equal educational opportunity. They are: to create a national foundation program to be supported by federal, state, and local funds to be distributed to schools according to need;[21] to give equal grants to students with no requirement of state or local effort; to award equal grants to pupils which require state and local effort in proportion to their ability; and a combination of the first and second plan (PCSF 1972). Boulding comments:

> ...Any major changes in the educational industry will
> have to be a combination of financial, organizational
> and technical changes. Of these...financial and
> organizational changes will have to come first." "...
> a change in methods of finance to one that subsidizes
> the students rather than the school might set off drastic

189

changes in the organization of the whole industry
(Boulding 1970).
Boulding comments also on the anticipated character of the
change by observing the nature of the economic structure into
which schools have been placed during these two decades of
change...from the "exchange sector" of the economy to the
"grants sector." On this shift from school dependence on local
contributions and control to what he calls the national "grants
economy," he says, "...the demand for education, therefore, is
likely to depend more on what is happening in other parts of the
grants economy...than it is on what is happening to income and
expenditures in general." (In the case of the public schools,
local school district or state capacity (Boulding 1970).

The reawakening of concern for education in the
executive branch of the federal government has thus had a
profound effect on the reorganization of educational agencies
and on the breadth and rate of school change. The processes of
decision making are rational and knowable; they are based on the
collection of data about schools and executive and federal
legislative intent. Through the power of the executive mandate
and federal legislation, through the requirement that schools
respond to concerns of national scope rather than local ones,
through a multi-focal approach to innovation, and through a
widespread revision of the organization of the educational enterprise creating pre-conditions for change, federal intervention
has set in motion modifications in school decision making so
impactful that the effects, both intended and unintended, cannot
yet be assessed. Federal control of curriculum, instruction,
personnel and materials is forbidden by law; however, if one
could identify the nature of the decision making units of
government and some of the national priorities likely to influence decisions which affect local districts, he might be able
to predict the general character of changes in these areas as
well. Some such influences are mentioned in the following
section.

An Emerging Service Orientation in the School

Schools appear to be more and more characterized by a
developing service orientation (NERC 1970). Whatever the
complex seeds for this change were, some identifiable facilitators in this process may be located organizationally in the
unique make-up of the new federal office in which educational
responsibilities are located; and they are supported by the
character of the grants economy on which the schools have become
increasingly dependent. Given the rational approach to educational decision making which has characterized school innovation
during the past two decades, a third influence is mentioned...
that of the growing dominance of service industries in the
market for human skills. Together, these developing themes

190

appear to be leading to a service-providing school, with a service-using population, and a curriculum which can produce increasingly larger numbers of service oriented personnel for the future.

An important organizational influence on school change has been the combining of functions of health, education and welfare in one agency of national scope.[22] Its first important influence has been to broaden and redefine the legitimate purposes of schools from "the transfer of knowledges and skill from one generation to another" (DHEW 1971a:Chap. I) to "activities in the general welfare."[23] As a result, the combined duties of this agency have resulted in "comprehensive planning," rather than educational planning per se (DHEW 1971:Chap. I); and influences on compulsory age schooling may be found as components of housing, health care, welfare or law enforcement legislation, as well as in that devoted to strictly educational concerns.[24] Secondly, this consortium of agencies has also been responsible for the direction of school change by defining "target populations" (the poor, Spanish surname youth, the blind, deaf and physically or mentally handicapped) as priority educational populations, or by identifying specific social problems as the basis for necessary curricular innovations (poverty, law enforcement, rehabilitation (Toffman, et al. 1971:28, 95).

An example of the effect on educational programming of non-educational legislation may be found, for instance, in the Community Mental Health Legislation of 1963.[25] Among its other provisions, it is directed toward the prevention of mental illness, and it identifies the "community" as the agent responsible for the development of mental health as well as the arena for the selection, diagnosis and treatment of the mentally ill and retarded. Whether such programs developed under related legislation will succeed in their present form or not, they have had a lasting influence on the school. The impact of Community Mental Health legislation is found in the requirement that schools assign Social Security numbers to children on entry into first grade so that longitudinal records may be kept,[26] in the increase in clinical treatment staff in schools, and in the use of emotional stability as a criterion for advanced education.[27] It is certainly responsible for the inclusion of a large variety of mentally and physically handicapped children in public school facilities and for the development and availability of "affective curricula" (NCERD 1970:Chap. II). Its more general and more important influence on the schools is found, however, in the assignment of responsibility for the solution of social problems to the community through the use of publicly controlled, and publicly evaluatable existing agencies. As the only compulsory, community based, normal social setting, the school has thus come to be viewed as an arena for preventing the development of mental illness.

The school may also be used as an arena to distribute

public services (e.g. recent plans for school finance include, in addition to conventional teaching and supportive services, such additions to school budgets as hot breakfasts and lunches, periodic physical examinations, remedial visual and auditory services, dental care, disease treatment and clothing allowances, at no cost to children from low income homes (PCSF 1972). The school is also viewed as an available agency to solve social problems by "recycling" improperly socialized individuals from a variety of different contexts...e.g. to resocialize the poor to lead productive lives (Welfare eligibility requirements may now provide assistance to mothers receiving Aid to Dependent Children when they are furthering their educations) (DHEW 1970) or to rehabilitate criminals (half a dozen cities now sentence juvenile law offenders to educational rehabilitation or to combined psychiatric-employment-educational rehabilitation,[28] and two cities provide for the education of convicted prostitutes).[29]

Despite the fact that these broadly based efforts which are built into a wide variety of federal legislative efforts may be expected to be relatively lasting in their general import at least there is little effort to study their effects in the school. The impact of multiple health, education and welfare objectives on the school and their concern with "target populations" for instance, is largely unresearched. We do not know how the temporary reversal of priorities in the school...the objectives of unequal financial support to schools (greater) for unequal children (economically, physically, emotionally or educationally handicapped) will affect pupil status systems in them, or at what cut-off point, the increase of clinical staff over teaching staff may influence the curriculum or modify the theories of learning which undergird them. Although comprehensive planning has been responsible in part for some of the more radical modifications in conventional classroom management, we do not know at what point these modifications will become models of effective schooling, rather than efforts directed toward their original purposes. The point is that, although using a compulsory community agency like the school for the delivery of a wide range of public services is obviously an efficient method for distributing them, it cannot be expected not to have a lasting effect on the curriculum. At the least, this type of service program may be viewed as producing an un-researched infra-curriculum in the school directed toward the school production of "service users."

A common denominator in all of HEW provisions is that educational agencies have become part of a complex service delivery system, the major concerns of which have been blended. Within this context of multiple service delivery, comprehensive planning has made it possible for funds and decision makers, service staff and service populations to move relatively freely across what were once institutional boundaries. As the only compulsory, normal social setting in communities, the school has become the nucleus of activities. It is, therefore, no longer possible to talk of educational curricula in limited terms. Educational agencies now provide "services in the general welfare," the purposes of which cannot help but be reflected in school objectives.

The nature of the "grants economy" appears to be another important influence on the developing service orientation of the school. Little research appears in this area despite the fact that, in 1970, the "grants sector" was responsible for 7% of the Gross National Product and was rising...i.e. it represented a larger proportion of total economic activity than did agriculture. One of the characteristics of the grants economy is that a school's continued involvement in it requires rapid shifts in focus and programming. "The total sum of grants is likely to be more stable than any participating component of it" (Boulding 1970). Provisions for such flexibility are departures from traditional efforts to insulate schooling from immediacy of response and from the influence of special interest groups, but they do characterize service providing agencies. Although the tendency has been to view these shifts as the frequent abandonment of older objectives for newer ones, this has not been the case. When viewed in larger perspective, funds for given populations or for the solution of specific social problems have remained relatively stable, despite the abandonment of individual programs which have appeared less productive than others (PCSF 1972). The flexibility requirement for participation in the grants economy did stimulate the spread of appropriate administrative provisions in school such as flexible programming, modular scheduling and team teaching (DHEW 1971a).

Not only does participation in the grants economy require a flexible orientation to school innovation, but also, as it is described by economists, it has many of the qualities of Polanyi's "redistribution economy (Polanyi 1957). One unique characteristic of this type of large-scale social organization is the absence of the link between producing and consuming which characterizes alternate notions of their "reciprocity" and "exchange" economies.[30] Individuals may consume as a right, rather than in exchange for other goods and services. This break in exchange relationships is not only a stated effort of the legislation of the last two decades, but it is also a distinctive characteristic of ideally designed service systems. In brief, if the similarity between the grants economy and the redistirbution notion can be empirically demonstrated, at some point, participation in the grants sector would require a qualitative modification of the social expectations of the school over older "exchange" mechanisms, and the subsequent modification of inter-personal expectations and role definitions within it.[31]

A third important theme in educational change is the

qualitative shift in the dominance of one type of industry over
another in the employment market for which schools provide basic
skills. In 1956 (these same two decades) the United States
became the first major country in which less than 50% of its
non-farm laborers were engaged in secondary industry, dominance
having shifted to service industries with an increasing involvement of fourth sector industries (Freeman 1967). The terms,
"primary," "secondary," "tertiary" and "fourth sector" industries
are used in similar fashion to that in which economists use
them. Primary industry produces materials which are used as
they come from Nature as in farming, fishing and logging.
Secondary industry produces tangible items which require many
processes to take place on them before they are ready for market.
Third sector industries provide services, and fourth sector
industries produce intangibles like creative art and music,
basic research, recreation and planning (Rostow 1960).

As the high levels of differentiation and specialization
associated with the dominance of secondary industry were reflected in the school, it is expected that those methods of
social organization which characterize the service industries
will find their counterparts in the socialization settings of
the school as well. For instance, observers believe that only
secondary industry requires the high levels of differentiation
and specialization and interdependence which characterize them
to function optimally. In addition, their purposes were to
utilize the services of many different kinds of functionaries,
with different levels and different kinds of education, to lead
different styles of life and to receive differential rewards.[32]
Since equalization is a central theme in the legislation of the
past two decades, it would appear that these high levels of
differentiation in the school for large segments of the population now in school will no longer be appropriate. Further,
school systems which are charged with the responsibility of
developing "human capital" are faced with a duty to find and
develop progressively smaller numbers of children with secondary
industry skills and increasing numbers of individuals with
service relevant skills, and to modify its classroom organization
and curriculum appropriately (DHEW 1971c).

This impact may be felt in the scheduling of tasks.
Only secondary industry appears to require the complex task
rhythms which characterize it. That is, although the scheduling
of primary industry was closely related to the rhythms of
natural phenomena (day and night, the weather, the seasons)
secondary industry developed task-rhythms (Bowen 1964), tied to
the controlled flow of goods, machinery and personnel. They
were unrelated to natural phenomena, or for that matter, to
human needs or satisfactions. The dominance of third sector
industries suggests a new theme. Although the demand for
services may be artificially stimulated or depressed, service
agencies function optimally on a schedule of human needs and

194

demands however these are defined...they are subject to "rushes" of demand or need with large limbos in between (Bowen 1964). A projected dominance of fourth sector products--intangibles--may be seen to further break down the importance of task rhythms. Since fourth sector products are frequently the products of imagination and creative urges, they cannot be induced to occur by pre-planning, and the high levels of interdependence and pre-planned time schedules may be completely dysfunctional. Associated with the decreasing importance of secondary industry in the past two decades, modifications in classroom organization have, in fact, included many programs explicitly designed to regroup children and teachers, curriculum and study units, in an effort to reverse the trends toward differentiation, classification and complex time scheduling (DHEW 1971c). Open classrooms and school without walls may be viewed as more extreme examples of this phenomenon.

Still another difference marked by this shift in the employment market for human skills is found in newer cognitive requirements. Primary and secondary industry produce tangible products: They, therefore, require an object orientation among their workers. This object orientation has, in fact, been associated in time with the dominance of primary and secondary industry, and it is found in objective form in standarized tests of intelligence and achievement (Cohen 1967). Third and fourth sector products, however--services and creative enterprises--require the development of inter-personal and intra-personal orientations (Menaker 1965). A school system to serve an employment market with a growing dominance of these latter kinds of expectations then, could reasonably be expected to develop subject-oriented curricula which are substantially different from more traditional object-oriented ones. The spread of "affective curricula" is an example of this regard.

It is of note that there has been no pervasive shift in the use of such modifications in classroom management or curricula as those mentioned above. In general, where they are provided, they appear side-by-side with the more conventional classrooms and curricula. Open schools or schools without walls may appear in the same school districts as do more conventional ones; and open classrooms and affective curricula appear in the same schools on the same grade levels as other styles of schooling (DHEW 1971c). If the objectives of the two types of schooling are as consistent with occupational involvement as they appear to be,[33] in choosing one or the other, parents are at the same time not only reflecting their own interests and occupational concerns, but they are also selecting in which sector of the economy their children will be engaged as adults.

The conclusions of this section are, then, clear. Organizationally, educational functions have been placed within a service context. It both provides services, and, in addition to its other objectives, it is expected to produce service

personnel, and service users in increasing numbers. The unique
consortium of agencies which make up the Department of Health,
Education and Welfare has influenced this purpose by redefining
the objectives of educational agencies; by multiple, combined
programs; and by the use of the school as an arena for service
agency intervention. The character of the "grants economy" on
which schools are increasingly dependent, is also consistent
with this effort in requiring the flexibility and the change in
interpersonal relationships which characterize service systems.
In addition, in these past two decades a shift in the dominance
of the employment market for which human capital is developed
has occurred, one in which secondary industry has lost its
dominance, and service and fourth sector industry are increasingly influential. The trend seems to indicate that the conditions under which educational institutions, in providing
services, may effectively be able to produce services users and
service personnel as well.

Changing Education Expectations

The spread of certain types of innovations in classroom management and curricula have been marked. Some reasons
for their widespread application may be found in the national
scope of educational decision making and in its rational
methods.[34] Federal concerns have focused, in part, on the
involvement of previously school-deviant pupil populations and,
in part, on stimulating the development of service skills among
children to meet changing occupational needs. The use of "open
classrooms" in addition to conventional discussions, and the
use of "affective curricula" as well as "cognitive (Analytic)
curricula" are, therefore, relevant innovations. If empirical
associations between group organization and the organization
of cognition remain reliable (Cohen 1967), and if the affective
curricula are as different from traditional curricula as they
appear now to be, such innovative programs may be expected to
produce children who are qualitatively different from those in
traditional classrooms. If in addition, the social cognitive
expectations of open classrooms and affective curricula are
used as sole standards of effective education, they may
qualitatively redefine dominant educational expectations. On
the other hand, if such school modifications remain as alternatives only to traditional schooling they may enlarge the
bases of innovation among pupils and increase the adaptability
of society to change.
An example of the close association between the
organization of the classroom and the organization of thought
may be found in the relationship between the formal style of
the conventional classroom and its formal, or Analytic, requirements for cognitive performance. For example, to the
extent that one can speak of school organization as typical,

the typical 1950's school may be viewed as a "formal" organization in the same sense that one speaks of a business as a formal organization. Among its other characteristics, roles had been formally and impersonally defined; there were clear career paths into various positions in an organizational plan; and the patterns of social change characteristically had proceeded in a formal fashion in the direction of greater differentiation and specialization of functions and toward the increased specificity of status-role expectations. Curricula had also proceeded through the process of differentation and specialization of subject matter; teacher training programs had differentiated and specialized, producing teacher specialists to accomodate the differentiating curriculum; textbook manufacturers had produced progressively differentiated and specialized teaching materials to accomodate the programs; pupils had been differentiated and homogeously grouped; and school buildings had been designed with walled-in cubicles so that classified subjects could be taught to classified pupils by classified teachers using classified materials, without undue interference. Where pupils populations were small or not so varied, the degree of differentiation in their schools was less than where pupils populations were large and varied, but the formal organization of the school and its patterns of change had remained reasonably constant for several generations. The similarity of the social organization of the school to that of dominant occupational settings had been so marked that, until the 1950's, schools were called "factory model schools" (NYEFLR 1968).

Not only had the social organization of the school been formally organized, but also its cognitive expectations for the performance of pupils had been "formal." In other studies, this formal structure of cognition has been called the "Analytic conceptual style," (Cohen 1969) or by other authors, a "logico-analytic" approach to problem identification and solution (Gardner, et al. 1959). Formal expectations has been embedded in standardized tests of intelligence and achievement, in curriculum construction, in less definitive expectations for pupil behavior, and in the identification of "self" and "referent others" (Cohen and Hartley 1969). Formal expectations had been reflected also in the value placed on the use of Standard English (Cohen 1967).

Rules of the formal or Analytic conceptual style are also rules of Standard English as well as the rules of formal social organization. Attributes of objects or stimuli have formal, long lasting or relatively stable meanings; in Standard English, words and parts of speech also have these characteristics as do status-roles in a formal social organization. Each has a similarly formal, long-lasting and relatively stable set of relationships with other attributes, words or parts of speech, and other status-roles. The process of change in each of the above frames of reference--cognitive, linguistic or social organizational, has been toward greater specificity of their definition. In cognition, the greater the differentiation of a concept, the more specific the lower level concepts; in social organization, the greater the status-role specialization, the greater the specificity of role expectations. The same or similar rules had appeared in multiple contexts and they had had a tendency to reinforce each other in processes of thought. That is, the rules of social organization, the rules of language use, and the rules for cognitive performance had produced a coherent set of formal expectations in the school (Cohen 1967). But if any reinforcing context were to change--the organization of teachers and pupils, the structure of the curriculum, the requirements for language use or the cognitive expectations for performance--at the least, the capacity of that context to reinforce the formal conceptual style would have been lost. At the most, if any context for reinforcement had been radically altered, depending upon the kind of alteration, a conflict of reality organization might be induced in pupils, or the creation in them of another conceptual style.

Requirements for the Analytic conceptual style had been identified long before these two decades of change; they were the bases on which the rational planning of materials and teaching methods had been based.[35] But during the late 1950's and early 1960's the rules of three additional styles were identified: the Flexible, Concrete, and Relational styles. Each of the non-Analytic styles was similarly associated with and appropriate within non-formal styles of social organization; each style was associated with an unique language style among its users; and each conceptual style was associated with related kinds of behavior patterns (Cohen 1971a).

Conceptual styles, appear to be important determinants of behavior, beliefs and values (Cohen 1967). They appear to determine the possible and permissible relationships among objects and peoples, among people and among objects. They also control the perceptual distance between the observer and the observed, thus controlling the subjectivity-objectivity of individuals, and regulating their sense of control of, or powerlessness within, different kinds of environments. Since the conceptual styles were so closely associated with the styles of social organization within which they were appropriate, it was believed that, should the style of social organization of a group change, the conceptual styles of the individuals who participate in it would also change. Such changes have in fact been observed, both in natural contexts and in experimental ones.[36]

The rules of conceptual organization may also become institutional definitions of acceptable pupil performance and pupil deviance. Individuals who use the different styles tend to produce "anti-other" discriminators out of the rules of their styles--objective methods for devaluing individuals who are carriers of different styles, and who, therefore, have different behavioral characteristics. This phenomenon of producing objective "anti-other" discriminators was most marked among the carriers of the mutually incompatible Analytic and Relational conceptual styles. The carriers of the two styles could verbalize distinctive feelings of disgust and rejection for both the cognitive output and the behavioral characteristics of individuals who used the other styles (Cohen 1971b).

When "anti-other" discriminators have been depersonalized and established as performance criteria in a given setting, they may be viewed as "institutional anti-other discriminators." The pre-1950's schools had, indeed, established the Analytic conceptual style as its standard for cognitive performance, and the set of Analytically related socio-behavioral characteristics of its carriers as its model for conforming behavior among pupils. In doing so, it had at the same time identified alternate styles of conceptual organization and social performance as "deviant" by institutional definition. The Analytic cognitive expectations of pupils had been built into quite objective, standardized tests of intelligence and achievement, and into teaching materials and teaching methods. The socio-behavioral correlates of the Analytic conceptual style had similarly been built into less structured, but no less stringent, social requirements like attendance, punctuality of general citizenship expectations. Both the cognitive and socio-behavioral characteristics of individuals who were carriers of non-Analytic styles, separately and together, had been devalued in the school, by institutional definition (Cohen 1971b).

The extent to which such formal definitions of appropriate behavior were consistent with non-school expectation for behavior is reflected in settings other than the school. For instance, in a study of correctional institutions for youth, only a handful of pupils in them were carriers of the highly valued Analytic conceptual style;[37] and in a community employment skills center directed toward the rehabiliation of the poor, none was a carrier of this style.[38] The institutionally defined "anti-other" discriminators of the important Analytic style and its related formal social organization of individuals around tasks had acted, thus, as important facilitators for highly Analytic individuals, and important barriers to the involvement of individuals who were carriers of non-Analytic conceptual styles.

A major direction of innovative school programming in the past two decades has been toward the inclusion of many Analytically defined deviants into school contexts, by so modifying classroom organization that what had previously been considered deviant pupil behavior could be accommodated. The "open" classroom, "schools without walls" and "invisible schools" were efforts to do so. The choice of "affective curricula" over

Analytic curricula has been a similar effort (DHEW 1971). If
the suggestions of earlier research can be supported with large
numbers of children, i.e. if a change in any of the independent
learning contexts of the school (classroom organization, cognitive, language or behavioral expectations for performance)
were to change from those defined as formal, the conceptual
styles of children schooled in them could be expected to change
as well--then the characterisitcs of pupils who learn in the
"open" classroom with "affective" curricula could be expected
to be cognitive and behaviorally different from those who emerge
from schools of a consistently formal type.

The impact of a given style of classroom management on
cognition is complex.[39] For instance, in addition to the cognitive requirements of the formally organized school, other,
more subtle, social requirements had been expected to be
internalized by pupils as well. One such expectation was that
children will develop a boxed-in notion of personal space. This
personal space notion is taught subliminally by school architecture which separates learning space into areas and rooms
devoted to certain classes or uses. In the classroom, each
pupil has a personal space circumscribed by his desk or his
chair. The door to his personal space faces the teacher who
may enter at will; but casting his eyes sideways or backwards,
i.e. assuming other doors, is severely discouraged.[40] The
notion of classified physical spaces is intended to be reflected
in the classified conceptual spaces occupied by certain subjects and subject units.

This structural infra-curriculum is drastically revised
in the "open classroom." The "open classroom" not only provides
for the breakdown of barriers around the personal spaces of the
pupils and classes, but for their dissolution around subject
areas and units of study as well. The personal spaces of pupils
are assumed to have no rigid barriers i.e., they may be entered
by anyone from any direction by glances, gestures, by verbal
expression or by personal contact. Similarly, the mode of
thinking promoted by these social rules leads away from formal
classification of thought, in the direction of free association
and the flexible reformulation of subjects and units. In the
open classroom, also, the definitions of conforming and deviant
behavior are reversed over those previously held. The loner in
the open classroom is viewed as deviant, as are those who hold
to a preplanned course of action or thought.[41]

A second kind of subliminal influence of the formal
school is related to its intricate but formally designed time
schedule. Despite its complexity, it has a rhythm of its own
which is unrelated to natural rhythms e.g. the weather or the
seasons. Circular patterns of Monday-Wednesday-Friday classes,
Tudesday gym, Auditorium every other Friday, Midsemester and
final examinations and so forth, create an internalized notion
of pattern-on-pattern time scheduling, all Analytically or

formally defined, and planned for optimum school performance. Certain aspects of highly rationalized micro-teaching provide for an even more intricate patterning based on intervals of seconds in teaching. Certainly, syllabus units are rhythmically planned as well. One of the important characteristics of the formally organized school is the teaching of this intricate time schedule, and some schools (and factories) of the past decades were designed without windows so as to more completely isolate these task rhythms from outside influences.

Task rhythms control the level of stimulation in the school as well as its organization (Office of Education 1966). The more heterogeneous the population and the more varied its curriculum, the more complex its time scheduling and the higher its level of stimulation. Pupils who enter large urban schools from the less differentiated time patterns of the rural school may be unnerved by the high level of stimulation in them; conversely, pupils who move from highly differentiated urban schools to those in rural areas may find them boring. These reactions are entirely unrelated to the quality of the curriculum or of the teachers. Pupils apparently become socialized to a complex time schedule and a controlled level of stimulation governed by pupil heterogeneity and curriculum differentiation (structural characteristics of the school) as well as to its content.

Without changing the basic nature of the curriculum, then, the open classroom drastically alters these rhythms. Without increasing pupil heterogeneity or curriculum complexity, because they provide for open personal and curriculum spaces, "open classrooms" breakdown the rational task-rhythms of the formal classroom, and, they increase the level of stimulation. This phenomenon is even more marked in "schools without walls.[42]

A third subliminal component of the traditional school has been its objectivity. The important relationship promoted by the school has been that between the pupil and his task. School architecture and methods of classroom management has been designed to promote this relationship, and the teacher appeared mainly as a tool of the learning process. The "open classroom" and its expectations for the development of interpersonal relationships shift this focuses toward greater subjectivity and interpersonal sensitivity.

The shift in focus from objectivity to subjectivity is made explicit in the "affective curriculum" (NCTE 1969). The "affective curriculum," as its name suggests, provides for the development of pupil sensitivity to inter-personal cues and for the increase in pupils' knowledge of a wider range of their own emotional responses as well as those of other pupils. A simple example of affective study units is that of the widely used "I-units" of study. They allocate instructional time and syllabus units to practice in sending and receiving "I messages"--verbal expressions of feelings. Affective curricula require modified teacher preparation, the evidences of which are found in the increasing concentration of Regional Laboratories on sensitivity group activity as an important aspect of the learning process, and in the increasing use by teachers of Workshops which provide for increased skills in manipulating group processes. Clinical staff which are provided through the linkages of health and welfare agencies with the school are now more needed and much more widely available, than they had been two decades ago, for a wider range of pupils.[43]

Affective curricula are intended to develop subject-oriented children--a major departure from the required objectivity of two decades ago. The "open classroom" and "affective curricula" together can be expected to decrease the perceptual distance between the observer and the observed in pupils, over that developed by Analytic curricula; to increase inter-personal sensitivity through requiring their response to non-verbal cues; to require the verbalization of feelings and motivation; to increase stimulation in the class from sources unrelated to the cognitive syllabus; and to the breakdown of the barriers around pupils, classes, subject matter, and curricula.[44] At the least, these changes in classroom organization and curriculum objectives fail to reinforce the formal expectations which are built into Analytically designed curricula and expectations. At the most, they may be expected to produce, in pupils, one of the subject-oriented conceptual styles.

The particular characteristics of cognitive processes mentioned do not represent merely the choice of pupils not to use Analytic cognitive skills, but, rather, the positive requirement of one of the subject-oriented styles. In addition, it is not surprising that subject oriented styles with their inter-personal or intra-personal rules are associated with many service and fourth-sector occupations. Each of the four styles had apparently served for some time as a medium both for self-selection into, and as selection criteria into, various kinds of occupations. Carriers of the Analytic and Concrete, object-oriented styles, had selected themselves into, and had been selected into, object-oriented occupations; and the Flexible and Ralational style carriers (self-and other-oriented individuals) had selected themselves into and had been selected into, interpersonally demanding settings, even with educational level and occupational skills held constant. Highly Analytic individuals had been found most frequently in the basic sciences and in larger, more highly differentiated, commercial enterprises; Concrete style carriers were found in the applied fields or in settings where work is done alone, as in small businesses, as postmen and craftsmen, or in rural settings. Flexible style carriers were found in the helping professions and in personal service occupations (and, of special interest, mostly among females); and Relational style carriers were found most often in the creative and performing arts, in sensitivity group leader-

202

ship, and in many deviant occupations (Cohen and Hartley 1969).
These relationships would suggest that certain kinds of occupations and occupational settings both expect and reward the
use of certain definitive kinds of cognitive and social skills
for role performance, and that the requirements of the work
and social settings in which work is done are valued by individuals who seek satisfaction in their work.[45] Such curricular innovations, then, as the open classroom and the affective
curricula are functional counterparts of a developing service
orientation in the school, and the provision of such alternatives for learning in the school is consistent with the recent
shifts to third and fourth sector dominance of the employment
market. They are undoubtedly supported by increasing numbers
of service staff who are now available in school because of
the health and welfare linkages with educational agencies; and
they appear broadly appropriate to the inclusion of service
pupil populations (e.g. handicapped, or emotionally disturbed)
in the school. It is for reasons like those mentioned above
that such innovations as the "open classroom" and "affective
curricula" are viewed as significant themes in school change.

Questions which remain involve the impact of these
alternative methods of schooling on the culture of the school,
and on the dominant culture of the population at large. If
the objectified rules of the subject oriented cognitive styles
were to become institutional anti-group discriminators in the
school, for instance, i.e. if they may be expected to define
conforming and deviant behavior in similar fashion to the
manner in which the Analytic criteria were formerly used--one
could anticipate a growing anti-intellectualism as its product.
One could also anticipate the breakdown of formal methods of
social organization around tasks (the breakdown of bureaucracy)
and a reversal of the status systems which now exist. However,
so long as both alternatives to schooling are available to
children--the formal and the open classroom--so long as both
types of curricula are available--the formal and the affective--
each with equal value, so long as social and behavioral science
research will continue to produce research concerning the
rational development of relevant curricula and methods for all
alternatives in schooling and the intended and unintended
consequences of each, such alternatives in classroom management
and curricula may serve the changing purposes of a rapidly
changing society.

Conclusions

During the past two decades, schooling processes have
undergone widespread and sometimes radical changes. Because a
major impetus toward school reforms emanates from the executive
branch of the federal government, change has been rapid, impactful, broadly based and rational. Some of its major direc-

tions have been determined by the tri-part post which combine the purposes of health, education and welfare agencies, by the character of the "grants economy" on which schools have become increasingly dependent, and by a shift in the employment market from a dominance of secondary industry to that of third and fourth sector industry. These multiple influences have stimulated the spread of certain kinds of school innovations like the "open classroom" and "affective curricula." If behaviors associated with these innovations should become sole standards of effective schooling however, they may mark a major school redefinition. To the extent that they may replace earlier models of education, they may also redefine institutional definitions of conforming and deviant behavior in such a way as to influence the character of the dominant culture. When alternatives in the social and cognitive requirements of schools are presented, however, they may be viewed as serving multiple purposes, increasing the bases of innovation among pupils, and when used in life occupations, increasing the capacity of society to adapt to change.

NOTES

1. See National Educational Finance Project Reports, Washington, D.C., NEFP, 1970 and 1971. See also the Report of the Educational Policies Committee, Washington, D.C., 1956. See also Intergovernmental Relations and the Governance of Education, Washington, D.C., 1970.

2. Elementary and Secondary Education Act Amendments (20 U.S.C. 1232a) Enacted April 13, 1970, P.L. 91-230, Title IV, sec. 401 (a) (10), 84 Stat. 169. "... no provision... shall be construed to authorize any department, agency, officer or employee of the United States to exercise any direction, supervision, or control over the curriculum, program of instruction, administration, or personnel of any educational institution, school, or school system, or over the selection of library resources, textbooks, or other printed or other published instructional materials by an educational institution or school system, or to require the assignment or transportation of students or teachers in order to overcome racial imbalance."

3. See U. S. Government Organizational Manual, 1970-71, Washington, D.C.: Office of the Federal Register. Regulations codified under "Office of Education - Code of Federal Regulations," Title 45, Chapter I.

4. Acts, March 2, 1867, ch. 158, sec. 2, 14 Stat. 434.

5. (20 U.S.C.1) Enacted June 22, 1874 as R.S. 516, 18 Stat. 84 (18 Stat. 85 rev. ed.).

6. Title XI, "The Department of the Interior," Chapter IX, sec. 516.

7. Prepared by the President and transmitted to the Senate and the House of Representatives in Congress assembled

April 25, 1939, pursuant to the provisions of the Reorganization Act of 1939, approved April 3, 1939, effective July 1, 1939. Reorganization Plan No. 1. Federal Security Agency, secs. 201 - 211.

8. Reorganization Plan No. 1 of 1953, prepared by the President and transmitted to the Senate and the House of Representatives in Congress assembled, March 12, 1953 pursuant to the provisions of the Reorganization Act of 1949, approved June 20, 1949 as ammended. Department of Health, Education and Welfare Sections 1 - 9, effective April 11, 1953.

9. Publications of the Education and Labor Committee, U.S. House of Representatives. A compilation of Federal Education Laws is printed and distributed for each Congress by the U.S. Government Printing Office for use by the House Committee on Education and Labor. See also Manpower Reports of the President, 1961 - 1963, Washington, D.C., in appropriate years for history.

10. See Reports of the Secretary's Committee on Mental Retardation, U.S. Dept. of HEW in appropriate years or under individual programs.

11. No state may make laws which are contrary to federal law or which limit the power of the federal government.

12. Executive Order 11513. Economic Opportunity Act, 1964. See also EOA Amendments of 1969, P.L. 91-177, Dec. 30, 1969, 83 Stat. 827-833. This kind of equalization is sometimes called "fiscal neutrality."

13. This approach is not new. A Presidential Committee on Economy and Efficiency was first established by an Act of Congress, approved June 25, 1910.

14. An approach to this effort is found in Schultz, J. W., "The Human Capital Approach to Education," in Johns, R. L., Goffman, I. J., Alexander, K. and Stollar, D. H., (eds), Economic Factors Affecting the Financing of Education, Washington, D.C., U.S. Government Printing Office, 1971. It deals with 1) human capital economics, 2) economic accounting for schools, and 3) economics of discrimination.

15. The sense in which "marginality" is used in this literature has none of the social system or reference group connotations of the social sciences. It refers only to continum measures on which school costs and measures of educational attainment are placed. Those school districts whose fiscal capacity falls below an arbitrary cut-off point below which schools cannot offer minimal educational services, or below which a given proportion of pupils cannot attain minimal levels of performance, are viewed as "marginal."

16. The Serrano Decision, California Supreme Court, 1971. U.S. District Courts in Texas and Minnesota and the Superior Court in New Jersey also questioned the sole reliance of schools on local property taxes as they affect the raising and distribution of funds for schools, but the suits were struck

down.

17. See also Public School Finance; Present Disparities and Fiscal Alternatives, Report for the Pres. Comm. on School Finance, 1971.

18. See also federal legislation concerning the strengthening of support to state educational agencies. ESEA Title V (20 U.S.C. 862) Enacted April 11, 1965.

19. See federal legislation concerning public appropriations to non-public schools for limited purposes.

20. See Education of the Disadvantaged, Wash., D.C., U.S. Government Printing Office, 1970, an evaluative report on Title I, ESEA, and Financial Implications of Changing Patterns of Non-public School Operations in Four Cities. Wash., D.C., USGPO, 1970.

21. Possibly the widely discussed possibility of a National Institute of Education.

22. Department of HEW, legislation cited in footnote 8.

23. A statement in this regard from the Presidential Commission on School Finance, constituted under Executive Order 11513 (March 3, 1970) was as follows: "The interrelationships among governments, institutions and people...must, and do, provide means for reform...The Constitution makes no reference to education as such, implying without question that it is a responsibility retained by the States. But in its Preamble, the Constitution seeks to 'promote the general welfare,' and 'secure the blessings of liberty to ourselves and to our posterity.' In that way, it assigns the Federal Government a significant role in education, which surely is an ingredient of 'the general welfare."

24. An example of efforts to control both the size and the social composition of schools through residential requirements may be found in the Newtown experiments. Through residential controls requiring that Newtowns include all age groups, an effort is made to provide for a steady flow of pupils into the community schools without overcrowding; and residentially controlled interracial and interclass populations are to provide for similar social mixtures in the schools. See legislative framework emerging from the Office of Research and Technology, Department of HUD, 701 (b) of Housing Act of 1954, as ammended 40 U.S.C. 461.

25. Public Law 88-164, Senate 1576. 88th Congress, October 31, 1963; Mental Health Centers Construction Act of 1963. It arose out of the President's Message to Congress, U. S. Congressional Record, 88th Congress, 1st session, 1963, CIX, Part 2, 1744-49 and as H. R. Cec., 1963.

26. A social Security measure which went into effect the first of the year requires that each child be issued a Social Security (identification) number when he enters school. Numbering is to begin in 1974 and to completed by 1980.

27. The experimental personality assessment form in

use now by the National Association of Secondary School Princi-
pals includes "emotional stability" as a criterion for recommen-
dation for higher education. The form is filled out by teachers,
and the principal interprets the assessment and signs his name.

    28.   Most states have accelerated Rehabilitation Dis-
position programs administered by State Supreme Court Criminal
Procedures Rules Committees. They are often expressly adopted
for pre-trial case dispositions.

    29.   Portland, Oregon, and Detroit, Michigan.

    30.   Using two variables, symmetrical or assymentrical
units and back and forth movements or one-sided movements of
goods and services, the authors describe three types of economic
systems, Reciprocity, Exchange and Redistribution. One empty
cell completed a two-by-two chart. The characteristics of the
Redistribution arrangements and those of the empty cell were
similar in the one-sided movements of goods and services,
representing a dissociation between producing and consuming.

    31.   The reader is referred to the bibliography attached
to the Boulding article.

    32.   Most significant is the high level of interde-
pendence which secondary industry requires. For instance, ore
is taken from the ground, smelted, mixed with other ore, made
into "pigs," rolled into sheets, combined with rubber, plastic,
glass, paint and so forth and made into hundreds of different
articles in hundreds of different places. Between processes,
transportation moves materials multiple times both internally
and externally, requiring a widely distributed clerical, commercial, industrial complex of tasks. Secondary industry
requires multiple operations, performed by individuals with a
variety of special skills and abilities, widely distributed
over space, but linked together in an intricate pattern on
pattern of activities, highly time-schedulled in such a way
that each operation or combination of operations may flow-
charged to completion. Yet no one in the complex of activities
can be rewarded for his efforts until the final products are
completed and marketed. This structural interdependence is
reflected in the school.

    33.   The reader is referred to the following section
on conceptual styles.

    34.   The point is that, given the rationality of
decision making for the schools, the development of those
skills which are in greatest need in the employment market
will continue to be supported and rewarded in program developments.

    35.   Any standard text on curriculum theory makes the
linkage explicit.

    36.   Many observations of changes in conceptual styles
under natural and experimental conditions have been reported in
program documents by Wynona Hartley and her associates at the
Greater Kansas City Mental Health Foundation and the University

of Kansas Medical School as well as by the author.

37. Five out of 450 boys and girls, ages 9 to 17 in 1969. Youth Development Center Study, Penna. Department of Corrections Grant to the Graduate School of Social Work, University of Pittsburgh, 1969, unpublished paper.

38. Opportunities Industrialization Center Program Documents reporting the analyses of data concerning all students in selected programs in a two year period from 1968 - 1970.

39. The following observations are drawn from yet unpublished studies by the author comparing subliminal effects of traditional and open classrooms on cognition among elementary school pupils.

40. The notion of personal space among individuals is not unique to the school. Similar notions of the bounded social spaces of the classroom and its subject matter are found in occupational settings in the ideas of "work space," "desk," "position," "job," "professional turf," and in health care settings as "specialization," "condition limited cases," "heart ward" and so forth.

41. Unpublished study of private schools using affective curriculas as sole standards of pupil performance by Cohen, Rosalie, MS.

42. Refer to footnote 39.

43. See evaluation of programs developed and disseminated by the Philadelphia Regional Laboratory, Research for Better Schools, Philadelphia, Pa.

44. Analysis of early outcomes of open classrooms and affective curricula suggest that both of the above processes may be taking place. They indicate that the open classroom results in greater responsiveness on the parts of pupils and more social involvement, but also in greatly reduced depth and length of concentration, less objectivity, less structured curiosity, decreasing confidence in the ability to tackle intellectual tasks alone and a growing dependence upon group. Of special note in the observation of such pupil differences is the work of Joseph Bogen and his associates at the Ross-Loos Medical Group in Los Angeles. They call Analytic thinking and the alternate subject-oriented styles "Propositional and Appositional Thinking" and find that the two styles of thought arise from the stimulation and development of different hemispheres of the brain. An exemplary citation is "The Other Side of the Brain II: An Appositional Mind," Bulletin of the Los Angeles Neurological Societies, Vol. 34, No. 3, July, 1969.

45. The four styles are also associated with a wide variety of socio-behavioral correlates in their users which had acted as criteria for "belonging" in the groups in which they were appropriate.

REFERENCES

Boulding, Kenneth
    1970   Factors affecting the Future Demand for
                    Education In Economic Factors Affecting the
                    Financing of Education, R. L. Johns, I. J.
                    Goffman, K. Alexander, and D. H. Stollar, eds.
                    Washington, D.C.

Bowen, Hugh M.
    1964   Rational Design. Darien, Conn. Dunlap and
                    Associates.

Cohen, Rosalie
    1967   Primary Group Structure, Conceptual Styles and
                    School Achievement. Monograph of the Center for
                    Psycho-Social Studies, Learning Research and
                    Development Center, University of Pittsburgh,
                    Study 1.
    1969   Conceptual Styles, Culture Conflict and Non-
                    verbal Tests of Intelligence, Amer. Anthro-
                    pologist, Vol. 71, No. 5.
    1971   Conceptual Styles and Measures of Learning
                    Ability, American Anthropologist Special Issue
                    on Race and Intelligence, S. Tax, G. Gamble and
                    J. Bond, eds.
    1971   Anti-Other Discriminators As Derivatives of
                    Conceptual Rules, mimeo.

Cohen, Rosalie and Wynone S. Hartley
    1969   The Role of Primary Group Structure in the
                    Development of Values, Paper read at the
                    American Sociol. Assoc. meetings.

Department of Health, Education and Welfare
    1966   National Education Finance Report. Washington,
                    D.C.
    1970   Welfare Eligibility: A National Survey.
                    Washington, D.C.
    1971a   National Educational Finance Report.
                    Washington, D.C.
    1971b   People Serving People. Washington, D.C.
    1971c   National Educational Research Report.
                    Washington, D.C.
    1972a   1970 Annual Report. Washington, D.C.
    1972b   People Serving People, Washington, D.C.

Freeman, Orville
    1967   Malthus, Marx and the North American Bread-
                    basket In Foreign Affairs, p. 587.

Gardner, Riley, P. S. Holzman, G. S. Klein, H. B. Linton and
D. P. Spence
    1959   Cognitive Control: A Study of Individual
                Consistencies in Cognitive Behavior, Psy-
                chological Issues, 1, 4.

Goffman, Irving, J. R. Davis and J. F. Morrad
    1971   The Concept of Education as an Investment In
                Economic Report of the President. Washington,
                D.C.

Menaker, Esther and William
    1965   Ego in Evolution. New York: Grove Press.

National Center for Educational Research and Development
    1969   Educational Research and Development in the
                U. S. Washington, D.C.
    1970   Educational Research and Development in the
                U. S. Washington, D.C.

National Commission on Teacher Education
    1969   Provoking Change in Education. Washington, D.C.

National Educational Research Conference
    1970   Proceedings. New York.

Office of Education
    1966   Education in the United States: Structure and
                Organization. Washington, D.C. U. S. Printing
                Office.

Polanyi, Karl (ed.)
    1957   Trade and Market in Early Feudal Empires,
                New York: Free Press.

President's Commission on School Finance
    1972   Schools, People, and Money: The Need of
                Educational Reform. Neil McElroy, Chairman.
                Washington.

Rostow, W. W.
    1960   The Stages of Economic Growth. Forge Village,
                Mass., Cambridge University Press.

ON THE EVOLUTION OF EDUCATION[1]

H. Clyde Wilson
University of Missouri-Columbia

Indeed, education as practiced in a given society and considered at a given moment of its evolution, is a totality of practices, of ways of doing things, of customs which constitute perfectly defined facts and which have the same reality as other social facts -- Emile Durkheim.

Introduction

The task of this essay is to develop a framework for a study of the evolution of education. To this end I shall attempt to establish a set of criteria upon which the evolutionary stages of education may be established and to trace in broad outline a sequence of evolutionary stages of education from the least developed cultures to the most advanced. The basic concepts underlying this study were stated by Durkheim (1956:95-98) over fifty years ago:

Educational practices are not phenomena that are isolated from one another; rather, for a given society, they are bound up in the same system all the parts of which contribute toward the same end: it is the system of education suitable to this country and to this time. Each people has its own, as it has its own moral, religious, economic system, etc. But on the other hand, peoples of the same kind, that is to say, people who resemble one another with respect to essential characteristics of their constitution, should practice comparable systems of education. The similarities in their general organization should necessarily lead to others of equal importance in their educational organization. Consequently, through comparison, by abstracting the similarities and eliminating the differences from them, one can certainly establish the generic types of education which correspond to the different types of societies... Once the types were established, we would have to explain them, that is to say, to seek out the conditions on which the characteristic traits of each of them depended, and how they have emerged from one another. One would thus obtain the laws which govern the evolution of systems of education. One

211

would be able to perceive, then, both how education developed and what the causes are which have determined this development and which account for it.

Durkheim's grand program for a study of the evolution of education has not been realized; this paper is only an initial step toward his goal.

Several concepts underlying this study must be discussed in order to provide a background for understanding the development of the evolutionary stages of education as attempted here. These are the nature of culture, the nature of evolution, and the nature of education.[2]

The Nature of Culture

'Culture' is defined here as a class of phenomena dependent upon man's ability for articulate or symbolic speech (White 1949:139-140). This class has four characteristics which are important for the problem at hand. First, culture is considered to be "superorganic," and, therefore, a distinct order of phenomena analytically separable from the biological factors of man (Kroeber 1917; Kroeber and Kluckhohn 1963:289; White 1949; Durkheim 1938). This means, without denying the importance of that part of psychological theory which has its roots in biology, we may proceed with this study with the assumption that the physiological bases for learning, perception, and so on, do not vary from population to population and are not factors in explaining cultural variation. Further, this point of view emphasizes the role of the cultural tradition in determining human behavior and minimizes the role of the individual: "There is no man who can make a society have, at a given moment, a system of education other than that which is implied in its structure, just as it is impossible for a living organism to have other organs and other functions than those which are implied in its constitution" (Durkheim 1956:94).

Second, culture is transmitted from one generation to the next by symbolic behavior and, therefore, must be acquired or learned anew by each generation from the preceding generation. This characteristic of culture has probably impressed anthropologists the most. It was stated explicitly in Tylor's classic definition of culture and has been emphasized repeatedly in later definitions (see Kroeber and Kluckhohn 1963). If a cultural tradition is continued, then every aspect of that culture must be transmitted in detail to the succeeding generation. The means by which this transmission is accomplished is the point where the interests of the anthropologists and the educationalists are as one. In this paper the fact of cultural transmission will be an important consideration in defining "education" and in establishing criteria for a typology of education.

Third, culture is cumulative; each successive generation

builds upon the past. This allows the next generation to begin
where the last generation left off. This characteristic should
be manifested in a tendency for the number or types of education
to increase with time. Another implication of this characteristic of culture is that emergent cultural forms are determined
to a large extent by the preceding cultural forms: "Our most
fruitful innovations consist very often of casting new ideas in
old molds, which it is sufficient to modify partially in order
to adapt them to their new content" (Durkheim 1956:145-146).

The fourth characteristic of culture to be considered
is that culture is an adaptive mechanism. Man like other
animals must adapt to his environment. While other animals
adapt primarily by biological mechanisms, man adapts primarily
by culture. Selection is inherent in any adaptive process, and
the implication here is that the particular types of cultural
adaptation are finite and knowable; therefore, the types of
educational systems are finite and knowable. Further, given
the requirements which must be met in the adaptive process, the
types of educational systems which would meet these requirements
would fall into a narrowly determinable range.

The class "culture" may be divided into three parts --
objects, acts, and ideas (White 1949:130-140; Parsons 1951:4;
Huxley 1958:437). A number of social scientists, beginning
with Alfred Weber in 1920 and including Murdock, MacIver,
Kroeber, and White, have suggested these three divisions of
culture make-up the three sub-systems of a cultural system --
technology (objects), society or social organization (acts),
and ideology (ideas) (Kroeber 1952:152-166; Kroeber and Kluckhohn 1963:182-190). Studies of culture may concentrate upon
one of these sub-systems, some combination of two of them, or
attempt to deal with all three as a total cultural system.
This paper will be concerned with only two of these sub-systems,
technology and society. Technology is regarded as that part of
culture which is most immediately involved in the adaptive
process between man and his environment. If technology is not
the primary determinant of the other two sub-systems of a
culture, as White (1959:33-57) has strongly argued, it at least
sets definite limits upon the range of variation possible for
society and ideology. A consideration of technology had the
additional advantage in that in establishing levels of cultural
development, technology appears now to have the greatest possibility of being objectively quantified or ranked. The classification of levels of cultural development used in this paper
is based to a large extent upon technological factors (Beardsley
et al. 1956:134).

If technology is the primary means by which man,
through the use of objects (e.g., tools) adapts to his environment, then society is the primary means by which human relations
are organized to carry out this adaptive process. This adaptive
process of society includes such obvious things as a division of

213

labor and means of controlling production, distribution, and consumption, to less obvious things such as the formation of social groups from rules of descent, rules of marriage, and rules of post-marital residence. Education is primarily a set of social acts, a part of society, because it is through social interaction that the process of cultural transmission occurs. Thus, in this paper, both the definition of education and the criteria for establishing educational types are derived from the societal sub-system of culture.

The third sub-system of culture, ideology, will not be considered directly. This is not to deny the importance of systems of beliefs, sentiments, values, ethics, and so on, which are a part of ideology. Durkheim (1956:70-71) considered the transmission of ideas to the child one of the primary functions of education. Further, throughout all of his works he emphasized the role of "collective ideas and sentiments" in maintaining the social order and in providing a basis for the continuation of the social order from one generation to the next. Problems arise, however, when one attempts to apply an evolutionary scheme to the sub-system of ideology. I know of no generally accepted evolutionary order for ideology comparable to those used for technology and society. Developmental schemes relating society or technology to ideology deal with only limited aspects of ideology rather than ideology as a whole. Swanson (1964) and Gouldner and Peterson (1962) deal with certain aspects of society and technology in relation to religious beliefs in primitive societies, and the classification of Beardsley et al. used in this study limit their discussion of ideology to a category that they label "ceremonialism." In light of these considerations I have chosen to limit my study to the technological and social sub-systems of culture.

The Nature of Evolution

The concept 'evolution' has had a long and varied career in cultural anthropology (vide White 1945, Harris 1968, and Sahlins 1960). Much of the recent discussion of 'evolution' has attempted to distinguish the concept 'evolution' from the concept 'history' and to differentiate between such terms as unilinear and multilineal evolution, general and specific evolution, and so on. The distinction between 'evolution' and 'history' is of major importance for this study; a "history of education" is not the same thing as an "evolution of education," and a study in one of these frameworks should not be judged in terms of the other.

The difference between 'history' and 'evolution' depends upon different concepts of 'time.' History is concerned with a temporal scale which is independent of the events which might be placed on that scale. Thus, we say the peace treaty was signed at Ghent before the Battle of New Orleans because the

214

first event occurred on December 24, 1814 and the second event occurred on January 8, 1815. These two dates on our time scale would be there if these two events had not occurred. Evolution, on the other hand, is concerned with a temporal scale which is dependent upon the ordering of phenomena on some basis other than temporal. This statement requires further explanation since it varies from our usual concepts of 'time.'

Evolutionary schemes for ordering cultures are based upon such criteria as complexity of social organization (Naroll 1956), or the amount of energy used by cultures (White 1949), or different types of settlement patterns (Beardsley et al. 1956), or increased structural differentiation and functional specialization in social organization (Durkheim 1933). After the cultures have been placed in an assumed evolutionary sequence on the basis of these criteria then a temporal order is imposed. Beardsley and his co-workers can say the Australian aborigines represent an "earlier" type of culture than the Plains horticulturists because the latter groups are placed "later" on the basis of their settlement pattern. We say, therefore, that the temporal dimension is dependent because it is imposed upon an already existing ordering of the phenomena.

There are two major advantages to evolutionary sequences for understanding cultures. First, it allows us to group cultures into classes on the basis of their similarities in structure and then to place these classes in relation to each other in a temporal order. Thus, all hunters and gatherers can be compared, as a class, to all horticulturists, and generalizations can be derived about what changes occur when hunters and gatherers become horticulturists. The second advantage for evolutionary sequences is that it allows us to study "earlier" cultures using contemporary examples. This is particularly important if we wish to study aspects of culture, such as education, which are not adequately represented in the archaelogical record. We do not know much about education in the Upper Paleolithic if we limit ourselves to the archaeological evidence; however, by studying contemporary cultures which have technologies like those of the Upper Paleolithic we assume we can learn something of what education must have been like over 12,000 years ago.

The methodology for establishing a sequence of evolutional stages of education will be carried out in three steps. First, an acceptable evolutionary classification of cultures established by other investigators will be used as an independent variable. Second, a classification of education based upon evolutionary criteria will be established. Third, an attempt will be made to correlate tentatively the stages of cultural evolution with types of education. However, first I must make clear the nature of education as it will be regarded in this paper.

The Nature of Education

'Education' may be regarded as a class of events
ranging, at one extreme, from anything which has ever happened
to an individual to, at the other extreme, that which happens
to an individual in a classroom in the presence of a teacher.
While it is true that one may consider 'education' anything he
wishes, the usefulness of a concept depends, at least in part,
on its having some reference to more commonly understood
meanings. This places a limitation on the nature of 'education.'
Another limitation is that the nature of 'education' must be
suitable to the purpose at hand, in this case, must have
meaning in terms of an evolutionary sequence. A third limitation is that 'education' must be defined in a way which makes
it likely that the activity will be described in a typical
ethnography. An acceptable definition can best be developed by
isolating varying degrees of specificity.

Everything that happens to an individual I shall call
'experience.' This includes 'things' biological such as being
male or female, the color of one's skin, body size at different
stages of physical development, the order of birth in relation
to siblings, and so on. It includes 'things' which happen to
an individual quite aside from his participation in a society
such as falling into a river, hearing a mocking bird at night,
smelling a grass fire, seeing a tree struck by lightning, and
so on. It also includes all of those 'things' which happen to
the individual as a consequence of social interaction.

Everything that happens to an individual involving
interaction with another individual I shall call 'social
awareness.' This includes such 'things' as being pushed in a
crowded subway, catching a fly ball, being smiled at by a girl,
and so on. It also includes less direct social interaction
such as reading a book, seeing a movie, and listening to
records. Finally, it includes those social interactions which
have the consequence of equipping the individual for effective
participation in his society or some segment of his society.

Everything that happens to an individual involving
social interaction which equips him for effective participation
in his society or a segment of his society I shall call 'socialization.' This includes such things as playing house, dressing-
up in adult clothes, playing nurse, and so on. It also includes
mowing the lawn, being president of the neighborhood club,
taking care of a younger sibling, and so on. Finally, socialization includes social interaction involving two or more
people where at least one of the actors has as his purpose the
instruction of at least one of the other actors.

Everything that happens to an individual involving social
interaction where at least one actor has as his purpose the
instruction of at least one other actor I shall call "education.'
This includes such things as one friend telling another about

sex, an older brother showing a younger brother how to hit a
ball, a senior showing a freshman how to fill out a classcard.
It also includes a mother showing a child how to dress, a
Sunday School teacher telling a Bible story to a class, a
plumber showing a helper how to open a clogged drain, a
mathematics teacher explaining the binomial theorem.[3]

This increasing degree of specificty could be continued. For example, we might consider informal and formal education, private and public education, primary and secondary
education, and so on. However, further specificity would tend
to defeat the second limitation of a definition of education; it
would soon become too specific to be useful for comparative
purposes where a wide range of cultures and types of education
are involved. On the other hand, the basic concept of education
would appear to meet the first limitation; that is, it conforms
to the general meaning of 'education.'

The third limitation or restriction on the definition
of education can also be satisfied by this definition. 'Purpose,' as used in the definition, should be interpreted to mean
intent or direction manifested in the behavior of the actor.
Purpose, then should usually be expressed in the ethnographies
by use of such active verbs as tell, show, demonstrate, instruct,
teach, and so on. Activity of this type will normally be reported in a general ethnography.

Some implications of the above definition of education
should be made explicit. First, all learning is not education.
It is clear that learning may and does occur at all levels more
general than the level I have called 'education.' One learns by
'experience:' Fire burns. One learns 'social awareness' through
the most casual interaction: Others are polite, rude, or indifferent depending upon differences of age, sex, social status,
and so on. And, 'socialization' is by definition a learning
process. Education, then, is not characterized by learning, but
by teaching. Also, what is taught, that is, what is a part of
education, may vary from one culture to the next. In Western
civilizations children are usually taught toilet practices; in
many non-Western societies one learns toilet practices when he
becomes old enough to imitate adults or older children. Many
essential aspects of culture are not taught at all; natural
speech is taught only in a few cultures where emphasis upon
early childhood performance prevails, and in many cultures
techniques necessary for survival, for example, techniques of
hunting, are not taught. On the other hand, many aspects of a
culture which on the surface appear to be trivial, for example,
formal court etiquette, are taught with the greatest of care.
A classification of cultures in terms of what a given culture
selects as being important enough to see that it is taught to
the next generation, as opposed to what is regarded as something one learns on his own, might provide an important key to
understanding the role of education on culture. However, this

task is outside the aims of this paper.

Social interaction as used in the definition of education is not limited to face-to-face interaction. As technology has advanced, the limits of interaction through both time and space have been greatly extended. This advance has been characterized by the development of writing, the printing press, mass production of paper, mass distribution of printed materials through a market system, telephones, radios, photography, movies, recorders, television, machine translators, and so on. To exclude, for example, textbooks and educational television from any definition of education would be to place such a restriction upon the definition as to render the concept almost meaningless.

In the preceding three sections I have discussed the concepts necessary for a study of the evolution of education. Culture was defined as a class of phenomena dependent upon articulate speech. The four characteristics of culture -- super-organic, transmitability, cumulative, and adaptive -- were discussed. The class culture was divided into three sub-classes which were termed technology, society and ideology. Evolutionary studies were defined as studies which are concerned with the temporal dimension and compared with historical studies which are concerned with both the temporal and spatial dimensions. Education was defined as social interaction involving two or more actors where at least one of the actors has as his purpose the instruction of at least one other actor. The next obvious step is to bring together and correlate culture and education in an evolutionary framework. The critical problem is a classification of culture of stages and educational types:

> It is impossible to speak of the objects of any study, or to think lucidly about them, unless they are named. It is impossible to examine their relationships to each other and their places among the vast, incredibly complex phenomena of the universe, in short to treat them scientifically, without putting them into some sort of formal arrangement (Simpson 1945:1).

A Classification of Cultures

There are many classifications of culture, society, or some aspect of culture. Many of these classifications were devised for a special purpose and would not be suitable as a general type of classification we seek. Recent and general classifications have been offered by Oberg (1955), Steward (1948; 1955), Naroll (1956), Hester (1962), Service (1962), and Beardsley et al. (1956). It would not be useful in this paper to offer an evaluation of each of these classificatory schemes. The classificatory scheme of Beardsley et al. used in this paper will be explained, however.

The classificatory scheme of Beardsley et al. is meant to be a general universal classification:

The fitting of all cultures in the world, living and
extinct, into a single scheme, means that the definition
must be in general terms, although it is remarkable how
detailed they can be and still remain widely applicable.
The details are not those that characterize and contrast
distinct historical traditions, but those that distinguish
culture types (1956:133).

The single most important criterion used in this classification
is community mobility, and the names of the various classes
reflect this interest. However, the criteria are extended to
include "the organization of economic, sociopolitical and
ceremonial interrelationships within a community" (Beardsley
et al. 1956:134). Not only is this classification general,
as we desire, but it also has evolutionary applicability: "We
have tried to develop a classification of cultures that is
usable with both ethnological and archaeological data and that
has functional and evolutionary as well as historical and
descriptive significance" (Beardsley et al. 1956:133). Further,
the classification contains the technological bias referred to
earlier in this paper:

We have further assumed that the primary factor in the
dynamics of cultural advance from one category to another
is an improvement in subsistence, although we recognize
that on some occasions socio-political organizations may
be an important consideration in accelerating or retarding
this advance. We have taken it for granted that in
general sedentary life has more survival value than
wandering life to human race, and that, other things
being equal, whenever there is an opportunity to make
the transition, it will be made. (Beardsley et al. 1956:
134).

This classification, then, contains those four things we consider most essential: a consistent set of criteria, a set of
general classes, and evolutionary framework of the advancement
of the classes, and a technological explanation of the cultural
advance of the class from one stage to the next.

The classification of Beardsley et al. contains ten
classes. Three of these are special classes which apply only
to pastoral nomads and will not be considered further in this
paper. Of the seven remaining classes, the first stage is a
hypothetical stage not represented by any ethnographic examples
and probably not represented by any archaeological examples.
Finally, the last stage in the development of the classification
probably does not reach the level of modern industrialized
societies. As Beardsley et al. says in a footnote:

This category includes a wide range of cultures, and it
may be necessary to subdivide it into Simple and Advanced
... With industrialization and the growth of scientific
method, certain changes take place in the community
integration... [W]e were not able to pursue the question

219

of whether these can be considered simply as more
intensive developments of preindustrial trends or
whether they should be separated and such cultures
be called Advanced Supra-Nuclear Integrated. (1956:
145)

In this paper we shall follow the suggestion of the authors of
this classification and add an additional class which includes
modern industrial societies. The six stages in the original
classification we are using and the one we have added will be
briefly described.

I. Restricted Wandering. "Communities that wander
about within a territory that they define as theirs and defend
against trespass, or on which they have exclusive rights to food
resources of certain kinds. Movement within the territory may
be erratic or may follow a seasonal round, depending upon the
kind of wild food utilized" (p. 136). The technology of this
stage of development is characterized by a seasonal variation
in the available food supply, a lack of adequate food storage
techniques, and an absence of domesticated plants and animals
with the exception of the dog.

II. Central-Based Wandering. "A community that spends
part of each year wandering and the rest at a settlement of
'central-base,' to which it may or may not consistently return
in the subsequent years" (p. 138). The technological base at
this level of development may be one of three types: "(1) a
storageable or preservable wild food harvest, such as acorns or
mesquite beans; (2) a locally abundant food, such as shellfish;
and (3) incipient agriculture producing a small harvest" (p.
138).

III. Semi-Sedentary. "A community, which can be
identified with a village, that establishes itself in successive
locations, occupying each for a period of years. The population
is stable and continuously sedentary, but able to be so only by
moving the village periodically" (p. 140). The technology at
this stage of development is characterized by "simple, exploitative agriculture in areas of average to poor natural soil
fertility. In the absence of restorative techniques to maintain productivity, or because of the perishable nature of the
crops, no surplus can be relied upon indefinitely from the same
fields or held against future needs" (p. 140).

IV. Simple Nuclear Centered. "A primitive center,
with or without satellites. The center may be a self-supporting
town, or a market or ceremonial place that serves as a focus for
surrounding villages or hamlets. The center is not strikingly
differentiated in content from its satellites except when its
character is primarily ceremonial" (p. 141). The technology at
this level is characterized by "agricultural techniques adapted
to the local environment, so that the effect is conservational.
Cultivated plants become the primary food source, reducing the
per capita area needed for subsistence maintenance or providing

a dependable surplus sufficient to release a portion of the community from the role of primary producers" (p. 141).

V. <u>Advanced Nuclear Centered</u>. "A community of homogeneous tradition differentiated into an administrative centered and satellites consisting of villages, hamlets, and scattered homesteads" (p. 143). Beardsley <u>et al</u>. suggest the technology may not be the primary factor in differentiating this level from the preceding level: "This type of community differs more in degree than in type from the preceding one. It probably develops from the Simple Nuclear Center as agricultural techniques improve and are able to provide larger surpluses. These increasingly come under the control of the upper classes. As the elite become stabilized, it is less affected by public opinion and the main deterrent to private accumulation of wealth is removed. What was essentially voluntary integration on the Simple level becomes more administrative and coercive on the Advanced level" (p. 143-144).

VI. <u>Simple Supra-Nuclear Integrated</u>. (The word "Simple" has been added to this heading to differentiate it, as Beardsley <u>et al</u>. suggested, from the "Advanced" stage characteristic of industrial societies.) "A community that integrates nuclear centers and other formerly independent units of heterogeneous tradition, typically by conquest and subjugation" (p. 145). This stage of development is characterized by a technological superiority to wage warfare and/or more intensive food production: "Conquest may be promoted by the increasing requirements of food, commodities, or raw materials for maintenance of the administrative or ceremonial superstructure, or the economic system in excess of what the members of the expanding Advance Nuclear Centered community can supply... Or, the ability to maintain the enlarged administrative and military structures required for territorial expansion may be considered as an expression of more intensive food production, which places a burden of subsistence provision on a smaller percentage of the population and frees large numbers of peoples for other tasks" (p. 145).

VII. <u>Advanced Supra-Nuclear Integrated</u>. (A description of the community pattern and technology for this stage is supplied for purposes of this paper.) A community that integrates nuclear centers and their satellites into a single, nationally homogeneous tradition, typically by political and economic interdependency. The technology at this stage of development is characterized by an increasing dependency upon the use of fossil fuels and a high concentration of productive equipment in areas adjacent to raw materials and/or primary routes of communication.

It will be necessary to return to further discussion of these classes when we attempt to relate the classes of culture to the classes of education. First we must establish a typology of education.

221

A Classification of Education

The method of devising a classification of education
will be to treat each variable as if the range of the variable
was limited to two polar types, that is, each variable is
classified as either A or non-A. While it is almost certain
that most of the phenomena in the universe do not come in nice
either/or categories it is often more economical, especially in
exploratory stages, to define the categories so as to exclude
the middle range. The next step is to identify variables of the
phenomena under consideration which, at least in theory, vary
independently of each other. The minimum number of classes
established by this method is 2^N, where N equals the number of
variables.

A classification of education useful to an evolutionary
framework must be based upon criteria which would reflect
differential levels of progress development. Durkheim (1933)
noted that a developmental scale for the division of labor within a society was characterized by an increase in the number of
occupations and greater specialization of activity. This
particular phenomena has been generalized into the statement
that cultural evolution is characterized by an increasing
differentiation of structure and greater specialization of
function (White 1959:142-204). The question is: What are the
indications of increasing structural differentiation and greater
functional specialization in education. One possible answer to
this question is that changes in structure and function in education will be manifest by (1) who is taught, (2) who teaches,
and (3) what is the goal of education?

Who is Taught? The two-fold classification is as
follows: All individuals are taught or some individuals are
taught. It must be understood, however, that "all individuals"
refers to individuals in a given age and sex category, and some
individuals refers to less than all individuals in a given age
and sex category.

Who Teaches? The two-fold classification used here as
follows: Someone either occupies a position of "teacher" in a
given setting or no position of "teacher" is found in a particular setting. These two classifications will be abbreviated
simply as teacher and non-teacher. It is assumed that in some
cultures there will be no specific position, on a spare time,
part time, or full time basis, designated as "teacher." In
other cultures such a position will be designated. It is
further assumed that where there is a position of "teacher"
there will also be a position of "student."

Goal of Education? The two-fold classification is as
follows: The goal of education is to equip the individual to
occupy a specific position in his society or to occupy a general
position in his society. A specific position is one which is
achieved in the sense that the attainment of this position is

222

not normally assigned at birth or its attainment is not a natural consequence of growth and maturation. A special position is structurally differentiated and functionally specialized in relation to the total society. Examples of special positions are chief, priest, blacksmith, and trader. As indicated by these examples, special positions are primarily, if not exclusively, occupational specialties. These positions are usually occupied by "some individuals" in a specific age and sex category; however, at least one position, that of warrior, is a specialized position which may be occupied by "all individuals" of a specific age and sex. A general position, on the other hand, is normally occupied by all individuals of a specific age and sex, or in large pluralistic societies, by all individuals in an identifiable social group--ethnic, religious, racial, social class, caste, etc. Examples are adult male, citizen, father, and taxpayer, for the total society, and Irish, Jew, Negro, lord, and untouchable for identifiable social groups within the total society. The two goals of education defined above will be referred to simply as "specific" and "general."

Assuming each of these three characteristics of education vary independently of each other, it is possible to set up a typology of eight nominal types of education. These eight types are, for ease of reference, listed below in the order in which they emerged, that is, from the first to the most recent evolved type of education:

1. Non-teacher -- all individuals -- general
2. Non-teacher -- some individuals -- special
3. Non-teacher -- all individuals -- special
4. Non-teacher -- some individuals -- general
5. Teacher -- some individuals -- general
6. Teacher -- some individuals -- special
7. Teacher -- all individuals -- special
8. Teacher -- all individuals -- general

We are now in a position to attempt to relate the types of education to the various levels of cultural education.

The Evolution of Education

The procedure in this section will be to return to a more detailed description of each of the cultural stages described by Beardsley and others. I shall then indicate which type or types of education would occur at each cultural level and briefly give a justification for making this assertion. Often the relationship between a cultural level and educational types is logically clear from the description of the cultural level: If there are no specialists and all individuals are members of the same types of social segments, then there are no teachers, and all students must receive an education to equip them for general positions in the total society. However, the situation is not always as clear-cut as this, in which case I shall resort to information about specific cultures, examples of which are supplied in the monograph of Beardsley et al. and elsewhere. The relationships and propositions established by this method are obviously tentative; establishing these relationships upon a firm empirical basis is the task of a more extensive project.

The various cultural levels will be discussed in the same order as they were given in the section "A Classification of Cultures." The relationship between types of cultures and types of education is summarized in Table 1.

I. Restricted Wandering. At this level we find the basic social concrete structure to be the nuclear or extended family which may, at least for part of the year, be combined into bands. If there is a leader of the band, he has no coercive power. There may be minimal status differences or none at all "Puberty rites or other group ceremonies may be absent, sporadic, or well developed" (Beardsley et al. 1956:137). The only specialist, who may or may not be present, is the shaman. At this level of cultural development, there is no teacher position present, all individuals are taught some of the things they need for participation in the total society and, with one possible exception, the goal of education is general. The possible exception is that the position of shaman may be a special position that is learned. However, the presence of a shaman does not necessarily indicate that some individuals are taught to be shamans. At least in some cultures at this level all individuals in a society have shamanistic knowledge, but some individuals because of special visions or other factors tend to activate and emphasize this knowledge. In the event that shamanistic knowledge is taught as a speciality to some individuals through an apprenticeship with the shaman, then a second type of education would be found at this cultural level. Since it is uncertain whether or not this occurs, I have indicated this on the table by adding a question mark in the appropriate cell. Thus, Type (1) non-teacher--all individuals--general, education occurs at this cultural level. Type (1) education occurs in, at a minimum, the social concrete structure we refer to as the family. It is assumed that education, as it is defined in this paper, takes place in all families, whether it is teaching a boy to shoot a bow or drive a car. Since the family is universal in all cultures, we would argue that this type of education is found in all cultures at all cultural levels. Type (2) non-teacher--some individuals--special, if it does not occur at this level of culture development, almost certainly occurs at the next level of cultural development. Type (2) education also occurs in the most advanced cultural level (Advanced Supra-Nuclear Integrated) level of cultural development, for example, the apprentice-master relationship which may prepare a student for special positions such as plumber or movie director. Type (2) education seems to occur

224

WILSON: ON THE EVOLUTION OF EDUCATION

Table 1

Type of Education

Type of Culture*	Non-Teacher All Individuals General 1	Non-Teacher Some Individuals Special 2	Non-Teacher All Individuals Special 3	Non-Teacher Some Individuals General 4	Teacher Some Individuals General 5	Teacher Some Individuals General 6	Teacher All Individuals Special 7	Teacher All Individuals General 8
I. Restricted Wandering	X	X?						
II. Central-Based Wandering	X	X						
III. Semi-Permanent Sedentary	X	X	X					
IV. Simple Nuclear Centered	X	X	X	X				
V. Advanced Nuclear Centered	X	X	X	X	X	X		
VI. Simple Supra-Nuclear Integrated	X	X	X	X	X	X	X	
VII. Advanced Supra-Nuclear Integrated	X	X	X	X	X	X	X	X

* Based on Beardsley, R. K. et al. Functional and evolutionary implications of community patterning. Seminars in Archaeology: 1955. Memoirs of the Society for American Archaeology, 11, pp. 131-157 (1956).

from the second level of cultural development to the most advanced.

II. Central-Based Wandering. This cultural level, except in mobility pattern, is very little different from the preceding level; and in fact, most classifications do not distinguish between these two levels. As in the preceding level, there is no occupational division of labor "although certain families may have hereditary preeminence in crafts that are practiced to some degree by all" (Beardsley et al. 1956:138). However, based upon information of some of the ethnographic examples cited by Beardsley et al., e.g. the Eskimo, at least the position of shaman seems to be a speciality that one must learn. For this reason we have attributed Type (2) education to this level without any question.

III. Semi-Permanent Sedentary. Increased structural differentiation is clearly marked at this level of cultural development. "Village or tribal specialization in the manufacture of ceramics, basketry, manioc graters, or similar products occurs, with consequent regulation of trade relations. Within a community some individuals may be recognized as superior craftsmen, but their creations are rarely considered preferable for daily use. The basic skills involved in weaving, pottery making, and other crafts are known to all... Clans and/or moieties are typical..., although extended family organization is also relatively frequent at this level. Some individual is usually designated as the head man or chief, but his powers depend more upon his personal qualities than upon status vested in the office... Social differentiation ranges from incipient to well developed, with warfare and shamanism the primary means of acquiring prestige... Group ceremonies, featuring masked dancers and 'folk drama' are held to promote success in agriculture and other food quests important to the community as well as puberty and other events in the life cycle. Shamans are characteristic, and sometimes wield considerable power by virtue of their connections with the spirit world" (Beardsley et al. 1956:140-141). Another social segmentation found at this level of cultural development, although not mentioned in the description, is age-graded societies (see Eisenstadt 1956). Type (1) education is found at this level associated with the concrete social unit, the family. However, Type (1) education is also presently associated with other concrete units such as the clan and moiety. Within the clan or moiety setting, Type (1) education takes on two further aspects which differ from the family setting. First, education for the first time becomes somewhat formal in that it is often associated with ceremony and ritual, and the termination of the period of education is usually marked by acceptance of the newly initiated individual into the clan. Second, for the first time individuals are segregated into educational groups; that is, an individual is taught the ritual, ceremonies, customs, rights and obligations of his particular clan or moiety. However, the goal of education is the same for all individuals regardless of clan affiliation, and the difference in content is certainly qualitatively less than the differences between a college and non-college curriculum in a modern high school. The process of education is the responsibility of a priest or community elder who occupies that position and not the differentiated position of a teacher. While education in the clan setting has been typed with education in the family setting, it seems important to point out that this difference in setting anticipates changes in education which become increasingly important at higher levels of cultural development.

Some puberty rites, although not all puberty rites as Har (1963) indicates, found at this level of cultural development are also classified as Type (1) education. Many puberty rites, of which the female puberty rite of the Jicarilla Apache is an example, do not involve education as defined in this paper; these are rituals marking the transition of a change of status for an individual and his relations. No new knowledge, skills, or information are transmitted during these rituals. The knowledge necessary to occupy the new status is something the individual has learned since early childhood. The individual is not told how to do something, he is now expected to do it as part of the requirement of the new status. However, other puberty rites do transmit to the individual knowledge, information, or skills not formerly known, and these puberty rites fall into Type (1) education.

Type (3) non-teacher--all individuals--special, education is introduced at this level of cultural development with the presence of formal age-graded associations or with formal military associations whether age-graded or not. Military associations and many formal age-graded associations serve the purpose of training "all individuals," that is, all males of a given age, to occupy the "special position of warrior. That this is a special position and not a general position in the total society is demonstrated by the special skills and knowledge learned by the warrior class, by the fact the warriors are often set apart in special houses or clubs, and by the rights and obligations attributed to the warriors but denied non-warriors (e.g., the warriors may be excused from normal adult male productive activity, but are not allowed to marry). We would expect all adult males to be warriors if this were a general position in the total society. Such is not the case. After a specified period as a warrior, the adult male ceases to occupy this position and advances to the general position of adult male participating in normal productivity activity, acquiring a wife and children, and so on. An individual learns the warrior position by participation with and instruction from those in the advanced age-grades or who already occupy the warrior positions. No position of "teacher is associated with this training.

227

I know of no other example of Type (3) education. It is found in Type (IV) cultures and probably in Type (V) cultures; it is not found at higher levels of cultural development. However, the obvious modern descendant of this type of education is universal conscription for military training.

In summary, several important advances are made in education at the third level of cultural development. First, Type (1) education is associated with concrete groups other than the family, it takes on some formal aspects, and individuals are segregated for purposes of education. Second, Type (3) education emerges at this level; it disappears at higher levels of cultural development to be replaced by another type of education which will be discussed below.

IV. Simple Nuclear Centered. At this cultural level "full-time occupational specialization is characteristic of some part of the population, either in administration, ceremonialism, or technology. These specialties typically are hereditary... kinship-based organization continues to be important, but is overlaid to some extent by differential status within or between families. Incipient to well-developed social stratification is correlated with an increase of ascribed over achieved status. The chief acts to some extent in his own interest or the interest of his class, and usually has power to coerce subjects, particularly as individuals or as members of the lower class. His power is related to the size and distinctiveness of the upper class, however, and where the social stratification is minimal, the chief's role is little different from what it is in Semi-Permanent Sedentary communities... Religion is formalized and externalized in temples, ritual, prayers, and offerings... Both increase in community size and specialization of religious ritual seems to be responsible for the allocation of part of the community to an audience role rather than the participation characteristic in Semi-Permanent Sedentary and in Wandering Groups" (Beardsley et al. 1956:142). Specializations are clearly evident at this level especially in terms of occupations, administration, and religion. However, indications are that the specialization is still of an apprentice-master form, Type (2) education. Also clearly evident is that social stratification is now developed to the point that different social manners, beliefs, attitudes, skills, and so on must be taught to members of each distinct social class. We assume that this involves Type (4) non-teacher--some individuals--general, education. This type of education is characteristically carried out in the social concrete unit we refer to as the family. Such education is in addition to Type (1) education, which is also carried out within the family. However, it is probable that Type (4) education is carried out at other cultural levels in some social concrete units other than the family. Type (4) education will be found in societies that have social classes, ethnic groups, castes, racial minorities, and so on. More simply, Type (4)

228

education will be found in any society that is socially stratified. Thus, we attribute Type (4) education to every level above the Simple Nuclear Centered Stage of cultural development. An example of Type (4) education in an Advanced Supra-Nuclear Integrated culture is the type of education a Negro child living in the southeastern part of the United States would receive. The teachers would be parents or non-teachers, only Negro children or some individuals would be taught, and the goal of the education would be general, equipping the child for adjustment to a particular social segment of the larger society.

      V. <u>Advanced Nuclear Centered</u>. At this level of cultural development "surplus production, especially of food, may be acquired by the ruling class in the form of taxes, which seem to make their appearance at this stage. Well-developed specialization decreases family self-efficiency, and to the degree that goods must be acquired from others, distinctions in wealth and property are more pronounced. 'Earning' a living becomes possible for occupational specialists, and ability to devote full time to learning a craft results in proficiency and technological improvement. Public and temple granaries, filled by taxes, permit the priest or rulers to support labor for large-scale construction and to maintain a large body of retainers... Administration is carried out by the hierarchy of officials typically headed by a chief or king. Government assumes the task of social integration, law and politics supplanting kinship as the dominant regulator of interpersonal relations. Social classes are distinguished by dress and have different rights and privileges... Education is confined to members of the upperclass, and typically dispensed in the temples... Hierarchial ranking of priests parallels the civil administrative hierarchy... The priesthood is a depository of wealth and power" (Beardsley <u>et al</u>. 1956:144). Two different types of education make their appearance at this stage of cultural development. First, Type (5) <u>teacher--some individuals--general</u>, makes its appearance when the general education of the upper class is turned over to specialized teachers in the temples. Also, Type (6) <u>teacher--some individuals--special</u>, education makes its appearance with individuals devoting full time to learning occupational specialities. Presumably, some individuals devote full or part time to teaching these occupational specialties. Both of these types of education are found at the most advanced level of cultural development. Examples for the modern society of the United States are Groton for Type (5) and East Chicago Welding School for Type (6).

      VI. <u>Simple Supra-Nuclear Integrated</u>. This cultural level is characterized by large scale commerce. "Commercial attitudes are prevalent, and indebtedness may be punished by slavery. Wealth is accumulated in goods, land, or slaves... Goods, land, services and even people are bought and sold... Administrative procedure is similar to that developed in

229

Advanced Nuclear Centered communities. The major addition is
military organization, frequently including a standing army, for
international policing as well as external expansion. The ruler
may be identified with the gods and wield absolute power with
divine sanction. At the opposite extreme in the social hierarchy is a large lower class with a minimum of prerogatives, if
not actually reduced to slavery or serfdom... The religion of
the conqueror frequently becomes the state religion and is
imposed upon conquered groups... However, with the growth of
scientific knowledge, supranaturalism tends to change from a
coercive force to an ethical standard and ceases to be a major
mechanism of social control" (Beardsley et al. 1956:146). Type
(7) teacher--all individuals--special, education seems to be
introduced at this cultural level. One need for Type (7) education stems from the fact that at this stage of cultural
development standing armies are present usually with universal
conscription for all individuals of a particular age and sex
category. An example of Type (7) education in the modern
society of the United States is universal conscription for
military training.

VII. Advanced Supra-Nuclear Integrated. This stage
of cultural development is characterized by a high degree of
industrialization and occupational specialization. Occupational
specialization reaches the point where it becomes the major
criterion for determining social class, income, and other social
characteristics. The use of relatively untrained slaves and
serfs becomes highly unprofitable at the most advanced stages of
this level. There is a proliferation of associations, especially
voluntary associations. Social classes are less distinct than
in earlier stages and social mobility is relatively easy. The
population, initially derived from the heterogeneous segments
brought together in the previous stages of development, are now
welded into a social and political unit to the degree that
internal coercion is infrequent or absent. The state increasingly becomes concerned with the welfare of the general population
and for long term planning of social change. Individuals who
are not trained in any specialization or who lack the background
to become so trained are considered a liability to the society.
Type (8) teacher--all individuals--general, education is characteristic of this level of cultural development. A great deal of
the education at this level is carried out by individuals who
occupy a teacher position in the society; all individuals in the
society, including in some cases both sexes of a particular age
category, are educated; and the education is considered to be of
a general type to equip the student with knowledge and skills
for participation in the society-at-large. Type (8) education
is usually associated with a social concrete structure which we
call the public school. These schools are supported by the
society-at-large, and all students theoretically have a right,
in many cases an obligation, to attend these schools for a

230

certain period of time. Since this type of education is the primary interest of this paper, further discussion of Type (8) education will be reserved for a subsequent section.

A general overview of the foregoing attempt to relate types of education to levels of cultural development indicates there is some relationship between types of education and level of cultural development. The scale we have developed here is meant to serve as a model for further research, and there is no claim that it has been empirically validated. It is quite likely that a careful, detailed study of the ethnographic materials will indicate that some of the types of education developed either earlier or later than the stage with which we have associated it. Also, it may be necessary to change the general order in which some of the types of education have developed. Our task, however, is to see what this developmental scheme, regardless of how imperfect, contributes to our understanding of the nature of education.

General Trends in the Evolution of Education

In the foregoing section we attempted to empirically establish the relationship between different levels of culture and different types of education. Using the level of culture as the independent variable we determined an order in which the eight types of education evolved. We are now in a position to analyze and interpret the evolution of education.

The criteria for establishing types of education were selected to reflect increasing structural differentiation and functional specialization. Thus, the position of teacher becomes differentiated as a distinct and separate position, individuals become differentiated into separate educational groups, and the goal of education is differentiated into distinct and separate goals of equipping individuals to occupy special positions in the society. If increasing differentiation occurs in the developmental sequence, then we would expect the least differentiated forms of education to be found at the lowest level of cultural development. This does, in fact, occur where Type (1) education non-teacher--all individuals--general, is found at the first level of cultural development. Conversely, we would expect the most differentiated type of education, teacher--some individuals--special to be found at the highest level of cultural development and to be the last type of education to have evolved. This is not the case. The most differentiated type of education, Type (6), is found at the fifth level of cultural development, and the last type of education to evolve was Type (8), teacher--all individuals--general, which differs from Type (1) only in the differentiation of the position of teacher. How can these facts be reconciled with Durkheim's idea that increasing structural differentiation is characteristic of evolution.

231

The Nineteenth Century cultural evolutionists supposed
that any aspect of culture would manifest a unilinear progression, and this notion was applied to forms of marriage, rules
of descent and residence, kinship systems and so on. Modern
evolutionists take the position that cultures, not necessarily
sub-systems of cultures, follow a sequence from the least
differentiated to the most structurally differentiated. Thus,
Befu (1963:351) has suggested a five step sequence from bilater-
al-unilineal to unilineal to unilineal-bilateral to bilateral as
societies progress from the lower levels of development to the
most advanced levles. Service (1960) has shown that kinship
systems do not evolve in a unilinear fashion but that systems of
wider relationships do; and Greenburg (1959) says that systems
of communication become more structurally differentiated although natural languages do not. In fact, if we look at what
happens to specific parts of cultures in an evolutionary sequence
we find some parts disappear (the most as a form of defense),
some parts reach a certain level of development and do not
develop further (the long bow), some parts become less complex
(a modern flak suit as compared to a knight's armor), and so on.
Given these considerations, it is not surprising that the
specific forms of education did not follow the sequence suggested
in the paragraph above. However, when we examine education in
the broader context of the culture, we do find it is characterized by increased structural differentiation.

An inspection of the evolutionary sequence of education
shown in Table 1 lends the following four observations:

First, once a type of education emerges it tends to
persist and is found at higher levels of culture development.
The exception to this is that education Type (3) does not occur
after culture level V.

Second, it follows from the preceding statement that
new types of education are additive rather than substitutive.
The exception is that Type (3) is replaced by Type (7) at culture levels VI and VII.

Third, each culture level is associated with a new
emergent type of education. A possible exception is that education Type (2) may occur at culture level I.

Four, each culture level is associated with more types
of education than the immediately preceding culture level.
Culture level II may be an exception to this statement, and
culture level VI, where education Type (3) is replaced by Type
(7) is an exception. A corollary statement is that no culture
level has fewer types of education than the immediately preceding level.

These four observations indicate the increasing
structural differentiation of education as it evolved in the
context of the cultures at different levels of development.
The progression is an increase in types of education and the
emergence of new educational types with the development of new

cultural levels; culture level I is associated with one or perhaps two types of education while culture level VII is associated with seven types of education. This interpretation of increasing structural differentiation conforms to the interpretation of Service and others mentioned above.

If education becomes progressively structurally differentiated, then it would logically follow that it also becomes more functionally specialized. The supporting argument for this statement has been presented, in part, in our discussion relating types of education to levels of cultural development. However, all this argument says is that a type of education found at a given cultural level will be functional for that level of culture; and this is one of the premises upon which this study is based. The important question concerns the functional requisites at a given level of culture which would make a particular type of education necessary for that culture to exist. Space and time do not allow me to take up this question for each of the seven cultural levels. In light of this, and because other papers in this volume are primarily concerned with transmission and learning in national cultures, I shall briefly discuss the functional requisites which necessitate education Type (8) in modern industrial cultures. I shall limit my discussion to the public school since this is the primary social unit where Type (8) education is found.

The Public School: An Evolutionary Perspective

Advanced Supra-Nuclear Integrated cultures (VII) are characterized by a high level of technological development and a rapid rate of technological change. A prime functional requisite necessitated by this type of technology is a large number of occupational specialists trained to a high degree of specialization. The importance of occupational specialization to cultures at level VII can hardly be exaggerated. Individuals occupying positions requiring high degrees of specialization are rewarded with wealth and social prestige. The degree of specialization, in turn, depends largely upon the level to which an individual has been formally educated. Thus, there is a strong association between level of formal education, degree of occupational specialization, and social rank in modern industrial cultures. The chain of relationships finds, at one end, a technology requiring large numbers of highly trained specialists and, at the other end, the rewards of social rank and wealth for those individuals who meet these needs; in-between is formal education which is the means by which these needs are met. The argument follows that formal education meets the functional requisite for training occupational specialists for cultures at level (VII).

The public school in modern industrial cultures serves many purposes and it is pointless to argue that one purpose is

233

more important than another. Children must learn a great deal in the context of the public school since this is the place they spend most of their waking hours between the ages of five and 18, and many of the things formerly learned in the context of such social units as the family must now, of necessity, be learned in the school. It is pertinent, however, to ask what new educational requirements are demanded by modern cultures and to what extent these are met within the context of the public school. The argument in the paragraph above suggest occupational specialization as the primary factor in the development of public education. This argument has been presented most forcefully by Clark in his book, Educating the Expert Society. Clark's thesis is indicated by this statement:

> In the technological age, schools must perform more than a custodial function; for, more than ever, the young need a technical and cultural competence if they are to perform adult tasks--and, more than ever, as the schools take over the training function, personal capabilities must be developed through the school... The schools in previous eras might merely keep the kids off the streets and yet their graduates might function adequately in adult society. College might merely be a place for collegiate play and the graduate of the college might even be prepared for a place of business. But not today. The technological society makes the appropriateness of preparation less a relative matter of differing perspective. Below certain levels of literacy lies a deep and lifelong cultural incompetence. Below certain levels of skill lies the probability of unemployment and part-time work; there used to be a large number of jobs for unskilled laborers, but now a low-grade vocational education does not lead anywhere. Without long systematic preparation, the higher occupations are generally not open. Without a broad education in the sciences and the humanities, public and business leaders are without the perspectives and understandings they need. (1962:7-8).

I will not extend this line of discussion further, for there is another way, more immediately related to the topic of the evolution of education, in which we can approach the question of those functional requisites of modern industrial cultures that are met by the public school. To do this we must examine the part education has played in training occupational specialists at other levels of culture development.

In the culture levels I through VI there are four types of education which have the goal of training occupational specialists. Two of these, Types (3) and (7) are concerned with training for the special position of warrior. These two, as has already pointed out, have a direct lineal relationship in that Type (7) replaces (3). However, I have not been able

to see any relationship between these two types and the other
types of education concerned with occupational specialists;
therefore, I will not consider Types (3) and (7) further. The
other two types of education, Types (2) and (6), which are
concerned with occupational specialization, are directly related to each other and to Type (8) found in modern societies.

Type (2) education is the apprentice relationship that
may appear as early as culture level I. It is associated with
the part time position of shaman through level III. At culture
level IV full time occupational specialization first appears and
Type (2) education becomes important for providing specialists
necessary for the implementation of the technology. Apprentice
training can meet the requirements for training occupational
specialists as long as two conditions exist: (1) the number of
specialists needed in each generation is relatively constant or
increasing very slowly, and (2) the types of specialists needed
in the future are essentially the same types which are needed
in the present. I suggest Type (2) education meets these conditions at culture level IV. However, if either one or both of
these conditions change, then we would expect a new type of
education to meet these new demands.

At culture level V we find full time occupational
specialization characterize a large number of positions in the
society and "an ability to devote full time to learning a craft
results in proficiency and technological improvement" (Beardsley
et al. 1956:144). With an increase in the number of specialists
needed, the apprentice training can no longer meet the demand
for all occupations. Thus, the teacher, who can more efficiently train a larger number of individuals, takes on the task of
training some individuals in a given speciality. At this point
education Type (6) emerges to supplement Type (2). Type (6)
emerges to supplement Type (2). Type (6) education can meet the
requirements for training occupational specialists as long as
these two conditions exist: (1) the number of specialists
needed in each generation is predictable, even though this
number may be large, and (2) the types of specialists needed in
the future are known. Type (6) education meet these conditions
for culture levels V and VI.

At culture level VII both of the conditions met by
Type (6) education change; the technology changes so rapidly it
was no longer possible to predict the number of specialists
needed, and, most important, it became impossible to predict
what kinds of occupational specialists would be needed in the
future. However, these new conditions can be met with certain
changes or alterations in Type (6) education. First, the position of teacher becomes more specialized reaching the point
where several teachers are necessary to provide basic instruction. Second, the number of special topics taught is increased;
increased, in fact, to the point where it tends to lose its
specialized meaning and becomes instead a general education

235

which is requisite to further specialization. Third, education is expanded to include all members of the society within certain age groups with the result that the total adult population makes up a potential pool from which the required specialist may be drawn. With these three changes education Type (6) has been transformed into education Type (8); the latter meeting the educational functional requisites for a modern industrial culture.

The problem of training occupational specialists for modern industrial cultures is a problem common in both biological and cultural evolution. On the one hand, there is an adaptive advantage to increasing specialization; on the other hand, there are disadvantages to specialization in changing situation, for specialization reduces the flexibility to adapt to new conditions. A closer look at the public school shows how this problem was solved. What we think of as a general education is actually intensive instruction in a number of very specialized areas. Elementary school teachers are primarily instructors specialized in teaching reading, writing, and arithmetic. They teach other things, but a student's progress is determined by his ability in reading and mathematics. Once the student finishes the elementary grades, his instruction becomes the concern of teachers who are specialized in only one subject. The trend toward more and more specialization in instruction is demonstrated by changes in public education in the United States over the past five decades. Specialized instruction first began in the last three years of high school. Then it was extended to the last five years of school with the development of the junior high school. Within the last 25 years another year of school was added at the terminal year of the education so that specialized instruction extends through one-half of the public school education. Also, there has been an increasing tendency to use specialists in the first six grades. This apparently began with art and music teachers and is now being extended to include teachers of foreign languages, science and mathematics. Where specialists are in short supply, their effectiveness is extended by the use of television, tapes, radio and so on. Added to this is the search for more effective teaching methods, therefore making it possible to acquire a higher degree of specialization in the same amount of time. Finally, there is an interest in probing the limitations of the students, especially to see if they cannot acquire skills and knowledge at an earlier age so that specilaized subjects can begin earlier and advance further before the end of the public school education. All of these trends in formal education add up to a single outcome: all individuals in the society receive an education to higher levels of specialization in an increasing number of areas; at the same time, commitment to a single area is delayed. This is what Type (8) education is and this is the way it meets the functional requisites of a rapidly changing, highly developed technology.

Type (8) education gives all members of the society an education in as many specialties as possible and to the highest degree of specialization possible within the limited time of the 12 years of public education. This type of education solves the problem of having to train people for a wide variety of specializations. A student with a secondary education is in a position to specialize as a service station attendant in a few days or a psychiatrist in a few years. This means also that a great deal of education may be wasted insofar as it applies to the special position the individual will occupy; e.g., the courses in biological sciences taken by the service station attendant. This type of education also provides a basis for learning new skills and knowledge which have not been anticipated. A high school education provides the foundation for one to become an electronics technician even though this position did not exist during the period of high school education. Finally, this type of education provides for the transmission of new skills and knowledge to the contemporary generation. The teachers, being specialists, are in a position to be aware of the most recent developments in their areas of specialization. Thus one generation may be learning a foreign language by techniques which have been developed since the last generation of students. Type (8) education, a general education made up of a number of specialties, then, effectively meets the requirements of level VII cultures.

Conclusion

In the first section of this paper I quoted Durkheim's program for the study of the evolution of education. He suggested we could learn how one type of education emerged from another, the laws which govern the evolution of systems of education, how education developed, and the causes for this development. We have made only modest progress toward those goals. We have seen how systems of education have become more structurally differentiated in their development as the number of types of education increased with higher levels of culture development. We have tried to show how some types of education given warriors is replaced by another type of education for warfare. In a second case, the training for occupational specialization to implement the technology follows a sequence from apprenticeship, to teachers teaching some individuals a particular speciality, to several teachers teaching all individuals many specialized areas; and those three types of education are additive in that all three are found in cultures at the highest level of development. Finally, we sought to establish the causes to account for the emergence of Type (8) education, the formal education of the public school, in highly industrialized cultures. It would be claiming too much to say that we have obtained "laws which govern the evolution of systems of education;" however, it is not claiming too much to say that an evolutionary perspective of education provides us with insights and understandings about the nature of education which could not be obtained by other approaches.

NOTES

1. This paper is the product of a year long seminar in education at the University of Missouri. The objective of this seminar, in which both faculty and graduate students participated, was to establish a framework for studying education from the most specific to the most general levels of consideration. I was given the responsibility of establishing the most general level, and I chose an evolutionary approach as my method. I wish to thank Bruce J. Biddle, the director of the seminar, and Raymond S. Adams, Paul F. Green, Fred E. Katz, Paul C. Rosenblatt, and Richard Videbeck, for educating me about education. Support for this seminar was provided by Research Contract Number 2-20-004, Educational Media Branch, Office of Education, Department of Health, Education and Welfare.

2. Much of the discussion of these three topics will be familiar to anthropologists. I have included this information because I hope the contents of this paper may be of interest to other disciplines concerned with the study of education. I found that in the course of the seminar mentioned in the note above, that a great deal of effort was devoted to making the points that 'culture' was not simply ideas, the 'evolution' was not another name for history, and that 'education' was not limited to what occurred in a classroom.

3. See Cohen (1970) for another attempt to distinguish socialization from education.

REFERENCES

Beardsley, R. K., H. Preston, A. D. Krieger, B. J. Meggers and J. B. Rinaldo
  1956   Functional and Evolutionary Implications of
                Community Patterning. Seminars in Archaeology:
                1955. Memoirs of the Society for American
                Archaeology, 11.

Befu, H.
  1963   Classification of Unilineal-Bilateral Societies.
                Southwestern Journal of Anthropology 19:335-55.

Clark, B. R.
  1962   Educating the Expert Society. San Francisco:
                Chandler.

Cohen, Y. A.
    1971   The Shaping of Men's Minds: Adaptation to the
                    Imperatives of Culture. In Anthropological
                    Perspectives on Education, Murray L. Wax,
                    Stanley Diamond, and Fred O. Gearing, eds. New
                    York: Basic Books.

Durkheim, E.
    1933   The Division of Labor in Society. New York:
                    MacMillan.
    1938   The Rules of Sociological Method. New York:
                    Free Press.
    1956   Education and Sociology. Glencoe, Ill.: Free
                    Press.

Eisenstadt, S. N.
    1956   From Generation to Generation. Glencoe, Ill.:
                    Free Press.

Gouldner, A. W. and R. A. Peterson
    1962   Notes on Technology and the Moral Order. New
                    York: Bobbs Merrill.

Greenberg, J. H.
    1959   Language and Evolution. In Evolution and
                    Anthropology: A Centennial Appraisal, B. J.
                    Meggers, ed. Brooklyn, New York: Theo Gaus
                    & Sons.

Harris, M.
    1968   The Rise of Anthropological Theory. New York:
                    Thomas Y. Crowell.

Hart, C. W. W.
    1963   Contrasts Between Prepubertal and Postpubertal
                    Education. In Education and Culture, G. D.
                    Spindler, ed. New York: Holt.

Hester, J. J.
    1962   A Comparative Typology of New World Cultures,
                    American Anthropologist 64:1001-15.

Huxley, J. S.
    1958   Cultural Process and Evolution. In Behavior and
                    Evolution, A. Roe and G. G. Simpson, eds. New
                    Haven: Yale University Press.

Kroeber, A. L.
    1917   The Superorganic. American Anthropologist 19:
                    163-213.

1952   The Nature of Culture. Chicago: University of
            Chicago Press.

Kroeber, A. L. and C. Kluckholm
    1963   Culture: A Critical Review of Concepts and
                Definitions. New York: Random House.

Naroll, R.
    1956   A Preliminary Index of Social Development.
                American Anthropologist 58:687-715.

Oberg, K.
    1955   Types of Social Structure Among the Lowland
                Tribes of South America. American Anthropolo-
                gist 57:472-87.

Parsons, T.
    1951   The Social System. Glencoe, Ill.: Free Press.

Sahlins, M. D.
    1960   Evolution: Specific and General. In Evolution
                and Culture, M. D. Sahlins and E. R. Service,
                eds. Ann Arbor: University of Michigan Press.

Service, E. R.
    1960   Kinship Terminology and Evolution. American
                Anthropologist 62:747-63.
    1962   Primitive Social Organization. New York:
                Random House.

Simpson, G. G.
    1945   The Principles of Classification and a Classifi-
                cation of Mammals. Bulletin of the American
                Museum of Natural History 85.

Steward, J. H.
    1948   A Functional-Developmental Classification of
                American High Cultures. A Reappraisal of
                Peruvian Archaeology. Memoirs of the Society
                for American Archaeology 4.

Swanson, G. E.
    1964   The Birth of the Gods. Ann Arbor: University
                of Michigan Press.

White, L. A.
    1945   History, Evolutionism and Functionalism: Three
                Types of Interpretation of Culture. South-
                western Journal of Anthropology 1:221-48.

1949   The Science of Culture. New York: Farrar,
        Straus.
1959   The Evolution of Culture. New York: McGraw-
        Hill.

ELSIE CLEWS PARSONS PRIZE
PAPER FOR 1972

FRIENDSHIP: THE AFFECTIVE MANIPULATION

Carol Sue Holzberg
Boston University

... the proper result of good definition is to transform
argument over terms into disagreements about fact, and
thus open arguments to further inquiry.

C. W. Mills,
The Sociological Imagination

Introduction[1]

Anthropologists have realized that in order to abstract
social structure and provide an analytical model of sociocultural phenomena, they must focus on concrete social situations
and interpersonal relations. Underlying most structural investigations and analyses is a search for some sort of systemic
unity of parts and processes interconnected by a limited number
of activating principles (Van Velson, 1967). At best, however,
the structural mapping of a society (its formal groupings and
associations, as well as its enduring categories and institutional framework) is only a partial representation of societal
organization irrespective of whether the socio-cultural system
itself is simple or complex. In order to present the other
dimension of institutional reality and get at what Wolf has
characterized as the interstitial, supplementary, and parallel
structures of a society (1966:2), the researcher must concentrate on social process: on individual actors, changing align-
ments, ephemeral unions, non-corporate groupings, variations in
behavior which run counter to the structural regularities or
normative patterns, and especially on the optative or choice-
making dimensions involved in strategic interaction (Aronson,
1970:260).

Social interaction provides the dynamic matrix linking
individuals to one another in various ways. Mitchell has noted
(1969) that an analysis of the characteristic features of the
linkages involves a consideration of both the structural and
interactional aspects of the social relation.[2] This paper will
be concerned with both the structural and interactional dimensions of one kind of interpersonal relationship known as
friendship. Thus, for example, in speaking of a directed or
reciprocal friendship alliance from an interactional perspective

245

one would be interested in the <u>nature</u> of the exchange of material and/or non-material goods and services, while from a structural orientation one would be interested in the actual goods exchanged and the status-role of the participants. A friendship relation precludes a lack of reciprocity but may be characterized by an asymetry of exchange. This will be elaborated in another part of the paper.

It must be made clear at this point that there may be models other than the one suggested in this paper which would contribute to the analysis of friendship situations.[3] For example, the paper takes a special interest in the social dimensions of friendship and not the cultural-cognitive components. Concern with the latter dimensions would probably lead the analyst into an examination of individual psychological factors with a sharp focus on the nature of the affective element. As such, the psychological-cultural-cognitive components pertain to a level of analysis which is beyond the scope of this paper. However, in order to fully understand the complexities of friendship, it is necessary to explore the subject on many levels and with the aid of additional models.

The purpose of this paper is to set down an appropriate guideline that will facilitate analysis of friendship. It is becoming increasingly more apparent that what may have been traditionally labeled as friendship and described as such in the literature has not been guided by any consistent social scientific framework. Typologies and dichotomies were set up to describe a friendship relation but these models reflect ideal type situations rather than empirical reality. As a result it is exceedingly difficult to pin down operationally quantifiable and qualitatively distinct variables. Thus the paper will be essentially exploratory in nature, providing a review of the relevant literature, suggesting a new definition for a friendship relation, and offering a theoretical orientation which will facilitate further research.

*   *   *   *   *

Previous thoughts about friendship suggest a starting point for reexamining the literature and proposing a working definition for the relationship. Cohen, in his article entitled, "Patterns of Friendship" (1961b) presents data which focus on the social structural forces which tend to maximize or minimize predispositions to certain types of friendship. For Cohen, friendship consists of "those supra- and extra-kin relationships and bonds which are entered into voluntarily and/or which are culturally recognized" (p. 352). The implication is that friendship is a non-kin relationship, but since there are many different kinds of non-kin relationships (e.g. buyer-seller, patron-client, student-teacher) this definition is of little analytical utility. Furthermore, there is a conceptual problem

with the vagueness of the phrase "culturally recognized." If
two kinsmen choose to call each other friends (such as two
brothers-in-law in the United States) and are culturally recognized as such by others, to what extent is the relationship a
function of the kinship bond and/or external non-kinship factors
and motivations? Native categories may seemingly be incon-
sistent with those of the analyst who seeks to explain rather
than merely describe.

Wolf, on the other hand, in an attempt to describe
some of the informal institutions of a complex socio-cultural
system, distinguishes between kinship ties and friendship ties
by noting that "the primary bond in the friendship dyad is not
forged in an ascribed situation; friendship is achieved" (1966:
10). Thus, affective commitment and reciprocal exchange of
material and/or social goods and services between kinsmen does
not constitute a friendship bond but rather a relationship
extant by virtue of the consanguineal or affinal tie.[4] Furthermore, the significance of the bond is not the only component of
the social relationship. Friendship is an enduring, intimate,
and voluntary association based on particularistic, diffuse,
and affective commitments; preconditioned, solidified or sustained by the reciprocal symbolic or actual exchange of material
and/or social goods and services. It is manipulated by the
contractants either consciously or unconsciously as an alternative or adjunct to kinship for the purposes of affiliation and
relationship extension. This does not preclude the possibility
of an individual finding his friends within a universe defined
by the kinship system. In the rapidly urbanizing sectors of
Africa, for example, tribal membership often functions as the
necessary prerequisite for recruitment into a voluntary association. However, once introduced by a fellow tribesman to a
series of co-tribesmen, the migrant is left on his own to eke
out and establish friendship ties (La Fontaine, 1970).

In the light of the above review and suggested working
definition, it is now possible to consider various types of
friendship. Cohen draws up a typology in which he posits four
different types: inalienable, close, casual, and expedient.
However, even he points out that it is virtually impossible to
consider these types as discrete or specifically unique. As
such, the typology is loosely constructed. At what point does
a "casual" friendship stop being "casual" and become "close?"
Does casualness reflect frequency of interaction or content of
the relationship or both? Is it impossible to have a casually-
expedient friendship determined by the nature of the roles of
the participants such as for example, a professor-student
relationship?

Similarly, Wolf sets up a non-operational dichotomy
when he considers two somewhat opposing types of friendship:
expressive vs. instrumental. Denich (1970) notes the difficulty
involved in trying to make use of Wolf's dichotomy in her

analysis of friendship patterns among migrants in Yugoslavia, while La Fontaine (1970) makes almost the identical statement for friendship in Léopoldville.[5] These anthropologists are unable to separate the two levels in "real" situations. But for Wolf there are no inherent ambiguities. Emotional friendship constitutes a relation between an ego and an alter in which each satisfies some emotional need or deficit for the opposite member. Furthermore, this dyadic relation is found "primarily in social situations where the individual is strongly embedded in solidary groupings like communities and lineages, and where the set of social structure inhibits social and geographical mobility (1966:11)." In contradistinction to the emotional friendship, an instrumental friendship is not restricted to the dyad involved, but each of the participants serves as a potential connecting link to others external to the relationship. In addition,

> instrumental friendship may not have been entered into for the purpose of attaining access to resources --natural and social--but the striving for such access becomes vital in it ...however, a minimal amount of affect remains an important ingredient in the relation. If it is not present it must be feigned (1966:12-13).

It is the contention of this writer that Cohen's typology and Wolf's dichotomy are essentially meaningless in terms of operationalizing and quantifying the underlying variables. All friendships are in a sense instrumental but they also involve affective commitment. Resources both natural and/or social are always exchanged. The diacritica lie in the nature and direction of the exchange, who is doing the exchanging, and the degree of dramatization of the relationship.

To speak of an affective commitment as an independent variable or as the basis for a dyadic relationship lends itself to an analytical simplification. An illustration in point would be Gibbs' material on compensatory bloodbrotherhood among the Tanala of Malagasy. He writes: "Bloodbrothers choose each other because they like each other" (1962:71). But he has not provided any material on why two individuals like each other to the extent that they ritually solidify their relationship. He claims that a bloodbrother chooses his partner on the basis of a "particularistic quality" in order to strengthen the friendship tie, but he does not explain what the nature of the particularistic variable is, nor why the desire to formalize the tie is present in the first place. Esentially, his explanation is limited and does not aid us in our understanding of the transactional or social component of the relationship. One cannot sufficiently explain the system by merely looking inward. In this instance, it becomes necessary to search for nonpsychological factors as well.

Friendship is partly a voluntary transaction between two individuals. As such, it has a social as well as a psychological dimension. But focusing on the cognitive or affective components of the relationship runs the analyst into the "you just can't be too sure" syndrome. The analytical model which best represents and accounts for the essential variables incorporated in a friendship tie is the one utilized by Fredrik Barth in The Role of the Entrepreneur in Northern Norway (1963). For Barth, "All social activity may be analysed as the result of constrained choices, and thereby connected with the variables of 'value' or 'purpose' (1963:7). An individual brings to the relationship the sum total of his social characteristics, represented in the form of "social capital," that is, occupational standing, skills, experience, age, power, rank, wealth, information potential, familiarity with bureaucratic procedure, property holdings, access to strategic resources, potential source of network extension and linkage, etc. These characteristics may in a sense be regarded as an individual's "social assets." Clearly, however, individuals differ with respect to their attractiveness to others on the basis of their social capital or assets. It is important to note that social assets are not restricted to the specifically material and tangible formal representations but may take on any manifestation (e.g. the ability to give or withold affective commitment) in so far as they make possible the continuation of a social relationship. A person will be evaluated by another in the light of his "friendship potential" (la Fontaine, 1970:173) which simply means that his social assets and his social liabilities will be considered and assessed prior to the making of friendship overtures.

Just as the "entrepreneur's choice of enterprise is clearly a highly strategic choice, through which his chances of profit are significantly determined" (Barth, 1963:10), so too is the friendship transaction where both participants seek to manipulate the social capital, maximize the expansion of their personal assets, and minimize their losses.[6] If the social costs of the relationship outweigh the social rewards, it is highly likely that the relationship will be terminated. Barth emphasizes that: "Persons have commitments in specific social relations which hamper them in, or prevent them from, pursuing effective strategies. This type of cost can only be avoided by not partaking in such relationships or may be paid once and for all by the repudiation of the relationship" (1963:8).

The nature of the transactional perspective is not an unfamiliar one in anthropology. Often subsumed under the heading of "action" theory, it sees life in terms of a perpetual game in which every individual is engaged in trying to enhance his social assets and rewards by "perpetually scheming, struggling, and making decisions. Every action he contemplates is the outcome of a transaction in which the returns are at least equal to, if not in excess of the outlay" (A. Cohen, 1969:223). Although the term scheming may be somewhat value-laden, it nevertheless points to ego's constant maneuvering and manipulating. The establishment of a friendship dyad is seen as a favorable source for assistance in promoting an individual's interests.

Thus, to consider the maintenance and perpetuation of the friendship relation merely in terms of psychological variables, explaining it on the basis of sentiment without documenting the social implications, reflects an oversimplified and narrowminded focus. Why should A choose B over C? Why should C comply with A's overtures and commit himself to a diffuse, particularistic and time-consuming relationship? Are there other factors which must be taken into consideration such as the structural features of the environment or the social context of the situation? These external factors might influence, constrain, restrict, or promote the continuation of the dyadic relation.

Personality characteristics cannot be dismissed as essential components of the friendship relation; however, there are other components as well. The structural dimensions of a friendship relation consist of the following features: duration, direction, spatial propinquity, transaction (or exchange), intensity, and status role of the contractants. The intensity of the dyadic relation can be seen as a combination of two elements: the frequecy of interaction (contact) and the depth of sentiment (content) involved. (Epstein, 1969:124; La Fontaine, 1970:175; Mitchell, 1969:27). Frequency of interaction may be the result of role overlap within an institutional framework, like two individuals who work at the same job or attend the same university and who therefore share institutional membership and common interests or two individuals who live spatially near one another and are thus more likely to be exposed to one another by virtue of the physical contiguity and proximity than persons living further apart. But whereas the frequency of interaction is not difficult to quantify the depth of sentiment is.[7] Duration refers to the amount of time interaction is sustained; direction to who initiates the interaction; spatial to the amount of distance between the individuals.

Homans has set up a series of postulates relating sentiment to the frequency of interaction. He notes that the more often persons interact with one another when neither of them originates interaction with much greater frequency than the other, the greater is the tendency for increased mutual sentiment and the feeling of ease in one another's presence. "The oftener A and B do things together, the more they will tend to like each other. The more they like each other, the oftener they will tend to do things together" (1950:xv, 243). Similarly, in a more recent article by Chrisman, the argument put forward carries the same nuances. "Those who continue to interact have

250

the occasion to expand their relationships on a more personal level ..." (1970:253). Thus, we can see that expressive relationships are not only found in social situations where the individual is strongly embedded in solidary groupings but may become manifest in any social situation resulting from the nature of the content, intensity and frequency of interaction.

Every social relationship, friendship notwithstanding, involves exchange. Friendship, seen in the light of a social transaction carries with it some degree of reciprocity in the mutual recognition of the potential utility of the alliance, both symbolic and actual. It follows that the more frequent the sustained interaction, the greater the likelihood of mutual indebtedness as well as increased sentiment. Given the fragile nature of the achieved social relation, its maintenance and perpetuation requires constant recultivation through continous reciprocal exchanges of goods and services. Sometimes these goods and services may take the form of expressive sentiment-- the giving and receiving of emotional support. But Landé (1970)[8] sees the dyadic relationship as a system of barter between individuals who have access to differential resources. He writes:

> Each gives to the other something the latter cannot provide for himself. The dissimilarity of the two partners may be temporal or categorical. In the first instance two individuals who in other respects are alike have a surplus or shortage of the same commodity at different times: A lends to B when B is in need, and B returns the favor when A finds himself in short supply. In the second instance individuals who are categorically different supply each other what neither can supply for himself ... (p. 6).

Foster also alludes to the informal principles of reciprocity underlying the anthropological model which he calls the dyadic contract (1963, 1967). He notes that reciprocity between participants in the system is complementary over a long term "because each partner owes to the other the same kinds and quantities of things ... not formally calculated yet somehow weighed so that in the end both partners balance contributions and receipts" (1967:217). However, the friendship dyad does not conform to the model postulated by Foster. In the first place friendship may not be an informal tie. It may be highly formalized cemented initially by a public ritual (Hammond, 1971; Gibbs, 1962; Piker, 1968; Srivastava, 1960). Secondly, Foster explicitly states that an important functional requirement of the dyadic contract is that an exactly even balance between the two participants never be reached. "This would jeopardize the whole relationship since, if all the credits and debits somehow could be balanced off at one time, the contract would cease to exist" (1967, 217). There is no indication in the literature on friendship that an unbalance in either material or social resources constitutes a functional requirement for the maintenance of the tie. As long as there is a steady on-going mutual reinforcement of the reciprocal ties over time, it is of little consequence whether an exact balance is ever struck.

Friendship: Dramatized and Non-dramatized[9]

Categorically speaking, there are two types of friendship: dramatized and non-dramatized. In the first type, establishment of the association is formally initiated by means of a public ritual. Dramatization seems to mediate between the social structural reality and the intimate, particularistic and diffuse nature of the friendship idiom. Among the rural Thai, for example, dramatized friendship is called "friendship to the death" (Piker, 1968). The alliance is cemented by an initial swearing ritual during which the participants pledge mutual devotion and unconditional loyalty. "Such swearing rituals normally include one or two witnesses, and involve the use of holy water, special chants, and mutual blood-letting and mixing" (Piker, 1968:201). Similarly, among the Zande in Africa, "dramatized" friendship takes the form of institutionalized blood-brotherhood.[10] In a public ceremony, "the two blood-brothers cut gashes on each other's chests or arms and smear their blood on bits of wood which are exchanged, swallowed, and addressed in each others' stomachs" (Gibbs, 1962:72).

Srivastava has noted two broad types of "dramatized" friendships for tribal India: serious and non-serious. For the serious type symbolic ceremonial formulation finds its analog in a marriage ritual; for the non-serious, ritualization is analogous to a love affair (1960:247). Hammond discusses "dramatized" friendship among the herding peoples of East Africa. For the Jie of Uganda the relationship takes on the form of a "bond friendship" and is contracted by two individuals who exchange cattle under public scrutinance, signaling their agreement to provide mutual material assistance. Dramatized initiation cements the bond and friendship is usually maintained for life. One could ask the following questions. In dramatized friendships, when new structural positions and concomitantly new obligations and responsibilities in the form of specific rights and duties are activated, do some of these responsibilities persist even after termination of the relationship? If so, which ones and why? Non-dramatized friendship is not initiated by means of any public ceremony nor in front of any witnesses. As such, one could speculate that its institutionalization within a socio-cultural system is deeply embedded and that it might even involve many more diffuse obligations than the more functionally specific dramatized counterpart. However, as a consequence of non-dramatization, the relationship tends to be less stable and consequently less binding on the contractants. The importance of the relationship is not diminished by its lack of institutionalization.

Epstein (1961), Graves (1966), Gutkind (1965), and Hanson and Simmons (1968) discuss the instrumental importance of friendship relations for newly-urbanized migrants. Through interaction with others and often as a member of a voluntary association, the migrant familiarizes himself with the urban social structure, role prescriptions, and behavioral proscriptions. His new friend will serve as a mediator easing his adjustment to the demands and pressures of the new community. Often just a recently urbanized individual himself, the new friend understands the background from which the migrant comes and can acclimate him to the demands of the new situational context by serving as a focus of identification as well as a source of emotional support and technical assistance. The kinds of rewards he receives in return should be acknowledged as well. Some of these might be: potential network partner for future or current business transactions; knowledge and gossip about the home front; power accrued from having a personal following, etc. This particular kind of friendship continues to function only as long as concrete or symbolic benefits of assistance and protection are reciprocally exchanged. The migrant will eventually become highly selective of his friends, strategically basing his choices on their social capital. As his field of contacts expands, he opts from one kind of network to another. "Friends become enemies; enemies friends" (Gutkind, 1965:57).

Friendship as Exchange

With respect to the nature of the reciprocal exchange, it is suggested that dramatized friendship may be "typically" characterized by balanced reciprocity (Sahlins, 1965). As a result of the formal initiation ceremony, which is in itself a symbolic transaction, individuals become obligated to give for that which is received and the relationship takes on a somewhat functionally specific nature. In bond friendship as among the Jie, the association once formed is "held together by the steady, on-going mutual reinforcement of the reciprocal tie through the giving of property, time, attention, interest, and support, both emotional and social" (Hammond, 1971:185). Reciprocity entails mutual rights and obligations and an individual will retain his rights only as long as he reciprocates in kind.

In a non-dramatized friendship, the absence of any formal tie precludes the necessity of keeping a public image and the exchange often takes the form of generalized reciprocity. Altruistic gift-giving may be characteristic. Equivalence of exchange and the immediacy of repayment recede into the background making the expectations of the counter obligations indefinite. As Heider (1969) points out, generalized reciprocity involves behavior which is more functionally diffuse than the functionally specific behavior characterized by balanced reciprocity. In the former, transactions may impinge upon many other

253

cultural domains than the exchange itself, while the individuals concerned are maximizing more than just the exchange (p. 463). Nevertheless, it is important to realize that if one of the parties feels slighted or "used" to the extent that he sees his personal assets or social capital being depleted without replenishment, the relationship will probably terminate.[11]

This raises the important questions of what are the antecedent correlates or the concomitants of the two types of friendship and under what conditions have developed one rather than the other formal arrangement? Friendship ritualization is directly related to the relative integration of the sociocultural system in terms of "loosely woven" and "tightly woven" social structures (Embree, 1950; Gibbs, 1962). Loose and tight are variables which take into account the significant variation in individual behavior which is tolerated and given positive sanction and the emphasis on a rigid adherence to formal sociocultural patterns in human relations. Gibbs remarks:

Accordingly, I define a 'tight' society as one in which there is not a wide range of roles to select from and where roles are primarily ascribed, rather than achieved. Moreover, there is not much tolerance for individual variation in role performance, and deviance in role performance is regularly met with clear-cut social sanctions (1962:67).

A loosely-structured sociocultural system does not imply that the society itself is poorly integrated, nor does it follow that a tightly-woven sociocultural system is more integrated than a loosely structured one. Three variables which operate here, serving to define and constituting preconditions for the community type are: 1) the degree of solidification into corporate kin groupings 2) the level of technoeconomic adaptation, and cultural complexity and 3) the "scale" of the sociocultural system.

Maximally solidary communities are solidified into corporate kin groups and tend to be tightly structured by virtue of their corporateness. As a result of the spatial contiguity between households, the constitutent families of the localized communities are socially contiguous as well. Interaction takes on a face to face nature and is relatively stable over time. The stability is further accentuated by the exclusive kin ownership of land and the tendency to form associations and interact primarily with kinsmen. Another type of corporate kin unit is the unilineal kinship corporation known as the lineage. Often transcending the local, three or four generation descent group, it functions in a somewhat similar fashion to the local corporate grouping mentioned above. In both these types of corporate communities deviations from normative role behavior are often met with severe negative sanctions.

In the absence of corporate kin groupings, there is a tendency to find loosely-structured sociocultural systems.

Cohen (1961a and b) has characterized these societies as "in-dividuated social structures" and has noted that few if any institutionally significant statuses are ascribed. Physical mobility and change in community membership are two features which help to accentuate the individualistic nature of the society. Cohen remarks: "The individuated social structure is focused on individuated amassment and accumulation of wealth as an end in itself rather than as an intervening step or means to cooperative or competitive generosity" (1961a:317). Essen-tially, individuals compete for scarce resources and the competition for personal profit and success is carried out between kinsmen and non-kinsmen alike.

Moreover, it should be stressed that there is not a one to one correlation between tightness and corporateness. Whereas this is more obvious in a maximally solidary community or lineage where roles are primarily ascribed, societies of the type described by Banfield in The Moral Basis of a Backward Society (1958) can also be characterized as tightly woven. However, here it is the structure of the agricultural system (the techno-economic adaptation) which imposes severe limitations on behavioral variations, even though roles are primarily achieved rather than ascribed. This is often characteristic of peasant societies in general. Similarly, the notion of the "scale" of the sociocultural system should be included. This complex variable takes into account demographic factors as well as the intensity of intra- and inter-community social relations (Goldberg, u.p.). The greater the frequency of socio-economic and sociocultural interchanges between the specific community and its sociocultural environment, the larger the scale and the more likely the society to be loosely structured.

Friendship: The Affective Manipulation

Throughout this paper I have reiterated that friend-ship is essentially a transaction between two individuals based on the mutual exchange of material and/or social goods and services, sustained and perpetuated over time by the very nature of the symbolic or actual reciprocal exchange. It is funda-mentally maintained by the participants' awareness, either conscious or unconscious, implicit or explicit, of the relation-ship's mutual advantageousness. Affective sentiment may be useful for the establishment of the alliance, it may also be a critical factor for its perpetuation, but it is in the mutual interest of both parties that the relationship retains a some-what balanced nature and that neither asks for nor receives more than he can eventually give back in return.

It is hypothesized that "dramatized" or ritualized friendship tends to occur more frequently in tightly-woven sociocultural systems. Because kin relations in the corporate community tend to structure "the nature of social resources at

255

one's command in operations in the non-kin realm" (Wolf, 1966:9), extra-kin relations need the sanctioning approval of the kin network. Similarly, for extra-familial relations in communities of a tight but non-corporate nature, one can therefore see the initiation ceremony as a formalized arena in which positive social sanctioning takes place. The participants in a sense secure permission to contract an intimate, and particularistically-diffuse extra-kin tie which essentially takes on instrumental economic importance. Among the Mossi of Yatunga in Western Africa, for example, bond friendship functions as a mechanism by which two individuals can "increase their chances of keeping their gains secret from kinsmen with whom their responsibility to share would soon leave their small profits depleted ..." (Hammond, 1971:186).

Friendship to the death among rural Thai villagers takes on similar dimensions. Here, however, the community is of a tight but non-corporate nature. Piker gives a psychological explanation for the establishment of the relationship. He claims that the Thai peasant is desirous of, but unwilling to undertake binding relations with others in his own village by virtue of the "image of limited good" and that as a consequence of this ethos, more than 60% of the relationships were contracted with someone residing in another province. Friendships to the death thus make possible "a degree of vicarious, or fantasied gratification of desires strongly felt but otherwise largely frustrated in every day life" (Piker, 1968:203). As a result of mutual distrust and wariness of the intentions of others, the villager will not commit himself to a friendship relation in his own village. He will nevertheless seek out "affectionate, supportive, or trusting involvement" (Ibid:203) with individuals whom he doesn't see more than a few times a year.[12]

Although one cannot dismiss the psychological component of the relationship it seems apparent that a somewhat elaborated analysis of friendship to the death is required. Piker gives clues when he talks about the relationship, but these remain implicit. Thai special friendship entails mutual assistance "sporadically exchanged but occasionally of substantial proportions... Such assistance, if given, is normally economic and takes the form of money given outright or loaned without interest" (Piker, 1968:201). Thus, while affective commitment may be the peasant's rationale for contracting the relationship, it is obviously not the sole motivation. By securing a friend in a foreign village, the peasant provides himself with a network of contacts that he may call on for help and assistance while on a business trip away from home. As such, the instrumental quality of the relationship may take on implicitly unconscious priority. Whereas peasants living in the same village probably have access to the same resources, it is also possible that inter-village associations provide access to differential resources. Friendship therefore provides the framework within

which the peasant can manipulate social capital which may not
have been available to him by virtue of intra-village ties.

Whereas dramatized friendships can occur in loosely-
woven social structures, it is suggested that non-dramatized
friendships will be statistically more significant. Jacobson
(1968, 1970), for example, discusses the importance of non-
dramatized friendships among urban African elites. For the
elites friendship has both instrumental and expressive under-
tones and it is difficult to analytically separate the two
dimensions. From the instrumental perspective Jacobson notes
that "friendship is important in the elite's ideology as a mode
of expressing elite status ... [It] becomes critical in differentiating elite from non-elite ... They expect to interact with
and to have as friends only other elite Africans, thereby con-
firming their own status" (1968:125). Furthermore, since the
elites are highly mobile, being constantly moved around by the
government from position to position, it is of utmost importance
that they secure friends and establish a potential friendship
network from which they can draw material and social rewards.
From the expressive perspective, however, there is an emotional
commitment between friends. Friends are expected to be com-
panions and companionship entails such varied obligations as
talking together, drinking together, attending movies, lectures
or dances, etc (Ibid:126). As a result of the dual dimensions,
it becomes difficult to draw up an analytical distinction between expressivity and instrumentality. Both these dimensions
are complementary and are necessary for analytical purposes as
well as for the maintenance and perpetuation of the friendship
relation.

Informal non-dramatized friendship incorporates degrees
of both instrumentality and expressivity. The more formalized
non-dramatized friendship approximates a patron-client relationship and as Wolf points out, it comes about "when instrumental
friendship reaches a maximum point of imbalance so that one
partner is clearly superior to the other in his capacity to
grant goods and services ... (1966:16), yet a minimum degree of
affect must be present "to form that trust which underwrites the
promise of future mutual support" (Ibid:16). This is therefore
an added example of how the emotional-instrumental dichotomy as
a model to explain friendship is vague and difficult to make use
of.

Summary and Conclusions

Wolf's dichotomy and Cohen's typology as models have
no apparent definitive or explanatory properties. Perhaps this
is due to the fact that the typology is not made up of discrete
categories and the dichotomy distinguishes between two analytical
levels that are difficult to keep separate in the field. Emotional or expressive friendship lends itself more readily to a

257

psychological analysis, while instrumental friendship seems to be consistent with a sociological analysis, both structural and processual. But both levels of an analysis complement each other and should be considered. A new dichotomy was suggested: dramatized versus non-dramatized friendship and the theoretical orientation found to be most useful was transactional analysis. The importance of this particular social relationship is not that it solves conceptual puzzles by providing a model but that it gives rise to certain questions about intra- and inter-societal relationships.

The purpose of this paper has been to present a definition of and theoretical model for the analysis of friendship. Friendship is an intimate supra-kin bond based on the symbolic exchange of affective commitment, cultural material and/or social goods and services. Two individuals consanguineally or affinally related who sustain interaction and reciprocal exchange over a long period of time should be regarded as kinsmen and not friends.[13] If A and B contract and maintain an intimate, particularistic, and diffuse relationship, anteceded, cemented or sustained by reciprocal exchange such that the exchange is not to "maximize utility at the other's expense" (Sahlins, 1965), this social relationship can be designated as friendship. It is important to note that this relationship will continue only as long as reciprocal obligations are acknowledged and carried out.

In the past, there has been a consistent mishandling of the data dealing with friendship often based on analytical simplification and psychological reductionism. The basis for this analysis lies in a critique of Cohen's descriptive typology and Wolf's non-existent dichotomy. An illustration in point would be the friendship dyad per se. Wolf claims that emotional friendship remains dyadic. In contrast each member of the dyad in an instrumental friendship acts as a potential connecting link to others external to the dyad. But given the fact that individuals are embedded in may different kinds of social networks, friendship being only one of them, there is always the potential for extra-dyadic linkages. In socio-metric terminology, this potential has been called the co-friend bias alluding to the possibility that X targets on Y given that a third person Z exists who targets on both X and Y (Fararo and Sunshine, 1964: 26).

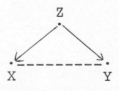

Affective commitment seems to have little to do with closure of the dyadic relationship.

In Barnes' classic paper on network analysis (1954)

friendship was viewed as a residual category, that is, as some kind of categorical remainder left behind after the formal structural relationships were considered. A secondary aim of this paper has been to point out how important residual categories can be. Friendship dyads by virtue of their morphological implications (who becomes friends with whom; what material and social goods and services are being exchanged) and their interactional dimension (the social context of the alliance, the nature of the relationship) are often highly structured and patterned and should not be regarded as residual properties of a dynamically operating sociocultural system.

NOTES

1. This paper derives from the writer's participation in a seminar on "Complex Societies" under the guidance of Professor Nancie L. González, spring 1971, University of Iowa.

2. Morphological (structural) features include: anchorage, density, reachability and range; interactional (processual) features include: context, directedness, durability, intensity, and frequency of interaction (Mitchell 1969:12). But it is clear that directedness, intensity, and frequency of interaction are characteristic not only of process. They may actually refer to the formal patterning of linkages.

3. I would like to thank David Plath and John W. Bennett for their clarifications on this point.

4. Professor Nancie González (personal communication) raised an interesting point pertaining to whether the affinal tie (marriage) under some circumstances may be considered a "legal" extension of the friendship relation between the sexes in that it too can be an achieved and voluntary association, based on the mutual exchange of goods and services and solidified by the procreation of offspring.

5. Denich writes: "In Yugoslavia, it is impossible to distinguish between affective and instrumental friendship, since both these aspects are combined in the operative concept of 'Friendship' (p. 136). Similarly, La Fontaine remarks, "... I am not entirely convinced that Wolf's types of emotional and instrumental friendship are analytically useful in undertaking the material discussed here (p. 170)."

6. Friendship differs from a buyer-seller or specifically entrepreneurial relationship in that it is more diffuse and is not characterized uniquely by a "movement of utilitarian goods from an area of plenty to one of scarcity" (Heider, 1969: 462).

7. Firth claims that expressive behavior is more of a cultural reality than a psychological reality because it is a visibly concrete phenomenon and not a state of mind which must be inferred and abstracted. He cites as his examples such things as inflections of the voice, the look of the eyes and

carriage of the head and intimate little movements of the hands and arms (Homans, 1950:241). However, it is not entirely clear whether these cultural manifestations mirror psychological reality or whether they reflect structural reality and are more a function of the frequency of interaction and the ability to feel at ease and relaxed in another's presence (that is, the result of sustained contact and/or familiarity with cue transmission). They may also be a product of the content of the relationship, i.e. the purposes of or interests in the on-going relationship by virtue of (for example) its religio-political obligations rather than a measure of expressive sentiment per se.

8. The author gratefully acknowledges Landé's permission to quote passages from a paper presented to the Southeast Asia Development Advisory Group of the Asia Society in a seminar entitled, Political Development Panel, March 20-21, 1970.

9. I would like to thank Professor H. Goldberg of the Department of Anthropology, University of Iowa, for suggesting these terms to me.

10. Institutionalized blood brotherhood falls into the realm of fictive kinship as does the Latin American compadrazgo or compadrinazgo which establishes a "friendship" relation between the parents and the godparents of the child. Compadrazgo statuses are ritually assigned during a fiesta. Persons holding the statuses need not be kinsmen to each other and the more characteristic style is for them to be unrelated. Individuals will make use of the compadrazgo to extend relationships and consequently their access to resources. Exchange may be both symbolic and actual, that is, there may be an exchange of affective commitment and political and religious support and/or there may be gift giving and mutual financial aid in agriculture or house construction. As Ravicz (1967) points out, "Compadrinazgo acts to bring separate families together in special relationships of a pseudo-kinship nature" (p. 241).

11. The author has not set up a dichotomy with institutionalized friendship: balanced reciprocity versus non-institutionalized friendship: generalized reciprocity as its components. Dichotomization does not appear sufficient and there may be other levels of abstraction with other variables to take into account. However, at the most general level and as an initial model, the dichotomy seems to hold true. It is anticipated that an elaboration of the model will follow in later research.

12. A similar situation can be found in many Latin American countries where institutionalized compadrazgo makes possible the establishment of a binding relationship between non-related individuals or an intensification of association between kinsmen. Again, Ravicz (1967) remarks: "Through the compadrinazgo, regional, ethnic, and local ties are established. When one is travelling, the padrino or compadre in another

community may be counted on for food, shelter, or information"
(p. 242).

    13. Again the affinal bond between a husband and wife
raises questions about the nature of "dramatized" friendship
which lie outside the scope of this paper.

REFERENCES

Aronson, Dan R.
     1970   "Social Networks: Toward Structure or Process?"
                   Canadian Review of Sociology and Anthropology,
                   7(4):258-296.

Banfield, Edward C.
     1958   The Moral Basis of a Backward Society. New
                   York: Free Press.

Barnes, J. A.
     1954   "Class and Committees in a Norwegian Island
                   Parish," Human Relations, 7:39-58.

Barth, Fredrik
     1963   "Introduction," in The Role of the Entrepreneur
                   in Social Change in Northern Norway. Bergen:
                   Norwegian University Press.

Cohen, Abner
     1969   "Political Anthropology: The Analysis of the
                   Symbolism of Power Relations," Man 4(2):215-235.

Cohen, Yehudi
     1961a   "Food and its Vicissitudes: A Cross-cultural
                   Study of Sharing and Non-sharing," in Yehudi
                   Cohen (ed.) Social Structure and Personality:
                   A Casebook. New York: Holt, Rinehart and
                   Winston, pp. 312-351.
     1961b   "Patterns of Friendship" in Cohen (ed.) op. cit.
                   pp. 351-396.

Chrisman, Noel J.
     1970   "Situation and Social Network in Cities," CRSA
                   7(4):245-257.

Denich, Bette S.
     1970   "Migration and Network Manipulation in
                   Yugoslavia," in Migration and Anthropology,
                   American Ethnological Society. Proceedings
                   of the 1970 Spring Meeting. pp. 133-149.

Embree, John
       1950   "Thailand--A Loosely Structured Social System,"
                    AA 52:181-193.

Epstein, A. L.
       1961   "The Network and Urban Social Organization,"
                    Rhodes-Livingstone Journal 29:28-62.
       1969   "Gossip, Norms and Social Network," in J. Clyde
                    Mitchell (ed.) Social Networks in Urban Situ-
                    ations. Manchester: Man. U. Press, pp. 117-127.

Fararo, T. J. and Morris H. Sunshine
       1964   A Study of A Biased Friendship Net. Youth Dev.
                    Center, New York: Syracuse University.

Foster, George M.
       1963   "The Dyadic Contract in Tzintzuntzan, II:
                    Patron-Client Relationships," AA 65(6):1280-
                    1295.
       1967   "The Dyadic Contract: A Model for the Social
                    Structure of a Mexican Peasant Village," in
                    Potter et. al. (eds.) Peasant Society: A
                    Reader, Boston, Little Brown and Co., pp. 213-
                    230.

Gibbs, James L. (Jr.)
       1962   "Compensatory Blood-Brotherhood: A Comparative
                    Analysis of Institutional Friendship in Two
                    African Societies," Proceedings of the Minn.
                    Academy of Science 30:67-74.

Goldberg, Harvey
       u.p.   "Historical Reconstruction of Tripolitanian
                    Jewry: The Statistical Significance of
                    Isopleths." (Paper presented at the AAA in
                    New York (1971) in the symposium on the
                    Ethnology of Traditional Jewish Communities.)

Gutkind, Peter C. W.
       1965   "African Urbanism, Mobility, and the Social
                    Network," International Journal of Comp.
                    Sociology 6:48-60.

Graves, T. D.
       1966   "Alternative Model for the Study of Urban
                    Migration," Human Organization 5:295-99.

Hammond, Peter B.
       1971   "Bond Friendship," in An Introduction to
                    Cultural and Social Anthropology, New York:

The Macmillan Co., pp. 185-187.

Hanson, R. C. and O. G. Simmons
    1968   "The Role Path: A Concept and Procedure for
              Analyzing Migration to Urban Communities,"
              Human Organization 27:152-158.

Heider, Karl G.
    1969   "Visiting Trade Institutions," American
              Anthropologist, 71(3):462-471.

Homans, George
    1950   The Human Group, New York: Harcourt, Brace
              and Co.

Jacobson, D.
    1968   "Friendship and Mobility in the Development
              of an Urban Elite African Social System,"
              SWJA 24:123-38.
    1970   "Network Analysis in East Africa: The Social
              Organization of Urban Transients," CRSA 7(4):
              281-286.

Kushner, G.
    1970   "The Anthropology of Complex Societies," in
              Bernard J. Siegal (ed.) Biennial Review of
              Anthropology, 1969, Stanford University Press,
              pp. 80-131.

La Fontaine, J. S.
    1970   "Friendship," in City Politics: A Study of
              Leopoldville, 1962-63, London, Cambridge
              University Press, pp. 170-177.

Landé, Carl H.
    u.p.   "Networks and Groups in Southeast Asia: Some
              Observations on the Group Theory of Politics,"
              (Southeast Asia Development Advisory Group
              (Seadag) discussion paper. Meeting of Seadag's
              Political Development Panel, March 20-21, 1970.)

Mitchell, J. Clyde (ed.)
    1969   "Introduction," in Social Networks in Urban
              Situations, Manchester: Man. University Press,
              pp. 1-50.

Piker, Steven
    1968   "Perspectives on the Atomistic Type Society:
              Friendship to the Death in Rural Thai Society,"
              Human Organization 7(3):200-204.

Sahlins, Marshall D.
    1965   "On the Sociology of Primitive Exchange," in
                The Relevance of Models For Social Anthropology,
                M. Banton (ed.) A.S.A. #1, pp. 139-237.

Ravicz, Robert
    1967   "Compadrinazgo" in Social Anthropology.
                Manning Nash (ed.) Vol. 6, Handbook of Middle
                American Indians, pp. 238-359.

Srivastava, S. K.
    1960   "Patterns of Ritual Friendship in Tribal India,"
                International Journal of Comparative Sociology,
                1(2):239-247.

Van Velson, J.
    1967   "The Extended Case Method in Situational
                Analysis," in A. L. Epstein The Craft of Social
                Anthropology, London Tavistock Pub., pp. 129-
                149.

Wolf, E.
    1956   "Aspects of Group Relations in a Complex
                Society," in Peasants and Peasant Societies,
                T. Shanin (ed.), Penguin Modern Sociology
                (1971), pp. 50-68.
    1966   "Kinship, Friendship, and Patron-Client
                Relations in Complex Societies," in M. Banton
                (ed.) The Social Anthropology of Complex
                Societies, A.S.A. #4 London: Tavistock Pub.,
                pp. 1-20.